In Praise of *Working with the Emotional Investor*

"Most successful investors have a contrarian streak. They buy when others are selling or, as Baron Rothschild put it, 'when there's blood in the streets.' But, for the vast majority of investors—the frightened herd—waiting for the proverbial 'marching band,' embracing the status quo, or even selling out serves as an emotional refuge. In *Working with the Emotional Investor*, seasoned wealth counselor Chris White offers his fellow wealth advisors essential advice on how to deal effectively with either type of client and with everybody in between! Indeed, he provides a critical roadmap to help advisors deal with investors who are influenced by a wide variety of conscious and unconscious emotions."

Arnold S. Wood
Co-chair, Investments, Martingale Asset Management

"Chris White gives us a treasure trove of well researched advice on wealth owner behavior, advisor bias, and a process for building a strong relationship with our clients. This book allows you to explore in depth some of your intuition about the business and gives you keen insight into how to engage with different personalities in your day to day work. An excellent contribution to the field of private wealth for decades to come!"

Sara Hamilton
Founder and CEO, Family Office Exchange

"Our human capacity for emotions plays a crucial (though often not fully understood) role in all the significant decisions in our life. The manner in which money is used in our society and has been used in the lives of the clients we serve has imbued this neutral form of exchange with very strong emotional connections. Therefore in order for a wealth advisor to become a truly 'trusted advisor,' it is vitally important to understand the client's unique emotional perspectives regarding financial choices. *Working with the Emotional Investor* provides a valuable resource for a wealth manager desiring to increase expertise in the intriguing field of behavioral finance."

Lee Hausner, PhD
Senior Vice President, Family Enterprise

"Finally, a paradigm shift in investment counseling. An approach that takes investor dynamics into account along with market dynamics. Brilliant!"

David Kantor, PhD
Psychologist, author of *Reading the Room*, and former professor, Harvard Medical School

"I have watched Chris in action, expertly leading an endowment committee through the treacherous waters of portfolio management. But not until reading *Working with the Emotional Investor* did I fully appreciate his profound understanding of the dynamics at play. Chris demonstrates convincingly that in *any* investment discussion, the numbers are important but managing the underlying emotions associated with investment decisions is essential as well. A critical read for wealth advisors everywhere!"

Eric Schultz
Former Chairman of the Board of Trustees, New England Historic Genealogical Society

"Few things are as intimate and poorly understood as the emotions surrounding money. Drawing upon psychology, behavioral economics, and neuro-economics as well as his own experiences advising high net worth clients, Chris White lays out a path both to understanding the emotional factors at play when people confront major financial decisions and working with these influences to best serve the client or, in the case of development, the donor."

Steve Rum
Vice President for Development & Alumni Relations, Fund for Johns Hopkins Medicine

"*Working with the Emotional Investor* captures a wealth of information about the psychology of clients, markets, and the advising profession. Chris White draws on principles of behavioral finance, client psychology, personality theory, and emotional intelligence to emphasize a clear message: advisors need to truly understand their clients in order to serve them well. For the psychologically-minded advisor looking for a book that resonates, *Working with the Emotional Investor* is a gem."

James Grubman, PhD
FamilyWealth Consulting

"When managing other people's money, constructing appropriate client portfolios is but one essential part of the advisory relationship. Building a strong psychological bond with the client is perhaps a more important factor in the advisor/client equation. In *Working with the Emotional Investor* Chris White illuminates the biases that investors often bring to the wealth management process and outlines powerful strategies that advisors can use to align investment goals with a client's unique personality, priorities, temperament, and risk-tolerance."

James L. Joslin, CFP
Chairman and CEO, TFC Financial Management

"In the process of developing professional relationships with clients, Chris combines his knowledge of intelligent investing with a deep understanding of the human factors that can drive, enhance, and complicate what a client wishes to achieve. He is an attentive listener and creative thinker, skilled at attending to clients' needs on many levels, and helping them to achieve their personal investment goals."

Mary Hope Dean
Licensed clinical social worker and client

"Noted investment advisor David Babson once said, 'If your investments keep you awake at night, sell them!' That's sound enough advice, but in his book, *Working with the Emotional Investor*, wealth advisor Chris White takes the conversation far deeper. He explores the reasons why we behave as we do when it comes to investing and how an aware investor and his or her advisors can manage investments better when we understand the emotional basis of our decision-making."

William M. Crozier, Jr.
Retired Chairman and President, BayBanks, Inc.

"*Working with the Emotional Investor* provides useful tools to comprehend one's true capacity for risk, and therefore pays the reader a great dividend!"

George W. Tall, IV
President, Burl Capital LLC

WORKING WITH THE EMOTIONAL INVESTOR

Financial Psychology for Wealth Managers

Chris White with Richard Koonce

Foreword by Bill Griffeth

PRAEGER™

An Imprint of ABC-CLIO, LLC
Santa Barbara, California • Denver, Colorado

Library of Congress Cataloging-in-Publication Data

Names: White, Chris (Wealth management advisor), author. | Koonce, Richard, author.
Title: Working with the emotional investor : financial psychology for wealth managers / Chris White with Richard Koonce ; foreword by Bill Griffeth.
Description: Santa Barbara, California : Praeger, [2016] | Includes bibliographical references and index.
Identifiers: LCCN 2016017511 (print) | LCCN 2016027384 (ebook) | ISBN 9781440845123 (hard copy : alk. paper) | ISBN 9781440845130 (ebook)
Subjects: LCSH: Investment advisor-client relationships. | Investments—Psychological aspects. | Portfolio management.
Classification: LCC HG4621 .W459 2016 (print) | LCC HG4621 (ebook) | DDC 332.6068/8—dc23
LC record available at https://lccn.loc.gov/2016017511

ISBN: 978-1-4408-4512-3
EISBN: 978-1-4408-4513-0

20 19 18 17 16   2 3 4 5

This book is also available as an eBook.

Praeger
An Imprint of ABC-CLIO, LLC

ABC-CLIO, LLC
130 Cremona Drive, P.O. Box 1911
Santa Barbara, California 93116-1911
www.abc-clio.com

This book is printed on acid-free paper ∞

Manufactured in the United States of America

Contents

Foreword by Bill Griffeth   ix

Preface   xiii

Acknowledgments   xix

Introduction   xxi

Part I   **How Human Psychology and Client
                     Emotions Drive Investor Behavior and
                     Decision-Making**   1

Chapter One   Understanding a Person's
                     Emotional Template   3

Chapter Two   The Psychology of Money and the
                     Emotions of Investing   21

Chapter Three   Introducing a Conversational Model You
                     Can Use with Clients   37

Part II   **Client Relationship Management**   **51**

Chapter Four   Understanding Your Client's
                     Engagement Style   53

Chapter Five   Heroes Rising: The Different Types of Clients
                     That Emerge in High-Stakes Situations   67

Chapter Six   Advising Clients Who Are Fixers   89

Chapter Seven   Advising Clients Who Are Survivors   109

Chapter Eight   Advising Clients Who Are Protectors   125

Part III   **Nurturing Client Relationships for
the Long Term**   147

Chapter Nine   Establishing Credibility and Building Trust
with Clients of *Any* Type   149

Chapter Ten   On Stewardship and Servant Leadership   171

Epilogue   181

*Appendix A: Thinking, Fast and Slow: The Differences in
Two Philosophies of Trading*   183

*Appendix B: Applying Principles of Behavioral Finance
to Understanding the Ups and Downs of Stock Prices*   187

Notes   191

Bibliography   199

Index   203

Foreword

In 1984, the year I turned 28, I fell in love with a car and with a stock. One relationship lasted several years and brought me great joy. The other did not. It lasted only a brief time, and it ended abruptly and painfully.

First, the car. I was born and raised in Los Angeles, where cars are an integral part of the lifestyle. When I was a child my brother Chuck, who is 16 years older than me, bought a 1963 Corvette Stingray. It was silver with white trim, and it was gorgeous. That was the car I would drive someday, I told myself, not realizing that by the time I was old enough to drive, it would practically be an antique. But it didn't matter, because by the late 1960s another car had come along that turned my head. It was Datsun's brand-new, sporty 240Z, which had lines very similar to my brother's Stingray. It stirred something in me as well, and I told myself: *that* is the car I will drive someday.

Fast-forward to 1978, when I was able to buy my first car with my own money. By then, the 280Z was being offered, but its $7,000 price tag was way beyond my means, so I settled for a Toyota Corolla two-door liftback, for which I paid $2,500.

Fast-forward once again to 1984. My wife, Cindy, and I had been married for a couple of years, I was three years into my career in TV news, and I needed a new car. Since Datsun was introducing a new model called the 300ZX, we figured we could probably get a good deal on any 280ZXs our local dealer still had in stock. I was very excited. Was I really going to be able to buy my dream car?

We explained to the salesman what we were looking for, and he walked us over to the 280ZXs on the lot. They were beautiful, and I was smitten. I sat in the driver's seat and gazed lovingly at the leather interior and the retro dials on the dashboard. Finally, I thought.

But then the salesman said something that changed my life.

"By the way," he mentioned casually, "we have one of the brand-new 300ZXs. Just came in last night, if you want to take a look at it."

I caught Cindy's eye. This had not been part of our plan, but I figured it wouldn't hurt just to look.

It was a revelation. First of all, the car was jet black. It sparkled in the mid-day sun. I sat in the driver's seat, which was roomier than the 280ZX. The upholstery was plush, and the all-electronic control panel cast an orange glow.

"Would you like to go for a test drive?" the salesman asked.

Boy, would I.

I will never forget that first ride. It was quiet and incredibly smooth, like floating on a cloud. And I had never experienced acceleration like that. The salesman turned the radio on to demonstrate the four-speaker sound system. I was hooked. My poor wife.

We drove it off the lot later that afternoon after having paid $4,000 more than we had budgeted. I have purchased some wonderful luxury and sports cars in the years since that day, but none have come close to stirring the emotions I felt for that 300ZX. I drove it more than 120,000 miles, until 1991, when I was hired by CNBC and we moved from L.A. to the East Coast. It was the automotive love of my life.

Now the stock. The Summer Olympics came to L.A. in 1984. A very exciting time. Several months before the opening ceremony, I saw a TV commercial for the long-distance company MCI Communications, boasting that it would be providing service to officials and athletes during the Games. I had already reported extensively about the epic break-up of AT&T into seven separate local phone companies, so I knew that Ma Bell was left to compete with upstart long-distance companies like MCI. This commercial got my attention.

It was a can't-miss deal, I told myself. Clearly this company was going places. If it was good enough for the Summer Olympics, it was good enough for me. I called Cindy and convinced her that we should invest $1,500. She reluctantly agreed. My poor wife.

I had never bought a stock in my life. My parents came of age during the Depression in the 1930s, and as a result they were very conservative with their money. They paid cash for everything, didn't have a single credit card, and they never, ever bought a share of stock. But here I was covering Wall Street, and I was excited about making my first killing in the market.

Big mistake. If I had done any homework, I would have seen a company with poor cash flow and too much debt battling for market share in a fiercely competitive landscape. Not a great recipe for success. By the time we sold our shares a year later, we had lost most of our original investment.

If only I had known Chris White back then. I could have taken him for a joy ride in my beloved 300ZX along Pacific Coast Highway, and he would have explained to me that the strong emotions I felt for my car should not be applied to my money management strategies. A more rational approach is more appropriate. But I had to learn that lesson the hard way.

My employment at CNBC prohibits me from investing in individual stocks. That's probably a good thing. At least I'm still free to buy fast cars!

Bill Griffeth
Co-host of CNBC's *Closing Bell*

Preface

You inherit your identity, your history, like a birthmark that you can't wash off.
— Hugo Hamilton, The Sailor in the Wardrobe

My late father, an investment advisor like myself, was a cold, distant, and emotionally unavailable man. Though I suspected as a youngster that he loved me, he seldom displayed any affection or warmth, even as I longed, as many young boys do as they are growing up and exploring and discovering their emerging male identities, for a close connection with my father.

Instead, my father prided himself on his logic, intellect, and discipline. Emotionally fastidious, he walled himself off from feelings, and disparaged their display in others. "You have hurty feelings," he once told me when I was a young boy, his words stinging me like garden nettles and making the young male psyche that was taking shape in me at that tender age feel an awkward mix of shame, embarrassment, and astonishment. How could someone who allegedly loved me talk to me that way? At the time I felt diminished, insignificant. Even foolish. Most of all, I felt *disconnected* from him. Didn't he know how much I longed for a close relationship with him as my father?

He never knew how much his words hurt me, although, on his death bed, he whispered to me, "Suffering, suffering."

Make no mistake. I grew up a child of privilege. My father and grandfather were descended from a long line of New York bankers, brokers, entrepreneurs, and financiers going back to the early 1800s. Their flinty resolve, steely discipline, and emotional reserve served them well in business in the early years of our country. I can remember, for example, my father telling me stories of how ancestors of mine from the Revolutionary War onward had been in the fur industry, based in Danbury, Connecticut. Beginning in the 1830s, my great-great grandfather began to crisscross multiple states, extending west to St. Louis by stage coach, steamer, rail, and foot, collecting on accounts and looking for new sources of high-quality animal pelts when his sources in New York and New England dwindled. It was a time when the U.S. banking system didn't exist as it does today, and he became a wary trader in local bank paper, avoiding notes issued by some banks while accepting bank paper from others. He thus became an arbitrageur of local bank paper across much of modern-day Virginia, Kentucky, Ohio, Indiana, and Illinois.[1] Later, he and other descendants set up a family bank that served still other states and did business overseas. All this set the stage for later descendants, my great uncles and paternal grandfather, to found and manage a Wall Street brokerage firm at the turn of the 20th century.

My family's business acumen over multiple generations blessed us with material abundance. As a child, I grew up with servants on a 75-acre parcel of land that had been a farm in New Canaan, Connecticut. My parents built a house there soon after World War II. It was a beautiful, formal home with nine bedrooms and eight and a half bathrooms. The rear part of the house was where the servants lived: a cook and butler, a chamber maid, and the governess. Dinner was served to us each night by our butler, William, who dressed in a bow tie and jacket. As one of five boys, I grew up spending my falls, winters, and springs running across hills, playing games in the forest and on the lawns, and fording streams. Summers were spent on the pristine beaches of Cape Cod, where my father indulged his passion for sailing, a passion I too embraced from the age of 4. It is one of the few pleasant memories that connects me with my father to this day.

Yes, growing up we were materially very comfortable. But in our household, emotional distance was the norm. Both of my parents were cold and aloof, which is why, at an early age, I formed a close attachment to a woman named Bibi, who was my governess. I absolutely adored Bibi, but when I was about eight years old my parents decided that Bibi and I had grown too close for my own good. Without any warning they fired her, unbeknownst to me.

I remember the day clearly even now.

Bibi had Thursdays off, and I typically came to her room Friday mornings to say hello. On one particular Friday morning in 1959, I remember my mother coming down the hallway of our house, her crisp, pressed cotton dress rustling as she walked. She came upon me as I waited to see Bibi and told me Bibi had been dismissed. I would never see her again. I was crushed! I'd grown so attached to Bibi, closer to her, in fact, than to my own mother, which she must have realized. So, she and my father had decided Bibi needed to be erased from my life forever.

"You'll never see her again!"

As my mother's harsh words echoed in my innocent, eight-year-old ears, time seemed to stop.

To this day, I still remember standing and staring at the plain, white door that led to the servant's quarters from our house, through which I always walked to connect with Bibi on Fridays. But now I felt unable to open it. In fact, what seemed to loom before me was not a door but an enormous chasm. I felt myself teetering, as if on the edge of a cliff, about to fall over.

Recalling that moment today, nearly 60 years later, I believe I was experiencing the first moments of grief, my mind racing as my eight-year-old psyche struggled to make meaning of what had just happened to me.

I'll never forget the images of that day. On that day, in that hallway, brute reality intruded into my idyllic childhood existence, and swept away someone very dear to me. In some respects, you could liken my feelings that day to the emotions that victims of hurricanes and tornadoes feel when they experience their worlds ripped quickly asunder—without warning or explanation. On that day, I felt the emotional umbilical cord of my life was cut. The moment proved to be a traumatic loss of innocence for me that led to several years of debilitating depression. Depression that was only gradually relieved by therapy, tears, and time.

A few years later, when I was 16, I was in the library of our home when our maid, Jenny, brought someone by to see me. Jenny told me it was somebody I'd known many years before. But when I met the surprise visitor I didn't recognize her. Only later did I learn that it was Bibi. After I failed to recognize her, I'm told that Bibi left our house, never to return. I also learned that when she left my parents' employ, she gave up working as a governess. That day, my non-recognition of her in the library must have left her as heartbroken as her departure many years before had left me.

Bibi's abrupt exit from my life proved, in retrospect, to be a foundational life story for me. This early and painful loss of "perfect love" affirmed in my young psyche the importance of relationships, stability, stewardship, love, and connection with others, and helped forge the "emotional template" that is the basis of the person I am today.

Bibi had abruptly left my life, but thankfully there was another person in my household with whom I could emotionally connect as a young person. William, our butler, perhaps intuitively stepped in and filled the void, becoming a surrogate father to me in the years that followed. He was *so* different from my father. My father had a dark side, a temper that could become volcanic, which on occasion was directed at me and my four brothers in the form of cold lectures, threats, and humiliating and shaming putdowns. At times he even whipped the family dog. For all these reasons, and the fact that he was seldom around, I never connected with him emotionally.

xvi   Preface

In contrast, William had a kind and steady way about him and was emotionally present to me in ways that reverberate to this day. It was not unusual for my parents to be gone during the day from our Connecticut house and for William and Jenny to be left to care for me and my brothers. In such instances I got to observe William up close and liked what I saw. William was, as they say, "a man's man." More hands-on than cerebral, he knew how to do *everything*. He knew how machines worked and how to fix things. He knew how to dress a turkey at Thanksgiving, as well as the fowl my parents brought home from their hunting trips in New York State. He knew how to get a carpet to lie flat. He even knew how to drive a car up a hill in deep snow without getting stuck. One year, he managed to retrieve our family car from a snow bank in our driveway, after my father ditched it there at the height of a blizzard.

Truth be told, I worshipped William as a boy, and secretly wished he was my father, just as I wished that Bibi was my mother. He held me in his thrall, and filled a tremendous emotional void. Always there, taking care of things. Taking care of me! He seemed the embodiment of responsible stewardship. His presence (like Bibi's earlier in my life) made me realize how important connections with other people were to me, and explains why stewardship (the "looking after of things") is a key theme of the work I do today as a wealth advisor.

At 14, I left home and went to Milton Academy, a boarding school just south of Boston. My first year there was difficult for me academically. I was at sea, and it was only through tutoring and generous teachers that I managed to pull myself up. I started at the bottom of my class but graduated in the top third! My Milton housemaster had a lot to do with this. He nurtured me and encouraged me, coordinating my efforts with my parents' concerns and love. In tenth grade, he introduced me to Quakerism. Its subsequent influence on my life, and his abiding care of me throughout my teenage years, further cemented my attraction to stewardship and helped to create a "protector" personality in me, whose traits I bring to my work with clients today.

Because of my unique upbringing with surrogate-like parents and my early childhood loss of "perfect love," I grew up with a deep longing for connection with others, and an intense desire to understand human emotions—both mine and others'. These interests led me to choose social psychology as my major in college, because I was fascinated with the nature of interaction between people (no doubt an outgrowth of what I had observed in my own family system growing up). I was looking for clues to understand my parents' emotional remoteness, my desires for closeness and connection with them and others, and the strong emotional pull I felt toward

Bibi and William as a youngster. Social psychology thus seemed like a perfect course of study. As a discipline, it sought to unpack and explain the emotional dynamics that exist between individuals and groups. And, it put a high value on human emotions and motivations as keys to understanding human behavior and actions.

Eventually, however, my interest in social psychology waned. It became too academic for me. I sought more "juice." So, I migrated to theater and drama, where I pictured myself exploring the world of human emotions and motivations in greater depth, and doing it on stage! Looking back on it now, I clearly was in search of an understanding of my emotional self, willing to try on roles crafted by playwrights to see if any resonated as being me. But in my school's theatre department I encountered more adolescent egos than insights into the nature of human nature. So, after a momentary stab at acting and writing plays, I moved on again, still searching.

It was then that I discovered geology. Geology had an absence of human actors (and egos), so it was refreshing! There was plenty of drama though. Think Continental Drift, glacial flows, lunar landings and moon rocks! Talk about theater! The physical world provides a dramatic stage for a geologist, and something in this world and work resonated in me at the deepest levels of my being.

At a deeper, emotional level, geology is about stewardship of physical assets (land); about conservation; about careful observation and data-gathering of what's in front of you, and about developing a careful frame of reference that respects not only what you observe on the surface of things but also what lies beneath. As a science it appealed to my analytical side in a very robust way. Geology also gave me the opportunity to work closely with private clients to help them with the stewardship of their land, to understand their needs and desires, and to act as a consultant in helping them achieve long-term goals from their (physical) assets. Thus, it appealed to the stewardship and servant sides of my personality.

I worked happily in the field of geology for ten years, but though I loved the work the pay wasn't good, and I started to wonder how I was going to send my three sons to college. Moreover, I was looking for deeper, more substantive ways to be of service to others and to form long-term relationships with people. Working as a contract geologist generally meant consulting relationships of limited duration, after which I'd move on without further contact with a client.

For all these reasons, I began considering what else I could do with my life other than be a geologist. It was about this time that my interest in social psychology reasserted itself, along with what had been a long-time fascination with financial markets. As a wealth advisor himself, my father had always dissuaded my brothers and me from careers on Wall Street. He called it "dirty work." But somehow I found the machinations and gyrations of the financial markets fascinating nonetheless. Moreover, investing was an activity that involved disciplined thinking (as geology does) and that encompassed the full suite of interests I had in social psychology, behavioral finance, and stewardship. The idea of being able to build long-term relationships with clients whose money I would manage was like icing on the cake!

My move over 25 years ago from a career in geology to one in business and finance was one of the best decisions I've ever made. For more than a quarter century, I've had some wonderful mentors who helped me chart a course first to business school (Columbia) and then to jobs at CIGNA; Shawmut Bank in Hartford, Connecticut; Boston Private Bank and Trust; Fiduciary Trust; and several other companies. Today, I am a senior portfolio manager at Hemenway Trust Company.

Human emotions and their role in driving investor behavior have continued to fascinate me since the day I entered the wealth advisory business. Rewardingly, I've built my entire career as a wealth advisor around understanding the role that emotions and human psychology play in investor behavior, both in low-stakes and high-stakes situations.

As wealth advisors, we must pay attention to the rich human dramas that reside in our clients and understand the experiences, stories, hurts, fears, and moments of love and triumph that make them the unique individuals they are as adults.

Don't be afraid to discover this treasured material! Taking the time to unearth these dynamics is essential to helping us better serve our clients and continually deepen our knowledge and appreciation of human emotions as a wellspring of people's motivations and actions.

Working with the Emotional Investor is intended to provide you with tools and insights I've gathered from a 25-year career in the wealth advisory business. It's my hope that this book will enhance your own approach to working with clients, helping you to understand the unique dynamics of human nature and how these factors inevitably influence peoples' thinking and decision-making about investment planning and wealth management.

Chris White
Pocasset, MA
Summer 2015

Acknowledgments

When I think of all that has gone into writing this book, my first thoughts go to my clients. They have taught me so much about what is in this book. Without them, there would be little I could say. You know who you are. Some of you are tucked into the case studies, although you have been blended in many, many ways with your colleagues. Client confidentiality is always the most prized attribute. How else would clients ever open up about the intimate details regarding their lives, their memories, and their ambitions? So, the stories that are embedded as an essential part of this book are often an amalgamation of stories, with names changed and places altered. But the attention and the care and the interest are all as valid and real as when I first heard the stories told. Thank you for your generosity and your trust.

Of course, none of this would have happened without my mentors and the firms where I worked and the bosses I had. Of the former group, John Beck clearly opened the path before me that allowed me to successfully transition from geology and farming to investments. In the firms, a few people stand out: the management at CIGNA, who generously guided me in polishing my research skills. Thank you, Jim Samuels, Jim Giblin, and post-humously, Dave Shinn. At Shawmut Bank, Jeff Marsted importantly urged me to share more of myself with my clients, thereby showing them I cared deeply about them. Jeff, your guidance is what has led me to being so open in writing this book. And at Boston Private Bank, Jay Henderson assembled a team of people, including Bob Everett, Trip Hargrave, and Bob Quinn, all of whom it was an honor to work with and build. My friends and colleagues at Fiduciary Trust, including sailing companions Tad DeMarco and Charles Platt, were always a source of inspiration and education. Finally, I am happy to be at Hemenway Trust Company. I have always been inspired by the quality of work at Hemenway as personified by Mike Elefante and George Shaw. My current colleagues teach me every day what it means to care for clients.

I am indebted to Sara Hamilton of Family Office Exchange (FOX) who, along with Lee Hausner, encouraged me to write this book and who then introduced me to Rick Koonce. It was as if she shined a light on the path, illuminating a closed gate. Then she gave me the keys for the gate! Rick has led me forward ever since. I am grateful to him for not only turning my turgid academic prose into something readable, but also to introducing me to my agent, Sheree Bykofsky, and through her, to my publisher, Praeger Books. Through all of this, Rick has become a dear friend. Near the end of the writing process, my eyes were opened to the creative artwork of Julie Sherman. Julie has brought to life through her art what Rick and I have described in words. This three-way collaboration has made the homestretch of creating this book a joy.

Speaking of dear friends, David Kantor, psychologist extraordinaire, introduced me to many of the concepts that form the systems thinking and modeling I describe in these chapters. As a wise man, dare I say a wise old man, David always knew when to push me and call me to stretch further, bringing my models into fuller blossom. His coaching work and his therapy are artfully intertwined, and he taught me how to love my clients more deeply than ever.

My parents, who play such a large role in the Preface, provided many life lessons. I know that they cared for me as only parents can, communicating the love they knew from their families of origin. While I may have harsh words in describing their behavior at times, I know they did the absolute best they knew how to do. For that, I thank them. There would be no "my story" without them. Together with my parents, I embrace Bibi Hurlbut, William Ryan, and Bill Lingelbach, all from across the grave, for so enriching my early life.

I thank my children and their spouses for their patience and support. Jen, Nate and Charlie, Gavin and Suz, and Henry, thank you. My greatest coach, my greatest confidant, and my closest friend is also my wife, Alice. How many times did she patiently stand by me as I struggled to write the next chapter, the next page, even the next word? She sees so much more in this book than I could ever hope to dream. Yet, isn't that precisely what I would want in my friend and my wife? She is always calling me to a higher level in her love, and for that I am eternally grateful. It is to her that I dedicate this book.

C.W.

Introduction

As an investment advisor, how much time do you take to truly get to know your clients as *people*?

I've been working as an investment analyst, portfolio manager, investment coach, and wealth management advisor now for over 25 years, and if there's one vital lesson I've learned over time it's that people—*individuals, couples,* and *families*—are both complicated and conflicted when it comes to issues of money, retirement, wealth management, and investment planning.

There are many reasons for this.

First, I believe that people's views about money (and security) can usually be traced back to early life experiences of pain and loss associated with family, friends, relationships, and love. These formative experiences deeply influence the development of a person's "emotional template" and shape how they think about their assets, risk-taking, and their ability (or inability) to control people and events later in life. For example, the person who experiences significant personal or emotional loss early in life may, later in life, display little trust in others, a high need for security and control, and/or little tolerance for risk-taking when it comes to making investment decisions. I've often seen such dynamics at play when I work with certain clients or meet new client prospects for the first time.

Second, peoples' attitudes about money can be profoundly shaped by what their parents, grandparents, or other authority figures told them about it when they were growing up. Was your client encouraged, from an early age, to be frugal and save for a rainy day? Or, did he or she grow up as the product of profligate parents? People often carry such "messages" about money with them into their adult lives.

Third, some people's attitudes and feelings about money are shaped based on whether they grew up with wealth or achieved it for themselves. Hence, the popular, if somewhat simplistic image of wealth creators as world-class penny-pinchers, and wealth inheritors as world-class spendthrifts.

Still other people's views about money are influenced by family dynamics, personal beliefs, college professors, religious faith, and philosophical convictions. Who made the greatest impression on your client as a child or young adult?

Finally, people's attitudes about money (and risk-taking) are frequently driven by primal emotions like fear, greed, guilt, discomfort, even a sense of inadequacy. Such emotions can literally sweep over them, immobilizing them from making clear and rational choices or acting in their best interests at critical times.

People Are Complicated!

Yes, when it comes to money, people are complicated! Thus, it's vital that we, as wealth advisors, understand our clients—be they individuals, couples, or families—as emotional and psychological "systems." These systems are characterized by various dynamics which manifest themselves in specific behaviors and attitudes we can observe. It may require considerable time, experience, sensitivity, and maturity on our parts to understand and appreciate our clients in this light. However, only by understanding our clients as unique human systems can we hope to effectively advise them about their wealth management plans and priorities.

But wait, there's more!

We, as wealth advisors, are complicated "systems" too. We too are shaped in our attitudes about money based on our life experience and internalized "scripts." We see the world through our own set of filters; hence the bromide: "We see the world not as it is but as *we* are." For example, if you, as a wealth advisor, grew up without a lot of money and find yourself counseling somebody who's had it in their family for generations, you may harbor a hidden envy or even resentment about that client that can color your advice. Conversely, if you grew up with wealth as the son or daughter of a wealth creator, you may or may not (based on the parenting you received) have a deep appreciation and understanding of the first generation wealth creator you are now advising.

Understanding ourselves as systems (with our own inclinations, biases, subconscious beliefs, assumptions, aversions, and attractions) is thus just as important to our success as wealth management advisors as understanding the psyches (emotions, needs, fears, concerns, hopes, etc.) of our clients.

Finally, the stock market in which we operate as advisors is a system as well. Its unpredictability spooks investors, defies carefully designed financial models and elegant predictive reasoning, and leaves the world of investing looking like a crap shoot, a shot in the dark, a roll of the dice—an activity not for the faint of heart!

Why I Wrote This Book

It's because of all the human and emotional variables at play in investment advisor-client relationships that I decided to write *Working with the Emotional Investor: Financial Psychology for Wealth Managers*. For, as the title of this book suggests, a client's investment and wealth-building decisions are invariably colored and driven by a welter of emotional and psychological factors and forces—some of them obvious and clear, others subtle and hidden from easy view. Whether visible or hidden, these emotions and dynamics invariably surface when it comes to discussing matters of risk tolerance with a client, especially in times of marketplace volatility or uncertainty.

In my view, it's our duty as responsible and ethical wealth advisors to educate ourselves about these forces and factors and how they drive all human behavior. It's also incumbent on us to become conscientious students and observers of human nature in general and of our clients in particular. This is essential if we are to advise clients effectively and customize client investment "solutions" based on their personalities and degree of risk tolerance. Wealth advisors who are trained, sophisticated, and astute enough to probe and gain understanding of the emotional make-up of their clients will be able to connect with clients (be they individuals, couples, or families) in ways other advisors cannot. Indeed, they'll be able to co-create investment strategies and plans with their clients that are custom-suited to each client's personality, priorities, goals, and temperament.

By reading *Working with the Emotional Investor* you'll learn the following:

- Why all investing and risk-taking by clients is *emotional*—driven by psychological factors such as early experiences of love and traumatic loss, and by powerful, sometimes very subtle family dynamics that a child experiences early in his or her life.
- Why all clients therefore can be thought of as unique psychological systems with certain observable qualities and traits that an advisor must be sensitive to, in order to fully understand an individual, and to accurately assess that person's risk tolerance when developing investment and wealth management plans.
- Why wealth advisors must understand themselves as human systems as well, because of the ways it impacts their approach to working with clients.
- Why every client, based on their emotional/psychological template, displays a unique personality type in the context of the client-advisor relationship, and why

this type can change based on perceived risk and on factors such as market uncertainty and volatility.

In *Working with the Emotional Investor* you'll also learn to:

- Use my unique client typology to identify different client personalities and then choose the best way to engage a client.
- Employ sophisticated client relationship management practices such as curiosity, appreciative inquiry, powerful questions, and other tools to understand clients' needs and drives at a deep, psychological level.
- Apply my client management approach with equal effectiveness to client engagements involving individuals, couples, and families.

Working with the Emotional Investor is divided into three distinct parts.

In **Part I**, I explain and elaborate on my theory of emotional templating and how it explains a client's appetite for risk and view of the world around them. I share deeply personal experiences of emotional loss from my own childhood as examples to support my thesis that all people are essentially emotional in their responses to the external environment. A person's emotional vulnerabilities become particularly evident in situations of danger or pressure, such as when an investor faces marketplace uncertainty and volatility as they set personal financial goals. Given such realities, I argue that the wealth advisor must develop finely tuned interpersonal skills to flesh out the emotional profiles of their clients and must understand them as fully formed human beings, shaped by their unique experiences.

In **Part II**, I lay out a systematic framework that wealth advisors can use to nurture, manage, and maintain strong relationships with clients. Based on years of working with my own clients, this framework includes a proprietary method for "contracting" with clients early in the client-advisor process; establishing rapport and trust; asking clients powerful questions; setting goals and expectations; defining metrics of success; designing investment approaches that align with the client's goals, values, and priorities; and monitoring and measuring success with financial performance over time. Also in this section, I discuss different types of clients that wealth advisors are likely to encounter in their work, and the importance of advising clients by cultivating a combination of agility, flexibility, creativity and humility. I draw heavily from the theories, ideas, and best practices of social psychology, systems thinking, neuroscience, and emotional intelligence to articulate a highly practical typology of client types that I have developed over the course of my 25-plus years in investments.

Finally, in **Part III**, I speak in depth about stewardship and the principles of servant leadership that I believe are critical for wealth advisors to bring to their work with clients. By adopting the principles of "servanthood" in our work with clients, we can keep our professional egos and agendas in check and ensure that the investment plans we co-create with clients are strongly aligned with their personal values, financial goals, and investment and wealth management priorities.

While much of my client work has been with high net worth individuals and families, this book has relevance and application for any wealth advisor who deals with the assets of others, whether those assets be $100,000, $1,000,000, $1,000,000,000, or even more!

Working with the Emotional Investor articulates a new, radical, yet highly practical approach to building and nurturing client relationships in the wealth management industry today. Some of what I say in this book you may find provocative. I hope you do! I hope also that you will see the relevance of the tools and case studies I present in this book to your own work with clients.

It's my conviction that by reading and reflecting on what is contained on the following pages, it will spark ideas and generate insights that will enrich your own relationships with current and future clients, resulting in "happy returns" for you both!

PART I

How Human Psychology and Client Emotions Drive Investor Behavior and Decision-Making

CHAPTER ONE

Understanding a Person's Emotional Template

Our current understanding of emotion lags far behind our understanding of nearly every other aspect of life. We can chart the universe and split the atom, but we can't seem to understand or manage our natural emotional reactions to provoking situations. We work with nutrition and exercise to increase our energy, but we ignore the richest source of energy we possess—our emotions. We are intellectually brilliant, physically resourceful, spiritually imaginative, but emotionally underdeveloped. This is a shame because emotions contain indispensable vitality that can be channeled toward self-knowledge, interpersonal awareness, and profound healing. Unfortunately we don't treat them as such. Instead, emotions are categorized, celebrated, vilified, repressed, manipulated, humiliated, adored, and ignored. Rarely, if ever are they honored.

—*From* The Language of Emotions *by Karla McLaren (Introduction)*

Emotions. We want to think (and believe) that they play no role, have no place, in the "rationally ordered" world of investing and wealth management. After all, as wealth advisors, we go to business school to study business and economics, not psychology. In our wealth management training we are schooled in the use of algorithms, fancy financial models, economic theory, and predictive reasoning to forecast future return rates. Indeed, one of the essential books in my coursework at Columbia Business School was *The Intelligent Investor* by Benjamin Graham.

But, in fact, much of the motivation for investing is rooted in *emotions*. Ours and those of our clients! It's critical to acknowledge this.

Thus, I've written this book, not to disparage quantitative tools and reason as they apply to investing, but to enlarge and broaden conversations about investing beyond the purely rational.

What exactly is "emotion"? It's hard to define. Remember Supreme Court Justice Potter Stewart's iconic 1964 freedom of speech case, when, referring to pornography, he penned, "I know it when I see it"? The same goes for emotion. Dictionary.com defines emotion as "a natural, instinctive state of mind deriving from one's circumstances, mood, or relationships with others." Further, it continues, it is an "instinctive or intuitive feeling as distinguished from reasoning or knowledge." I would argue vigorously (and will do so throughout this book) that even one's "reasoning" or "knowledge" can be colored by emotions and life experience!

Our Clients Are Psychological Systems Driven by Emotions

In the Introduction to this book, I noted that, as wealth advisors, one of the key principles we have to keep in mind is that every client we deal with is a psychological "system." And a unique one at that. We are composites of our life experiences of love, joy, pain, fear, and loss, ultimately forming the building blocks of our personalities, or what I like to refer to as our "emotional template." This template holds the DNA that explains who we are and why we act as we do. Think of this template as a kind of human software program that provides and sustains the basic functions of our personality. It is, in essence, the system that supports many of our basic and higher functions as human beings and is the source of our behaviors, beliefs, and human motivations.

The Formation of a Person's Emotional Template

As a lifelong student of social psychology and human behavior, I have always been fascinated with how people's emotional templates are formed. Evolutionary biology, of course, plays a huge role. So do the early formative experiences we have that establish the emotional and psychological response patterns that become fully formed in us as adults.

The study of people's emotional natures has been profoundly useful to me in helping me understand how best to work with clients on an individual basis, especially in high-stress or high-stakes situations.

As an advisor, I routinely observe clients and colleagues whose personal and emotional make-up strongly influences both their risk-taking tolerance (high or low) and investment style. In my own case, the loss of my beloved Bibi, whom I mentioned in the Preface, was a painful yet formative experience for me. I transmuted this experience of personal hurt and loss into a determination to protect not only myself but also those around me. Over many years, the concepts of stewardship, compassion, and commitment to others thus emerged and became powerful convictions for me, as I psychologically worked through issues of my own childhood. Today, these principles are among the most important tenets of my philosophy as a wealth advisor.

I am what psychologist David Kantor would call a "Protector" personality, having molded myself, in large part, after William and others whom I mentioned in the Preface. My "Protector" tendencies, which are at the heart of my emotional template today, display themselves daily in my working relationships with clients. Protecting the assets of my clients and being a good steward of people's hard-earned wealth are at the core of my being. This emotional core serves as my emotional, psychological, and ethical guidance system in working with individuals, couples, and families.

Peoples' emotional templates vary, of course, based on their early life experiences. One wealth advisor colleague of mine, "Jake," chooses today to work exclusively in the domain of private equity, with its ten-year holding periods and extended framework for resolving losses and gains from investments. Why does he specialize in this line of work? Jake would argue that having been abandoned by his father at an early age, and having had to deal with the trauma and pain of that experience, his personality is geared toward security, stability, and predictability. Kantor would describe him as a "Survivor" who dealt with his childhood experience of loss by adopting a profession and investment strategy that, as an adult, enable him to safeguard both his financial (and I would argue psychological) safety in anticipation of potential financial losses at a later time.

Another colleague of mine, "Jeremy," whose father was abusive and controlling, is today often personally abusive himself. Financial losses trigger deep despondency and grief in him, reminding him of the ignominy of loss and hurt at the hands of his abusive father. The intensity of Jeremy's emotional pain is only assuaged by the intense relief he experiences from occasionally winning with good stock picks. Not surprisingly, Jeremy likes to invest in value stocks that few others like and finds deep solace from being a loner and outlier. If his stocks eventually wind up doing well, he credits it to his brilliance and insight. If they don't, he has a tendency to beat himself up. He is what Kantor would call a "Fixer" personality.

Finally, still another colleague of mine, "Elizabeth," chose in childhood to react to her father's abandonment by striving to control and exert power over everything she can in life. Today, Elizabeth goes for broke in her investment work as a hedge fund manager. She, too, is what Kantor would call a "Fixer."

In the choices that I, and others, have made as adults, we are all attempting to work through and "work out" the losses of love and expectation we experienced in childhood. In doing so, our identities are shaped, in part, by the emotional bandages we apply to our wounds. Consequently, there's the "Protector," who safeguards the money of others; the private equity manager ("Survivor") who looks for solace and security in long-term investments; the stubborn value manager ("Fixer") who seeks validation of his brilliance and worth as a human being; and the hedge fund manager ("Fixer") who "goes for broke" in the investment decisions she makes for herself and others.

Both clients and advisors thus bring their emotional templates with them to client-advisor interactions. Throughout this book, I'll have a great deal to say about different personality types and how they show up in client-advisor relationships. For now, suffice it to say that understanding the psychology of your clients (and yourself) is key to navigating and negotiating the interpersonal dynamics that are always present in advisory relationships and that come clearly—and critically—to the fore in high-stakes situations.

Harvesting Insights from Psychology and Behavioral Finance

Today, the intersection of emotions, psychology, financial markets, and investing has become a topic of compelling interest to many writers, financial journalists, researchers, and scholars. New insights from behavioral finance, neuroscience, and brain research are helping us to better understand the psychology and biology of financial decision-making as never before, and this has tremendous implications for the work we do as wealth advisors.

Psychologists Daniel Kahneman and Amos Tversky were among the early pioneers and researchers in the areas of psychology, human behavior, and finance. Both men became fascinated with the application of psychological concepts to economics. Classic economics had always held that investors (indeed all consumers) experience financial gains and losses with equal degrees of intensity. In other words, a dollar gained would give the same amount of pleasure to an investor as a dollar lost would cause pain. Kahneman and Tversky doubted this hypothesis. In fact, through their research, first conducted at Hebrew University in Israel in the 1970s, they observed that the amount of pain subjects felt from a loss was TWICE as intense as the amount of pleasure they experienced from a gain. This breakthrough insight came to be known as "loss aversion." Loss aversion argues that a person who loses $100 will suffer twice as much pain from that loss as another person will gain satisfaction from a $100 windfall.

The roots of human loss aversion can be found deep in the forests of our evolutionary past. In such thickets "'sensitivity to losses was probably more [critical] than the appreciation of gains,'" according to Tversky. "'It

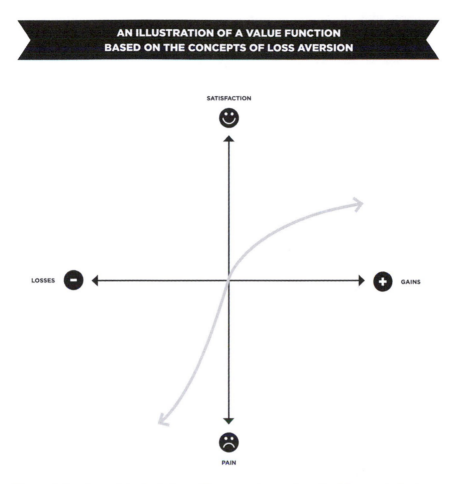

**AN ILLUSTRATION OF A VALUE FUNCTION
BASED ON THE CONCEPTS OF LOSS AVERSION**

SATISFACTION

LOSSES   GAINS

PAIN

Figure 1.1 A graphic depiction of loss aversion as described by psychologists Amos Tversky and Daniel Kahneman. The gray line above the x axis "flattens" to show that the experience of pleasure derived from a gain is only half as intense as the experience of pain sustained from a loss.

Source: Kahneman, Daniel, and Amos Tversky, "Prospect Theory: An Analysis of Decision Under Risk." *Econometrica*, XLVII [1979], p. 279.

would have been wonderful to be a species that was almost insensitive to pain and had an infinite capacity to appreciate pleasure. But you probably wouldn't have survived the evolutionary battle.'"[1]

Kahneman and Tversky's work helped to demonstrate that investing, because of the asymmetry of payoffs, is *emotional*. They noted that the anticipation of winning can be highly charged, the confirmation of winning slightly less satisfying, while the prospect of loss is *grievous!*[2] As a wealth advisor, it's critical for you to remember that such dynamics may be at work in the minds of your clients, even when the decision of what to do in a given client situation seems simple and straightforward to you!

The implications of Kahneman and Tversky's work were groundbreaking, shedding new light on what shapes investor and marketplace thinking. These visionaries helped to definitively explain behavioral attitudes toward risk and loss and to predict how investors often behave under conditions of uncertainty. The desire to avoid loss, for example, can be a powerful driver in investment decision-making and whether one "takes the bet" on an investment or not. In some cases, investors become frozen with fear and don't accept that they must take action to avoid losses that are on the horizon. In such instances, risk aversion overrides rational decision-making!

Thinking, Fast and Slow

Sadly, Tversky died before he could share in the honor of winning the Nobel Prize in Economic Sciences with Kahneman in 2002 for the work they did together. Kahneman went on to publish a book, *Thinking, Fast and Slow* in 2011, a book based in part on the work he did with Tversky that delves deeply into a discussion of how the brain makes decisions at one of two levels—the emotional or "fast" level (System One)—and at the purposeful, "slow" level of focused thinking, reflection, and concentration (System Two). System One thinking is generally effortless and almost automatic; people make decisions and judgments based on familiar patterns. System Two thinking requires more effort and operates in a logical and methodical way. Significantly, Kahneman notes that most people would say that they act primarily at a System Two level in daily life (exercising conscious reasoning, reflective thinking) when in fact they more likely operate at a System One level which is impulsive, automatic, and inclined to reduce life's randomness and complexities to simple truths. Keep Kahneman's typology of thinking types in mind, the next time you're trying to figure out what motivates a particular client in making investment decisions. What are the triggers? Under stress, is the client more likely to display System One thinking? Or System Two thinking? Or perhaps some combination of both?

Meanwhile, consider how "fast" and "slow" thinking differentiates the investment recommendations of the two investment advisors in Appendix A: "Thinking, Fast and Slow: The Differences in Two Philosophies of Trading."

Your Money and Your Brain

Another author whose work in the area of behavioral finance I admire and find highly useful in understanding client-advisor dynamics is Jason Zweig. Zweig has written an insightful book, *Your Money and Your Brain*, in which he discusses how scientists in the emerging discipline of neuroeconomics are making breakthrough discoveries about how the human brain assesses rewards and risks, and calculates the probabilities of gain and loss.

The Reflexive and Reflective Brain

Zweig and others have articulated compelling distinctions between what they call the *reflexive* brain and the *reflective* brain. The *reflexive* brain is driven by primitive, reptilian fears that derive from our evolutionary past. The impulses that emanate from this part of our brain are largely fear-based and hard-wired to our drive to survive. The reflexive brain is responsible for "everything from the 'startle reflex' and pattern recognition to the perception of risk or reward and the character judgments about the people we meet."[3] Thus, behaviors that emanate from this part of the brain may be driven by impulses to survive. Reflexive thinking processes tend to operate "rapidly, automatically, and below the level of consciousness."[4] In contrast, the *reflective* part of our brain is the part that behaves on a higher level, using reason and knowledge to curb impulses and to take deliberate, thoughtful action.[5]

Zweig notes that the growing use of magnetic resonance imaging (MRI) is helping to illuminate how the human brain operates in both these areas and showcases the unique evolutionary brain circuitry that becomes engaged when an individual engages in investing. He observes that when a person wins, loses, or risks money (in controlled laboratory experiments) it lights up the neural pathways of the human brain in remarkable ways, and activates strong emotions, including hope, surprise, regret, greed, and fear. "Understanding how those feelings—as a matter of biology—affect your decision-making [can] enable you to see as never before what makes you tick, and how you can improve, as an investor," says Zweig.[6]

Why Anticipating Gain Is More Intense Than Realizing It

Zweig notes that the human brain contains a region called the nucleus accumbens, which (amazingly) becomes more aroused when a person *anticipates* a profit than when he or she actually gets one. The reason?

A mechanism that researcher Jaak Panksepp of Bowling Green State University describes as the human brain's "seeking system." Over millions of years of evolution "it was the thrill of anticipation that put our senses in a state of high awareness, bracing us to capture uncertain rewards," says Zweig.[7] He cites the work of Paul Slovic, a psychologist at the University of Oregon, who says that our anticipatory "hard-wiring" includes "'beacon of incentive'" which "enables us to pursue rewards that can be earned only with patience and commitment."[8] Zweig wryly observes that if we received no pleasure from imagining riches down the road, "we would grab only at those gains that loom immediately in front of us."[9]

What We Think Can Be Both a Blessing and a Curse

The human seeking system operates "partly as a blessing and partly as a curse," according to Zweig. That's because "We pay close attention to the possibilities of coming rewards, but we also expect that the future will feel better than it does once it turns into the present."[10]

Zweig notes that a textbook example of this phenomenon occurred in the performance of the stock of Celera Genomics Group. Back in September 1999, Celera started to sequence the human genome. Through identifying the 3 billion molecular pairings that make up human DNA, the company stood to make a huge leap in human understanding of biotechnology. Thus, investors at the time went crazy with excitement and anticipation. The stock reached a peak of $244 in early 2000. Then, on June 26, Celera announced to the world that it had actually completed its work. The stock reacted by dropping 10.2% that day and another 12.7% the day afterwards. Zweig postulates that the most likely reason the stock tanked as it did is because anticipation of Celera's DNA breakthrough was so strong that actual accomplishment of the feat was a "letdown." "Getting exactly what they wished for left investors with nothing to look forward to, so they got out and the stock crashed."[11]

The Biology of Emotion

Zweig says that while scientists have found that a person's reflexive brain is highly sensitive to changes in the amount of reward at stake, it is less responsive to changes in the likelihood of getting rewards. Say you're in a lottery where the potential jackpot is $100 million and your odds of winning fall from 1 in 10 million to 1 in 100 million. Would you be ten times less likely to buy a ticket? Apparently not, because the prospect of winning $100 million sets off such a strong burst of anticipation in the reflexive parts of the brain that only later on does the analytical (reflective) part of the brain calculate the actual probability of a win![12]

The lesson in this mini-tutorial on brain chemistry? When you buy a stock or mutual fund your "expectation of scoring a big gain elbows aside your ability to evaluate how likely you are to earn it," says Zweig. Consequently, "your brain can get you into trouble whenever you're confronted with an opportunity to buy an investment with a hot, but probably unsustainable return."[13]

Emotional Styles

Yet another author whose work in the field of neuroscience research I admire and find useful is Richard J. Davidson, PhD, professor of psychology and psychiatry at the University of Wisconsin-Madison. In his book *The Emotional Life of Your Brain*, Davidson argues that every human being possesses a unique "emotional fingerprint" comprised of six "Emotional Styles" that relate to resilience, personal outlook, social intuition, self-awareness, sensitivity to context, and attention, and that this explains why some people recover quickly from setbacks while others get trapped in a downward spiral of despair and despondency. A person's "Resilience Style" has to do with how readily they can recover from challenges or setbacks. An individual's "Outlook Style" has to do with their capacity to maintain a positive mindset, even in adverse circumstances. An individual's "Social Intuition Style" relates to one's deftness at reading social cues and clues from those around them. A person's "Self-Awareness Style" refers to their awareness of how their thoughts and feelings affect their body. A person's "Sensitivity to Context style" refers to emotional self-regulation; in other words, how good they are at managing their emotions in a particular context. Finally, an individual's "Attention Style" refers to a person's ability to screen out unwanted or unproductive emotions and stay focused on a task at hand.[14]

"Everyone has elements of each of these dimensions of Emotional Style," says Davidson. "Think of the six dimensions as ingredients in the recipe for your emotional make-up."[15]

Davidson's work has helped to illuminate for me many of the elements that go into the formation of a person's emotional template, and how a person might reasonably and predictably respond in both low-stakes and high-stakes circumstances. While Davidson focuses on how the six Emotional Styles affect a person's overall health and wellness, I believe that understanding these dimensions of emotional response (particularly those related to Resilience, Outlook, and Attention) can greatly help advisors in understanding their clients and the motivations that drive people's investing and risk-taking behaviors, especially in high-stakes circumstances.

Dealing with Emotions in Our Clients

Thus far in this chapter I've discussed the biological and psychological basis of human emotions and behavior, which, I believe, is highly relevant to our work with clients. Now, I want to pivot to talk more about how we can best understand and respond to the specific emotions and behaviors that clients display in our presence, especially in high-stakes situations.

Clearly, every individual client we work with is unique. However, I have long observed that different kinds of clients operate by displaying specific behavioral traits, and that these traits fall into one of several specific categories. For quite a long time, I struggled to come up with a typology (and taxonomy) through which to understand and organize my observations of such behaviors, and to categorize clients (without dehumanizing them) in order to develop appropriate strategies to deal with different kinds of people in different situations.

Understanding Human Behavior: A Model and Taxonomy

Then, I discovered the work and theories of Dr. David Kantor, whom I mentioned earlier. Kantor, a Cambridge, Massachusetts, psychologist and consultant, is a major thought leader in the fields of social psychology and group dynamics. His work in the area of group dynamics has been especially useful to me in decoding human motivations and behavior, understanding how people act in different situations and circumstances, and organizing my understandings about people into a practical taxonomy.

Some years ago, Kantor devised a complex, multilevel model to explain how people tend to operate in the world, an adaption of which is shown in Figure 1.2. In my opinion, this model provides a nuanced way of understanding how people show up in group settings or in one-on-one interactions with others. But it goes beyond that. It also provides a basis for understanding not only how we behave and the personalities and interpersonal styles we adopt, but *why* we behave as we do.

If you look at the model in Figure 1.2, you'll see that Kantor's model of group and interpersonal dynamics ultimately derives from the formative childhood stories we all experience as we are growing up (Level IV in the model). Our childhood stories become the foundation for all that we then become, and they reverberate with implications throughout our lives, reflected in how we appear to others in the world, how we communicate

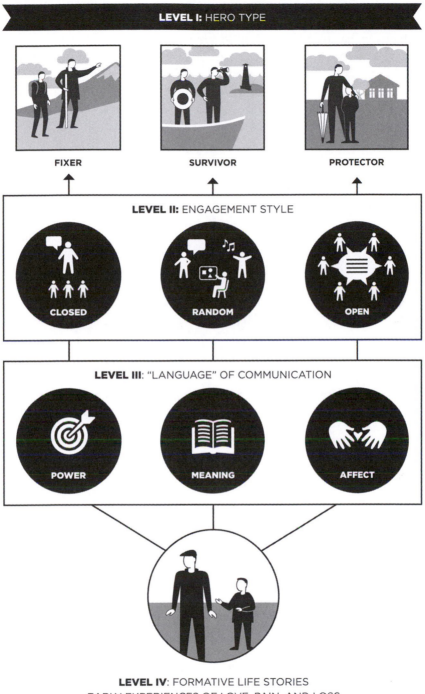

Figure 1.2 Understanding what contributes to the formation of an individual's emotional template.

with others, behave in the face of adversity and challenges, make decisions, and even in the conversational "stances" we take in conversation and group situations with others. By acquiring an understanding of this model, and how the various levels work together, it's possible to illuminate many aspects of a person's emotional template—or, as Kantor puts it, to understand a person's overall behavioral propensities profile (BPP).

So let's now look at each of these components of Kantor's model in greater detail.

Level IV: Childhood Stories

Kantor argues that much of a person's personality (emotional template) is formed as the result of childhood stories that become foundational in our development, first as children, then as adolescents and mature adults. The life "lessons" contained in our early stories (about love, loss, pain, hurt, power, powerlessness, etc.) become operating code for the development of our psyches and how we then see ourselves *vis a vis* the world. In Kantor's mind, the importance and centrality of early life stories, rooted in our first experience of the world around us, cannot be overestimated.

> We all gather stories about ourselves. From the age when we are first able to observe ourselves as objects in the world, we form and store our own experiences and identities in narrative form. Our identity and its support-ing stories shape what we say and how we react to what others say. To truly comprehend the structure of talk, we want to know as much as we can about our own underlying stories and those of others.[16]

Kantor's thinking is very much in line with what other psychologists refer to as "object relations theory"—a fancy term describing the process by which people relate to others and situations in their adult lives, based on experiences they have early in childhood.

Kantor says that the realm of "personal story and identity" is not an easy one to plumb, but by doing so, we can develop a deep understanding of human nature. That's because at any moment in life human beings "are hugely affected by their own identities, their self-told stories, and the state of their private lives."[17]

When I first read of Kantor's theories about personality development they resonated with me on many levels. They spoke to the importance of under-standing one's own emotional and psychological makeup, and committing oneself to the ongoing life tasks of personal development, self-actualization, and "meaning making" in all things one does. I also realized that by better understanding my own emotions, I could serve others more effectively in my capacity as an advisor.

Level III: Language of Communication: Power, Meaning, and Affect

Based on our earliest childhood experiences, all people develop preferred ways of communicating with others. Consequently, Kantor notes that all human beings tend to communicate in the "language" of *affect*, *power*, or *meaning*.

Consider how this could impact your work with clients.

Kantor says that people who communicate "in affect" tend to focus on their own feelings and those of others. Consequently, a client of yours who communicates "in affect" is likely to focus a great deal on the likely impact and implications for others of his/her investment planning or wealth management decisions.

In contrast, people who communicate "in power" tend to focus on getting things done. Thus, a client of yours who communicates "in power" is likely to be directive with you and focus on holding you to the specific investment objectives or targets the two of you may have agreed to. He or she tends to be task and results-oriented and puts more emphasis on completing tasks than on people or group process.

Finally, individuals who communicate "in meaning" are focused on the meaning and significance of their actions.[18] A client of yours who communicates with you "in meaning" is likely to focus on the logic and ideas behind specific decisions the two of you make, or to suggest and broach new ideas for the two of you to consider as part of your ongoing work together.

These "languages" of communication represent a person's overall orientation to the world and others around them, according to Kantor.[19]

Level II: Engagement Style

Just as every individual tends to adopt a specific "language" of communication, each of us also engages with others in specific ways, abiding by an "implicit set of rules" when in conversation or interaction with others. These "rules" govern how a person actually behaves, operates, and interacts with others in interpersonal and group situations.

Kantor identifies three specific engagement styles[20] that people typically display with others: open, closed, and random.

People who operate using an "open" engagement style tend to be highly social and interactive with others. They enjoy conversation, make decisions based on input from multiple sources, and work with others to achieve consensus around topics of discussion. Individuals (clients) who favor this engagement approach display a strong "give and take" attitude when interacting with others, including you, as their investment advisor. In considering investment options and plans, they're likely to want to explore many options, elicit input from you and others, and carefully weigh alternatives as part of making wealth management decisions.

People (i.e., clients) who operate using a "closed" engagement style tend to be more transactional than relational in their style of engagement with others. They're often very business-like, can dislike small talk, and focus most of their time and energy on concrete discussions of options and choices. They are disciplined decision-makers and won't be as focused on developing a relationship with you, as their advisor, as they will be on the results to be achieved by you on their behalf! A client who uses a closed system of communication with you may come across as somewhat rigid or regimented. He or she may look to you as the leader or authority in the relationship or may assume that role for themselves. In any case, when working with this kind of client it's important to explicitly "contract" around the way the two of you will work together so that expectations and roles are clear.

Finally, some people prefer to operate using a "random" engagement style. People who favor this engagement style tend to be great brainstormers. They love to kick around ideas, explore multiple options and are often highly creative (if also unstructured) in their approach to investment planning. Clients who display this preference may appear scattered, undisciplined, distracted, or unfocused in their discussions with you. It's important to meet this client where he or she is, and to provide the structure necessary to create a successful client-advisor relationship. I'll have much to say about engagement styles in Chapter Four.

Level I: "Hero" Types

Given that we are all shaped by early life experiences, our personalities inevitably take form and develop specific characteristics. Kantor says that human beings tend to exhibit one of several specific "hero types" in their daily existence, and that these can be observed both in low-stakes and high-stakes situations but are especially critical to understand in high-stakes situations. These "hero types" include the "Fixer," the "Survivor," and the

"Protector."[21] I briefly noted examples of each type earlier in this chapter. Each is characterized is by its own set of unique behaviors and motivations.

Fixers. Fixers are individuals who have an indomitable will that motivates them to overcome whatever obstacles come their way. It might be an enemy, adversary, or a unique personal challenge or threatening situation—a plunging stock market for example! Under normal, everyday (low-stress or low-stakes) circumstances, "Fixers" can be charming, even charismatic. In high-stakes situations, Fixers can change radically, becoming power hungry and overly controlling. Fixers generally operate in the language of "power." If you have a Fixer for a client, you generally know it. They like to be in charge and in control!

Survivors. Survivors operate largely in the language of "meaning." Strong belief—in causes, people, values, even specific approaches to investing—leads Survivors to be willing to sacrifice themselves, often "to the dismay of those they love," says Kantor.[22] Survivors often come across as martyrs or champions of noble (if sometimes) lost causes. If you have a Survivor client and the markets are in free fall, the Survivor is likely to say to you, "I'll get through this; I know I will!" Under extreme circumstances, Survivors dig their heels in. A cause can become a fanatical obsession. And when things don't go their way, they can often lash out at others, including you, as their financial advisor.

Protectors. Protectors operate primarily in the language of "affect." They use the language of feeling and emotion fluently, are focused primarily on the care of and consideration of those around them, and have a strong ability to empathize with others, even when faced with difficult decisions. If you have a Protector as a client you'll know it, because as part of their estate, investment, and retirement planning activities they are likely to talk in depth about others, including spouses, children, family members, and friends. They are guardians, stewards, and caretakers by nature.

Kantor says that the traits of each hero type become increasingly pronounced in an individual as the pressure or stress on a person increases, and they see themselves at risk or in circumstances of increasing stakes. From my professional experience, the traits of each "hero type" become abundantly clear in financial discussions with clients when markets become volatile or when a client suddenly has to deal with personal, financial, or family uncertainties and/or the threat or reality of financial losses. When a person's life circumstances change from low stakes to high stakes Kantor describes this as going from living in the "light zone" (low stakes) to the "gray" zone (intermediate stress or pressure) to the "dark" (or high stakes) zone—sometimes called the "shadow." As you'll discover in later chapters, when a client begins to operate in their "dark" zone (under circumstances of high pressure or stress) it can become problematic for an advisor to deal with.

Understanding Human Motivation and Action

The four-level model outlined by Kantor is a powerful framework through which to understand human emotions and behavior and provides an elegant way to comprehend and appreciate different behavioral styles/tendencies that you may observe in your clients. I like to think of it as a kind of "unified field theory" (theory of everything) that goes a long way toward explaining the nature and origin of all human emotion and action.

Later chapters of *Working with the Emotional Investor* will explore the various elements of Kantor's structural dynamics model in much more detail and provide you with strategies and insights for dealing with people who display the behavioral propensities of Fixers, Survivors, and Protectors in a variety of circumstances, but particularly in high-stakes situations.

For now, suffice it to say that I believe Kantor's BPP model provides a unique and rich way to look at the origins and nature of human emotions and motivations in both low-stakes and high-stakes situations. For us as wealth advisors, however, the practicality of the model's use in high-stakes client situations is particularly important.

Chapter Conclusions

In this chapter I've discussed the origins of the human "emotional template" (psychological system), which has its basis in both evolutionary biology and formative life stories that help shape our psyches as children, adolescents, and adults. I've also talked about how evolutionary biology and brain function shape human emotions and behavior—including risk-taking and investing—and have introduced a framework (Kantor's model) for understanding how our formative early life experiences (stories) go on to shape our psyches, emotions, behaviors, beliefs, and formation of "hero" types under situations of high stakes.

To be an effective wealth advisor today you must not only be a knowledgeable wealth management and investment planning expert but also a sensitive, self-aware, and discerning observer of human nature, behaviors, and motivations. By understanding all these factors, you'll be able to serve your clients in ways that your colleagues cannot. For you will bring the hugely important component of emotions and behavior to bear, not only to better understand your clients and what makes them tick but to work with them in a way that is aligned with their emotional nature and temperament. You will learn to observe, discern, and map courses of action with clients, based on your knowledge of their emotional template, and learn how this drives and shapes their behavior, beliefs, values, and goals in high-stakes situations.

CHAPTER TWO

The Psychology of Money and the Emotions of Investing

I can calculate the motion of heavenly bodies, but not the madness of people.
—*Sir Isaac Newton*

In Chapter One I briefly discussed why investing (making money and potentially losing it) is a highly emotional experience. I identified the powerful role that anticipation and fear play in such circumstances, and how they can light up the brain with neural activity. In this chapter we will discuss in greater depth:

- The complicated mix of emotions that investors experience, especially in times of high stakes and high stress.
- Beliefs about money and why these provide a powerful window into human nature and a basis for understanding human emotions and motivations.
- The potent power of loss, which we touched on with discussion of Kahneman and Tversky's model of "loss aversion" in Chapter One.
- How investing takes place in a range of emotional environments, just as it takes place in a range of market conditions, from the placid lagoon to the raging seas.
- The role that we, as advisors, need to play in high-stakes situations to help our clients successfully navigate what are often rapidly changing marketplace and personal circumstances.

The Brain-Biology-Belief-Behavior Connection

To get started, let's drill down more deeply into a discussion of emotions and how they can trigger an intense brain-biology-belief-behavior *connection*. In *Your Money and Your Brain,* Jason Zweig writes that scientists have determined that the brains of cocaine addicts who are expecting a fix have a lot in common with the brains of investors who are expecting a big pay-out from a risky financial move. "The similarity isn't just striking: it's chilling," he says, "Lay an MRI brain scan of a cocaine addict next to one of somebody who thinks he's about to make money, and the patterns of neurons firing in the two images" appear virtually identical.[1]

Love and Loss

So why does money—especially the loss or potential loss of it, have such a profound effect on us? Zweig notes that "financial losses are processed in the same areas of the brain that respond to mortal danger."[2] But there's more to the story than that.

It's been my observation, as I've worked with clients over the years, that loss is a grievous experience for people. I have certainly felt the emotional pain of financial losses myself. No money manager worth their salt would say otherwise. I believe that financial losses resonate deeply in us because of the experience of emotional losses (hurt) we have in early childhood. Remember, our emotional templates reflect conditioned responses based on early, always formative, and sometimes searing emotional experiences. Emotional losses that you or your clients might have experienced in childhood might not be obvious at first blush, but it's my belief that one's experience of financial loss as an adult triggers recall (almost like a flashback) of early experiences in the "emotional child" that still dwells in each of us.

So, why are these experiences so vivid? Because a child's world is *very* child-centric. In the emotional and psychological drive to make sense of his or her world, a child often seeks explanations to how the world works based on what he or she did or didn't do in a particular situation. This is foundational to the "meaning making" experience for a young psyche, trying to connect cause and effect in the world around him or her. It gets back to the issue of "object theory" that I mentioned in Chapter One.

For the investor (now a mature adult), the experience of financial loss in the market can evoke memories of past losses (and perhaps past fears) about "reality repeating itself." And, even though the mature adult realizes that he or she is no longer an innocent and uninformed child, the experience of loss (or the expectation of it) triggers "emotional tapes" from an earlier time and place. Such emotional scars, I believe, are underneath the dynamics of loss aversion as identified by Kahneman and Tversky.

What about gains? As noted, research shows that the anticipation of a gain is actually a more intense experience than realization of a gain. Researchers have found that "anticipating a gain, and actually receiving it, are expressed in entirely different ways in the brain, helping to explain why "money does not buy happiness!"[3] To piggyback on that, I would argue that there is a "thrill of the chase" component to our pursuit of gains that is biologically based, and that stems from our evolution as human beings. As noted in Chapter One, researchers such as Jakk Panksepp of Bowling Green University believe we are equipped by virtue of evolution with a "seeking system" that primes us to chase opportunities when they come into our view. In prehistoric times this might have been to give chase to prey (and that night's dinner). Today, that same impulse to give chase can come alive when we view the potential rewards of a big financial gain on the marketplace horizon.

But certainly, we've evolved since our days in the caves, haven't we? Or perhaps not! It's fascinating to see how unfulfilling the "gain side" of the financial equation is. Are we so addicted to the thrill of gain and the anticipation of gain that we strive for it again and again, without achieving ultimate satisfaction? John D. Rockefeller, one of the world's richest men of his time, was once asked by a reporter, "How much money is enough?" To which Rockefeller responded, "Just a little bit more."

Continental Insurance

It's 1983. The hit TV show *M*A*S*H* has finally wrapped production after 11 years (and 251 episodes) on CBS. On Broadway, the hit musical *Annie* has been performed for the last time, after 2377 shows at the Uris Theater in New York City. Sally Ride has become the first American woman in space aboard the Shuttle Challenger.

And in the insurance industry, things are bleak.

The prices that insurance companies can charge for their policies have been stagnant for years, and consequently many insurers are suffering financially. Among the underperformers is Continental Corporation, a New York–based insurer founded in the 1850s. In 1982 it is an unprofitable, unwieldy conglomerate of many businesses with a badly beaten down balance sheet. Its market share is eroding and cash flow is strained by shareholder dividends that exceed per share earnings. But top management seems unwilling or unable to change course and has become combative with investors and Wall Street analysts, who are increasingly critical of the company's performance.

Then, the company hires a dynamic new CEO, Jake Mascotte, an executive with no experience running a property/casualty insurer and, at 43, the youngest CEO in the industry. Soon, investors start buying up Continental stock. Acting with the impulse of sharks, they hope to cash in big-time if the company ever has a rebound from its near death experience. The chief strategist at a Wall Street brokerage firm makes a big bet on Continental, putting 2% (a significant market overweight) of his firm's assets into Continental stock and adding it to the firm's portfolio.

After just 19 months on the job, Mascotte hosts a meeting that is jammed with money managers and analysts. Unlike the previous CEO, Mascotte is affable and relaxed in front of the crowd. He welcomes everyone and acknowledges that, with most of his experience in life insurance (not property/casualty), he's clearly the new kid on the block. But then he goes on to firmly declare that as CEO, he will bring a fresh approach to managing Continental's beleaguered financials. He talks about cutting costs, rebuilding the balance sheet, and fields pointed questions with Midwestern sincerity. He beams broadly, is disarming, calls analysts by name, and impresses the attendees with his frequent use of all the buzzwords associated with corporate turnarounds.

As Mascotte speaks, a palpable excitement arises in the room. He is confident, even cocksure about his company's future, despite its currently dismal financials. The money managers have heard what they want to hear. Indeed, a "We can do it!" attitude seems to permeate the room, and for the first time in its history, Continental seems poised to buck the industry trend and, against all odds, recover and rebound.

But one analyst in the audience, a young woman just beginning her career in finance, is bewildered. She knows that Continental's future is troubled, even bleak. She calls her boss.

"I don't get it," she told him. "The people at this meeting today are all rational and logical people. But, by the end of the meeting, they'd all become very excited about Continental's prospects and felt that the CEO could walk on water."

Her boss chuckled. "I know; it's *not* logical. But, fact is, making money is always emotional. The only thing more emotional than making money is the *prospect* of making it," he told her. "Welcome to the world of emotional investing!"

Conquering Emotions: The Key to Investment Success

All of us have certain aphorisms that act as philosophical guiderails of our lives—both as human beings and wealth advisors. One of my favorites is Warren Buffett's suggestion that we "Be fearful when others are greedy, and greedy when others are fearful." Buffett's remark has particular relevance to me when applied to the markets. When the market's averages are selling at 52-week lows, it's a clear sign that people are becoming fearful about something, and if you check the headlines you'll probably see plenty of evidence of why the market has sold off and fear abounds. So, to agree with Buffett, that might be the very moment to put money *into* the markets, and look for opportunities to allocate capital to attractively priced stocks.[4] When the market is at all-time highs and greed abounds, the reverse is also true, of course. Then it may be time to quietly exit and place your money in cash instead of stocks.

When Fear Takes Over

Fear can push investors and advisors to act in ways that, in hindsight, they should not have. In early 2009, as the Bush administration was ending and the Obama administration was just beginning, the government was taking over more and more businesses. Banks were forced to take on massive government loans, whether they needed them or not. The U.S. government seized control of American International Group (AIG) by taking an 80% equity stake so the company could stabilize its various businesses. AIG later became a conduit for bailing out other financial firms with government money. Lehman Brothers went bankrupt in the autumn of 2008, and bank liquidity was almost nonexistent for several days that fall. General Motors and Chrysler were taken over by the U.S. government, and shareholders' equity was deemed worthless. These were dark days, fear was rampant, security prices fell, and it had to be the exceptional investor who did not sell but decided to buy.

The same can be said for the turbulence that briefly hit the markets in mid-August of 2015. Over concerns that China's economic growth was slowing (and that Chinese reports of previous expansion may have been falsified or at least "puffed up"), the Dow Jones had repeated days of triple-digit declines, accentuated by a 1600-point drop at one point, and swings of as much as a 1000 points on August 24 alone.

Fear and greed drive our emotional state into what psychologist David Kantor calls "high-stakes" behavior. Much of the time we, as investors, operate in low-stakes circumstances, when the world seems rational, and we have time to be reflective and logical about the decisions we make. As the perception of market risk rises, however, and the threat of loss increases, my experience as an advisor is that the stakes for investors rise quickly. Client emotions become stronger and stronger as stakes rise, and people often feel forced into a corner: their behaviors becoming increasingly stress-affected as they perceive their options to be narrowing and their choices being increasingly critical. Rational behavior and the sense of having broad options that characterize a low-stakes situation suddenly evaporate. People become tense, fearful, anxious, and easily angered. Sleepless nights make matters seem even worse! This doesn't always happen in such situations, but I've seen this scenario play itself often enough in client meetings. Not all people respond to high-stress and high-stakes situations in this way. Some people become emotionally distant in high-stakes situations. There's no "one-size-fits all" response that *all* individuals have to stressful, high-stakes situations, because people have different personality types that react to stress in different ways.

To use Kantor's taxonomy of hero types, Fixers, Survivors, and Protectors all move from operating in the "light zone" (normal, low-stakes circumstances) to a "gray zone" of intermediate stress, and from there to a "dark zone" in circumstances of high stress and high stakes. Later, we'll explore the specific behaviors that each hero type exhibits under circumstances of high stress or high stakes.

Beliefs about Money

People bring more than just their emotional makeup to wealth advisory discussions, of course. They also bring personal belief systems about money that impact them in both subtle and obvious ways. To many people, money is bound up with notions of status, entitlement, and family lineage and legacy. Others think about it in terms of hunger, satisfaction, scarcity, ability to accomplish things, security/insecurity, and comparisons and distinctions, among other things.

Sometimes people are confused or conflicted about money. We equate its pursuit to the pursuit of love. Indeed, for some people money becomes (regrettably) a *substitute* for love. How many people, for example, as they approach retirement after a successful career, suddenly realize that their marriage is in shambles or their relationships with children are hostile or nonexistent? Their stock portfolio may be healthy and their net worth in the top 1%, but their spiritual cupboard is empty. An individual may have achieved everything they wanted to achieve from a financial and professional point of view, but their relationships are shallow, barren of love, or even rife with recriminations and pain. In my view, it's no accident that the Bible counsels us that "The love of money is the root of all evil."

Sometimes, however, this aphorism is misquoted to say that "Money is the root of all evil." Consequently, some individuals, fearing the accumulation of money, spend everything they have in pursuit of new acquisitions or experiences rather than saving enough to retire in security and comfort. Because they see money as evil they set out to "lose" it rather than seeing its potential focus for good: as a means to provide for future generations or charitable causes.

It's only when a client develops a balanced relationship with money that he or she can begin to relate to it in healthy ways. Sometimes the client-advisor relationship becomes the perfect venue in which that can take place. It's one of the primary reasons why, on a regular basis, I ask clients and prospects to share with me their personal and family *values* surrounding money. What role do they see it playing in their lives? How do values about money influence their thinking about investment choices, portfolio planning, retirement, and their desire to pass on wealth to others, including heirs and charitable causes? Asking clients to talk about their personal and family values relative to money can also generate important insights into a client's personality, risk tolerance, and dynamics, such as family culture. In the case of inherited wealth, for example, how has money influenced the client's family culture, beliefs, and sibling and generational relationships among family members? Do people view wealth as an obligation, a curse, a privilege, a right, a gift?

And then, of course, it can be fascinating to see what emotions arise in individuals when they start talking about money and themselves. Did they have money when they were growing up? Or, were they the first in their family to build and acquire wealth? When I ask questions such as these, I pay close attention to people's body language and affect. Do they feel in control of their wealth and competent to manage it? Or do they feel it controls them?

This begs a larger question, of course. Do we want money to be in charge of us? Or, do we want to be in charge of our money? Having money in charge of us means that we are constantly fretting about outcomes, wondering if we've accumulated enough, or not trusting that we have made sound decisions in the first place about how to earn, save, and invest. If we are dependent upon money, then we give money a powerful position in our lives. Conversely, if we salt away enough of what we earn each paycheck and invest that money wisely, we will be happier and lead a more balanced life 20 years from now. We take control of our financial circumstances and are no longer dependent upon money to meet our day-to-day needs.

Why I'm a Behavioral Finance Guy

In the world of theories explaining how the financial markets work, I'm very much in the behavioral finance camp. Behavioral finance is a relatively new field that draws on insights from behavioral and cognitive psychological theory to help explain why people sometimes make highly unpredictable or irrational decisions about investments and risk-taking.

Conventional market theory would have you believe in the idea of efficient markets and would argue that most investors are rational actors and wealth maximizers. But in my experience, nothing could be further from the truth! There are just too many instances I've observed where people's psychological makeup acts as a driver of their risk-taking behavior. Their unique emotional template acts as a kind of operating system that determines how they behave both under low-stakes and high-stakes circumstances.

For us, as advisors, it's very important to become discerning observers of human nature, because doing so enables us to adjust our own behaviors and style of interaction with clients, based on the way they "show up" in particular situations. In Chapter One I introduced the various hero types that clients can take on in high-stakes situations. As you'll learn in future chapters, dealing effectively with a "Fixer" in the dark zone will require different skills and approaches than dealing with a "Protector" or "Survivor" in the dark zone. Your ability to "read the room" in such situations, and to intuit where your client is coming from behaviorally, will help you deal effectively with that individual under any kind of circumstance.

It's important for all of us, as we calibrate what kind of relationship to have with money, to be aware of the potential emotional baggage we carry around about it. I know for myself, having grown up in a wealthy family, that I can never match the lifestyle my parents enjoyed. Comparisons are ever present in how I live my life. I am never "good enough" to provide for my family in the same way. My initial response to this was to run away from my family's money to live in Vermont, and to pursue the kind of lifestyle (as a geologist and gentleman farmer) that would eventually have caused me to run out of cash. I had to make a mid-course correction to create a healthier relationship with money, where I was no longer so dependent on it. For me, establishing a healthy relationship with money meant "making peace" with my parents and the experiences of my early childhood. Money can be funny that way. Unpacking our feelings about it often proves to reveal a Rosetta stone with which we can then figure out the rest of our lives, or at least determine a new life trajectory to embark on. More than once I've seen clients of mine struggling with similar issues as they try to figure out their relationship with inherited wealth.

The Folklore of Finance

It's not only clients that get caught up in the emotions and psychology of money; so too do we, as wealth advisors and investment counselors! The State Street Center for Applied Research in Boston (www.google.com/#q=s tate+street+center+for+applied+research) has done some intriguing research on the so-called "folklore" employed by wealth advisors in advising clients. Folklore, of course, is not necessarily fact-based, but it is often embraced by large numbers of people as reliable truth. The Center has identified three specific types of "folklore"[5] that wealth advisors often employ in working with and advising clients:

- The Folklore of Time
- The Folklore of Knowledge
- The Folklore of False Comfort

All three pose potential traps for advisors and investors alike!

The Folklore of Time. Advisors who embrace the folklore of time subscribe to the belief that by examining backward-looking patterns and relationships among asset classes and industries, they can accurately forecast where future growth (and potential loss) is likely to occur. In this spirit, financial experts scramble to identify noncorrelating asset classes in order to pick and choose *future* asset classes and investment managers to build and manage portfolios. They employ expensive and complex software programs that delve into the history of asset classes (and outside investment managers) to build predictive models to forecast how portfolios are likely to behave under different risk scenarios, such as inflation, deflation, a strong dollar, a weak dollar, and so on. Once relationships between funds can be determined to produce low correlation, then "Presto!," the advisor (or firm) has identified a new candidate for addition to the client's portfolio! No matter that the analysts doing this work understand that the future is not like the past. But they can't predict the future, so they try to do the next best thing![6]

A second example of how investment advisors embrace folklore of time thinking is by focusing obsessively on quarterly results. As soon as a company announces its quarterly numbers, analysts have their research assistants adjust their earnings models incrementally and change their forecasts accordingly. After all, nobody wants to look like they weren't prescient! If a company beats earning predictions by two cents, it means the company can then trumpet this, implying an incrementally higher growth rate in earnings per share going forward. A miss of a penny in forecasted earnings can mean just the opposite, of course.[7]

A good way I've found to deal with the market's quarterly earnings craziness is to listen carefully to what corporate executives say to analysts during earning calls, and then to pay close attention to what a company does with its dividends. Companies hate to reduce dividends—ever! So, if after an earnings call, a company decides to increase dividends and announces it very publicly—as in, "We feel certain enough about business conditions and prospects to increase dividends by 8% this year"—it's a very good sign that company insiders are truly bullish on the company's growth prospects going forward. Such statements carry far more weight than whether the company just surprised Wall Street with a quarterly earnings "beat."

The Folklore of False Comfort. This is a second area of bogus (or at least sketchy) thinking that advisors tend to embrace in their work with clients.[8] The Center cites several kinds of false comfort thinking that wealth advisors and investment planning professionals embrace.

The first is the use of an ever-expanding array of ostensibly scientific indices which give wealth advisors a false sense of security about what really makes the markets work. These metrics can include measures of risk, such as value at risk (VaR), a widely used risk measure indicating the risk of loss on a specific portfolio of financial exposures, as well as fund ratings, ratings agency risk ratings, style boxes, and benchmark investment indices. At the risk of sounding conspiratorial, there is a very profitable cottage industry that has sprung up around having so many risk-related indices in the wealth management industry![9]

Indices, in fact, become highly profitable products for the firms that create them and then use them to design portfolios for clients. Rating agencies, fund analytical services, and risk assessment companies all peg their own market and company assessments to these indices. A false sense of security can develop, however, if investors believe they know just how much risk is embedded in their portfolios, based on the "insights" of various indices. The integrity of these indices is generally recognized until some cardinal assumption underlying a model gets violated (e.g., "Treasuries are totally risk-free."). Suddenly, what people always believed as gospel truth is no longer!

Although I'm generally skeptical about many of the popular, pseudo-scientific-based indices being used in the wealth management industry today, see Appendix B for information about one company, Market Profile Theorems (MPT) whose indices I do believe help illuminate the behavioral dynamics at work in the marketplace today, impacting everything from analysts' earnings estimates to stock prices to the behaviors of key marketplace actors at various points in a market cycle.

A second kind of "false comfort" arises when firms use outside managers to invest client money.[10] Many wealth management firms, to inoculate themselves against market downturns, enlist outside "experts" to handle most of their client portfolios.[11] The handmaiden to this practice is using consultants to help advise and choose the outside manager(s). Consultants can be very helpful. However, in my experience as the past chair of the investment committee for a local nonprofit organization, consultants can unintentionally create distance between the organization's investment committee, portfolio managers, and the markets. Moreover, consultants have their own agendas, so this represents a potential conflict of interest. There are also inevitable time lags between the end of the quarter when consulting firms conduct portfolio analyses and when the nonprofit's investment committee finally meets with consultants. Recommendations can grow stale, performance becomes dated, and what might have seemed like good investment strategy one to three months before is now no longer so "crystal clear." In the case of the nonprofit noted above, my colleagues and I normally found that the organization's performance was in line with the index benchmark, minus the double layer of fees we paid (to the investment manager and the consultant). Ultimately, we decided it was simpler (and less expensive) to manage our organization's money without a consultant, by allocating the funds to a group of managers we felt were well positioned to meet our organization's needs. Moreover, rather than be solely wedded to a market benchmark, we also decided to measure performance against inflation indices. After all, it is the corrosive effect of inflation that most adversely affects investors.

Putting too much faith in regulation and disclosure practices creates another kind of "false comfort"—for investors and advisors alike.[12] Investors and advisors tend to buy into the idea (perhaps subconsciously) that regulation and disclosure will effectively inoculate them against market downturns. But this clearly isn't always the case. In my opinion, the 2008 market downturn provides a stunning example of this. The causes of the 2008 market meltdown are still in dispute. Many people argue that it was the result of large banks and insurance companies selling people products that were faulty and dangerous and that propped up poorly written mortgages. From my perspective, however, one can make a convincing case that the seeds of these bad mortgages were planted back in the early 1990s during the Clinton administration, when Andrew Cuomo, the then Secretary of Housing and Urban Development, issued guidelines requiring banks, Fannie Mae, and Freddie Mac to increase the amount of subprime mortgages they wrote. Under the plan, banks that did not comply with these requirements would face a much more stringent approval process for mergers and acquisitions.[13]

This policy remained in effect through the 1990s and into the early 2000s. Efforts by banks to reduce or scale back this policy were met with howls of protest from influential politicians such as Representative Barney Frank of Massachusetts. Yet, when the whole financial system began to collapse under its own weight, Frank and Senator Chris Dodd of Connecticut spearheaded passage of a massive bill (Dodd-Frank) whose regulations identified financial institutions as being at fault. The sad part of this story is that, in retrospect, I believe that the Clinton administration's loan requirements for banks helped exacerbate banks' problems by forcing financial institutions and mortgage investors to take on questionable debt. If you buy this premise, the idea that government regulation will protect all of us from market downturns (or worse) isn't something we should "bank" on!

Still another way the financial services industry generates false comfort is in how it measures success, specifically by comparing what we desire (and achieve) against the performance of indices such as the S&P 500 Index. The State Street Center cites investors' beliefs that the S&P 500 embodies a universal goal for all of us to match or beat. However, in reality, nothing could be further from the truth. The S&P 500 is an easy-to-use, but potentially inappropriate, benchmark. As investors (and advisors) we all need to do the difficult work of identifying what we personally want to achieve in terms of portfolio performance, undergirded by the identification of specific goals and benchmarks that are important to our clients. We then need to determine how best to achieve those goals and monitor performance over time.

The Folklore of Knowledge (a.k.a. the Danger of Advisor Hubris). Yet another kind of folklore the State Street Center cites as damaging to the financial services industry is the penchant of investment advisors to claim good results from their stock picks as clear evidence of unique, special, or rare knowledge and skill on their parts. As an example, the Center cites the common pattern among portfolio managers of taking credit for successes that occur, while putting blame on others when things go wrong. Both are examples of unwarranted but perhaps inevitable "self-attribution bias."[14] "Investment professionals are caught in a double bind," notes the Center. "They need to feel conviction in their investment choices in order to reassure clients. At the same time, it is logically unreasonable to have high conviction due to the intrinsic uncertainty of investing." To counteract this, investors tell themselves stories to explain their success and failure, according to the Center. "These narratives are so compelling—whether they're playing the role of the hero or victim—that the story becomes the truth. And it does for their organizations and clients, as well."[15]

As an advisor, I know I am prone to this tendency myself. Mind you, it's always good to pat yourself on the back for a success. Who wouldn't? But when things go wrong, as they often do, I, like many of my colleagues, am only too happy to point fingers and assign blame. In fact, blaming is a particularly strong suit of my personality type when stakes are high, as you will see later.

Evidence of overconfidence by both investors and their advisors is often clear for all to see. Both wealth advisors and their clients often rank their investment abilities high, when, in fact, being more modest would be more financially prudent. Still, advisors and investors alike are often quite ready to commit capital—their own or others—to investments that may be riskier than they believe them to be.

The Lesson Here: Beware of Folklore Masquerading as Actual Financial Market Knowledge!

The impact of "market folklore" masquerading as hard knowledge or professional expertise is not to be underestimated, either by advisors or investors. Indeed, there are scores of biases that influence advisor and investor attitudes and behaviors. The State Street Center notes at least 28 different biases that often influence (consciously or unconsciously) advisor and/or investor behavior.[16] They include but are not limited to the following:

- Anchoring Bias
- Cognitive Dissonance
- Conservatism Bias
- Disposition Effect
- Emotional Quotient
- Gambler's Fallacy
- Heuristics
- Home Bias
- Loss Aversion
- Overconfidence Bias
- Representativeness Bias
- Self-Attribution Bias
- Status Quo Bias

- Availability Bias
- Confirmation Bias
- Decision Fatigue
- Endowment Effect
- Framing Bias
- Herding Bias
- Hindsight Bias
- Illusion of Control Bias
- Mental Accounting Bias
- Regret Aversion
- Self-Control Bias
- Short-Termism
- Value Attribution

Space precludes me from providing definitions for all these terms, but as a wealth advisor you are no doubt familiar with all of them.[17] Some of these biases are more easily identified in the rearview mirror once an error in judgment has occurred. All of these biases show up, depending on the personality types of investors and their advisors. Overconfidence is more common among those who are strong in "power and control." Herding (the tendency to make decisions about investing based on what others do) and value attribution[18] are things an advisor is more likely to see in clients that operate in "open and affect." The disposition effect, in which the investor tends to hold losing positions and sell his or her winners too early, is sometimes associated with people strong in "random and meaning."

The Responsibility of the Advisor

Besides analyzing stocks and managing portfolios, we, as advisors, need to be aware of where our professional knowledge and expertise begins and ends, and when we ourselves are prone to fall prey to financial markets and financial industry folklore, both in guiding and advising our clients, and investing for ourselves. The psychology of money—our opinions and embedded beliefs about it—is always at play—in some way, shape or form—in every interaction we have with clients.[19]

So what counsel do I offer here? In building and nurturing client relationships, it's important to keep the client's interests, priorities, and needs continually in mind. The relationship you have with a client ideally will be a co-created partnership in which the two of you work together to chart and draft an investment plan, determine strategy, and outline specific investment goals and objectives.

Early in any new client relationship, you need to take time to build rapport, chemistry, and understanding with individuals. Early "contracting" with clients—identifying client goals, expectations, personal and family values, and ways of working together—can help put a firm foundation of trust in place to help carry both you and the client through times of marketplace volatility when it's likely that the two of you will be having high-stakes conversations. (For more, see Chapter Nine.)

Become an astute observer of your clients. Understand what motivates and energizes them, what concerns them, and what makes them fearful and nervous. With knowledge of the client as a psychological "system," you'll be able to manage crucial conversations while maintaining and building trust, even in the most difficult of marketplace situations.

In chapters to come, I'll have much more to say about how to handle the psychological dynamics and emotions of money that are always present in client-advisor relationships, and which can become especially problematic in times of stress and high stakes. This is when it's important for you to remain grounded and to be confident in your ability to handle difficult conversations in ways that lead to productive and optimal outcomes.

CHAPTER THREE

Introducing a Conversational Model You Can Use with Clients

The real art of conversation is not only to say the right thing at the right place, but to leave unsaid the wrong thing at the tempting moment.

—Lady Dorothy Nevil

Being a wealth management advisor[1] is a tough and demanding job! It involves far more than simply a knowledge of the markets and of various financial and investment products. You must also be good with clients— the people stuff! And that means knowing how to cultivate client prospects and build strong and lasting personal relationships based on trust, mutual respect, discerning listening, and a clear understanding of a client's needs and wishes.

All this may sound straightforward enough to do, but in fact, it requires a deep and sophisticated understanding of human psychology—both that of your clients and of *yourself!* This will enable you to more deeply empathize with your clients, understand their needs, and anticipate their requests. You will begin to pick up on the unspoken agendas your clients may have had difficulty discussing with other advisers before you.

For that reason, this chapter delves deeply into the principles of interpersonal dynamics and explains how, by understanding these principles, you can gain a new and much deeper understanding of your clients.

I first mentioned interpersonal (group) dynamics and the work of Dr. David Kantor in Chapter One. In this chapter, I discuss his model of interpersonal interaction in greater detail because I have found it to be a valuable tool in understanding my clients and working effectively with them both in low-stakes and high-stakes situations.

What Exactly Are Interpersonal (Group) Dynamics?

Simply stated, interpersonal or group dynamics provides a way to understand the characteristics and patterns of interaction inherent in any conversational *system*. For my purposes here, a *system* can be as basic as the relationship you have with one individual client or as complex as the relationship you have with a couple or with all the members of a multigenerational family you are advising.

So what are the key elements of a conversational "system"?

In every human relationship, people have specific ways of talking with each other. They make statements and requests, for example, and ask questions. They also play specific roles.

Kantor has identified four principal roles or "action stances" that people play in low-stakes conversations. **Movers,** for example, tend to initiate action by offering ideas or suggesting specific courses of action to take. **Followers** are those who support what movers say and tend to keep conversations in a group moving forward. **Opposers** (not surprisingly) are those who challenge actions proposed by movers. They may resist the suggestions of a mover either because they disagree or because they want to provide an alternative perspective on the matter being discussed. Finally, **Bystanders** are those who observe the interactions among others in group settings. They offer up neutral comments or bridge the gap between what others say in conversation. They often aim to forge answers or resolution to problems based on different points of view that have previously been expressed by others. In doing so, Bystanders are active conversational participants.

Kantor describes this model as the Four-Player model of human interaction.[2] You may already recognize some of your clients as playing one or more of these roles in every conversation you have with them!

Taking a Closer Look at Client Roles (A.K.A. "Action Stances")

The **Mover** is the kind of client who is likely to say to you, "I want to examine my portfolio and consider making some changes in asset allocation." Or, "I like the performance the portfolio has generated in the last nine months, but I'd like to see what we could do to increase returns in the year ahead." As an advisor it's quickly apparent when a client is a Mover. He or she is likely to want to drive the conversational agenda when they meet with you (or at least match you in social assertiveness) and may even draw up the proposed agenda for the meetings you have with them!

A **Follower** on the other hand is somebody who may be inclined to defer to you, at least initially, in client exchanges, especially at the start of a client relationship or when discussing new wealth strategies and investment plans. In response to what you might suggest about portfolio rebalancing, for example, he/she might say something like this: "What you've said sounds good to me. Let's go with it!"

An **Opposer** as you might guess, is somebody who's likely to resist your suggestions or at least look for validation of recommendations you are making, or investment strategies and products you may be promoting. He/she may want to review written materials that support your point of view, or research that indicates market and investment trends in a particular direction. Opposers sometimes like to "stress-test" ideas; they look for supporting reasons to pursue a particular course of action, so you want to be prepared for this when you deal with them.

Finally, **Bystanders** are people who may, on the surface at least, appear a bit passive in client settings, although, in fact, they are simply paying attention to the dynamics taking place among others—or in the case of a one-on-one conversation, between you and them! A Bystander, in my experience, is an impartial observer of a social situation. I think of him or her as a sketch artist who captures not only the action going on in a "scene" of which they are a part but also the underlying moods and color of that scene. By then reflecting back to others the truth of their observations, especially as stakes get higher, the Bystander can be of great assistance in building the central points of agreement within a group. Indeed, he or she can help lay the foundation for group consensus. Having helped build consensus within a group, the Bystander can then adopt other action stances, including that of Mover, Opposer, or Follower, to help move the conversation along. From a group dynamics standpoint, it is very valuable and healthy if Bystanders are encouraged to offer their perspective in group settings (e.g., within a family), as they can often call attention to issues that others are not addressing. In some cases, they can help thwart bad or overly rapid decision-making within groups (or even when part of a couple).

How Clients Communicate Intentions to You

While individuals tend to assume specific roles in conversation, they also tend to communicate with specific (and different) intentions. These intentions typically are reflected in the "languages" of *power, affect,* or *meaning.*[3]

The person (of any type) who speaks in *power* has an orientation toward responsibility and getting things done. He or she is a person of action, whose goals are efficiency and completion of tasks. He or she is often quite easy to recognize.

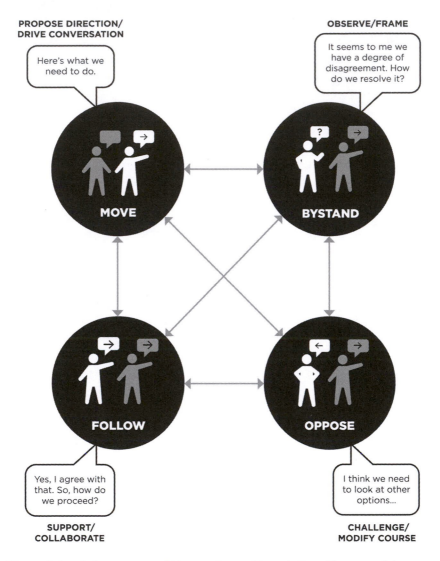

Figure 3.1 A Conversational Rosetta Stone: Kantor's Four-Player model provides a powerful lens through which to observe, understand, and manage interpersonal dynamics.

The person who speaks in *affect* is focused on feelings and relationships. His/her goals relate to nurturance, intimacy, caring, relationships, and connection with others, and he/she is typically concerned about people's well-being.

The person who speaks in *meaning* is oriented toward thinking, logic, and ideas. He or she is focused on the "search for truth" and integrating various ideas into a coherent, understandable, and philosophically complete whole.

So, let's pause here for a moment to review.

In your conversations with clients in low-risk situations, you're likely to encounter people who assume the "stances" of **Movers**, **Followers**, **Opposers**, and **Bystanders** in everyday conversations with you about investing. In so doing, they typically will engage with different intentions—in the "language" of *power*, *affect*, or *meaning*.

So, for example:

A **Mover** "in power" is likely to say something like this in conversation: "I'd like to use our meeting today to clarify investment goals for the year ahead. Our time is limited, so we need to be focused."

A **Mover** "in affect" is likely to say something like this: "I like what you're proposing today in terms of investment goals. I feel good about them. They will help build a stronger connection between my spouse and me. I'm concerned about the clock, so let's move forward on this."

A **Mover** "in meaning" is likely to say something like this: "Your suggested advice to me today about legacy gifting makes a lot of sense to me. I can see that this now becomes generational in nature. As such, I want it to be part of my wealth management approach for the future. Tell me more what you have in mind!"

A **Follower** "in power" is likely to say something like this: "I agree with your suggestions. They fit my priorities. Please go over your points in greater detail."

A **Follower** "in affect" is likely to say something like this: "I agree in principle with what you're saying. You know, it's very important to me to provide for my children and grandchildren. I appreciate where you're going with this. Go ahead with the discussion."

A **Follower** "in meaning" is likely to say something like this: "I resonate with what you're saying. It makes sense to me to plan systematically for the distribution of gifts over a ten-year period, keeping in mind the complexities of the tax code. I know you'll explore these intricacies as we get further into our conversation."

An **Opposer** "in power" is likely to say something like this: "I disagree for the moment with what you're saying. I couldn't agree to what you're suggesting unless I have more data on which to base a decision."

An **Opposer** "in affect" is likely to say something like this: "I'm not yet comfortable that this investment approach will meet my family's needs or wishes. I feel uneasy about this approach."

An **Opposer** "in meaning" is likely to say something like this: "I'm concerned that this approach isn't really in line with my investment goals and philosophy. You haven't proven to me the merits of what you've suggested."

A **Bystander** "in power" is likely to say something like this: "What you seem to be saying is in line with what you've recommended before. I see some confusion on your fifth point. Can you illuminate, please?"

A **Bystander** "in affect" is likely to say something like this: "What you're saying makes me feel good and corroborates assurances you've given me before. I note general agreement in the room with your proposal, although I see some discomfort with your fifth point."

A **Bystander** "in meaning" is likely to say something like this: "What you're saying seems very much in keeping with the philosophy and approach to investing that we've discussed before. Perhaps you can give me more detail on your fifth point as it seems to need greater clarification."

See the subtle differences in messaging in each of the preceding scenarios? An intimate understanding of interpersonal dynamics can help you "code" the conversations you have with clients and make determinations as to the roles and message styles of each of your clients. This, in turn, will help you decide on the role you too must play as part of conversational engagement with a particular client.[4]

So, for example, if you are dealing with a client who is a strong **Mover**, with a very clear point of view about something you're discussing, you may initially want to take the role of **Bystander** in conversation with him/her, listening to what they have to say, and getting them to articulate their ideas fully. At some point, you may then find yourself taking the **Follower** role, affirming and agreeing with what they say, and then suggesting a specific course of action to take (putting you in the **Mover** role).

In another client situation, a high-stakes situation in which a client is aggressively moving the conversational agenda along, perhaps too quickly, you may initially decide to play the role of **Bystander** so that you can fully discern the context of their concerns and observe the emotions that are fueling the intensity and energy of their words and interaction with you at that moment. Once you've read the situation correctly, you might conceivably adopt the role of the **Opposer**, perhaps to caution the client against taking action that is too rash and not well considered. Example: If he or she says "I want to sell my entire portfolio given what happened in the market today!" you might conceivably say, "I strongly advise against that. I think you'll regret that decision."

Given people's action propensities and the wide range of human personalities, the actual dynamics and *texture* of any specific human interaction are infinitely varied. And when you factor in people's engagement style (Closed, Open, and Random) and hero type, interpersonal dynamics become even more complex. These particulars will be covered in Chapters Four through Nine.

The Four-Player model provides a very good framework with which to enter and manage conversations with clients and to help them achieve their goals in both low-stakes and high-stakes situations. It takes a bit of practice to engage with clients this way, but once you master the principles of interpersonal dynamics it will take your wealth consulting skills to a new level and help you to be effective with clients, regardless of the circumstances in which you are counseling them.

Introducing the Behavioral Propensities Profile (BPP)

You may be wondering, "Where does the predisposition to take a particular stance in conversation come from?" As people mature into adults, they develop distinctive patterns (or tendencies) of behavior, engagement, and speech. These patterns became evident in the stances people take in conversational settings, in the words they choose when they speak, and in how they make decisions as conversations with others proceed. Together all these patterns represent a person's behavioral propensities and form the basis of their behavioral propensities profile (BPP), a personality construct created by Kantor.[5]

How is an individual's BPP initially formed? To a large extent it is forged in childhood, in early experiences of challenge, adversity, hurt, and loss. These early experiences of challenge, adversity, hurt, and loss form the basis of a person's "identity-forming" stories, which, to a very large extent, explain how a person "shows up" in life as an adult.[6] I first mentioned "childhood stories" as the foundation of Kantor's four-stage model in Chapter One. As Kantor notes, they play a critical role in an individual's early personal development:

> Stories are the primary means by which human beings make sense of the world and themselves in it. Each of us is a story gatherer—from birth observing and selecting images as basic references for our ideas about the world, what satisfies our hunger, makes us happy, brings us pain. Story is the device that allows us to store, organize, and retrieve meaning from the images we choose to remember. . . . Every individual's patterned behaviors, his or her characteristics in relationships . . . are based on these images.[7]

Every one of us walks around with a set of "stories" in our heads that forms the basis of our identity and existence—both to ourselves and to others. Taken in their rich and marvelous totality, these stories represent our connection to this world, to each other, and even to ourselves, helping us to understand who we are in this world. As wealth advisors, we do a great service to clients if we take time to hear and understand *their* personal life stories, for they hold the keys to comprehending a person's truest identity. With sensitivity and intention, the advisor who makes it a point to understand a client's personal life narrative (input that can be gathered at the beginning of a client relationship or during regular client meetings) can gain important insights into what motivates that client as an adult. He/she can begin to understand why they are the way they are, why they embrace certain values and beliefs, why they have a low-risk tolerance or a high-risk tolerance, why they display the behaviors, emotions, and attitudes they do, and why they take particular stances when it comes to discussing matters of money, wealth, life, retirement, and legacy.

When Conversations with Clients Become High Stakes

Up to now, I have outlined four conversational stances that clients are likely to display in low-stakes conversations with you or others. And we have touched on the various intentions (*power*, *affect*, and *meaning*) with which people speak in interaction with others. But what happens when circumstances change, and conversations suddenly become "high-stakes"?

This is when a client's predominant "hero" type (the Fixer, Protector, or Survivor) is likely to emerge in full array. While hero type characteristics are evident even in low-stakes circumstances, they became pronounced and can be problematic to deal with in high-stakes situations. There are many triggers that prompt a person to shift from operating in the "light" or "gray" zone (low-stakes circumstances) to operating in the "dark" zone (high-stakes circumstances.)

Consider the following scenarios:

- It's 2008 or 2009. The market is tanking and you have a client clamoring for advice about what to do next. She's bombarding you with voicemails and e-mails, asking for your thoughts on what should be done with her portfolio. You've told her to remain calm, but at the moment she's inconsolable and fearful she's going to lose everything.
- The husband of a wealthy couple with whom you've worked for years has died, and you need to offer the surviving spouse financial advice and counsel in the midst of her devastating grief. The situation is complicated because the widow's

children are now calling you, asking you to get more closely involved in the family's financial affairs.

- The son of one of your oldest clients is spending his inheritance like a drunken sailor and now the client has come to you for advice. He's desperate. What do you advise him to do, and what approach do you take?
- A highly successful entrepreneur has just sold his company and has become instantly wealthy. He has all kinds of ideas about what to do with his money in the next six months, and somehow you must get him to slow down before making any significant decisions about his financial future.
- You're working with multiple generations of a wealthy family, many of whose members loathe one another and don't communicate with each other very well. But somehow, you must act as convener and meditator to help them make some financial decisions that collectively impact them all.
- You're trying to manage the tension existing between a husband and wife around the degree of risk they are willing to take with their investment portfolio. It's tough because each has a different tolerance for risk, and you're trying to bridge the chasm between them.
- A client is recklessly overspending the annual budget that you and he agreed would help him sustain his wealth for the remainder of his lifetime. Now, you think you may have to become more directive in dealing with him, in order to stave off financial disaster. You're steeling yourself for your next conversation with him.

How Clients' Personalities Change under Pressure

Each of the preceding scenarios represents a high-stakes situation for a client. Under such circumstances, an individual's personality takes on new colorations and characteristics. As this occurs, a person's "hero type" (as a Fixer, Survivor, or Protector) comes into clearer view. The Fixer who was charming and affable in low-stakes situations now becomes demanding, controlling, arrogant, and rude. The Survivor who seemed so reasonable in low-stakes circumstances now seems stubborn and unreasonable, unwilling to listen to your investment advice as the market goes into a nosedive. The Protector, who was always so easy to talk to, and who wanted only the best for his/her family and loved ones, now becomes anxious, may feel like a victim, and even lashes out at you and others.[8]

Certain behavioral profiles often tend to predispose individuals toward certain heroic stances. The Movers who are oriented toward *power*, for example, will often reveal themselves as Fixers. The mantra of Fixers is "I will overcome, by sheer will, if necessary." In contrast, Movers who are oriented toward *meaning* tend to be Survivors and often display tremendous perseverance and endurance when facing challenging financial or personal circumstances. Meanwhile, the Mover who is a Protector is oriented toward

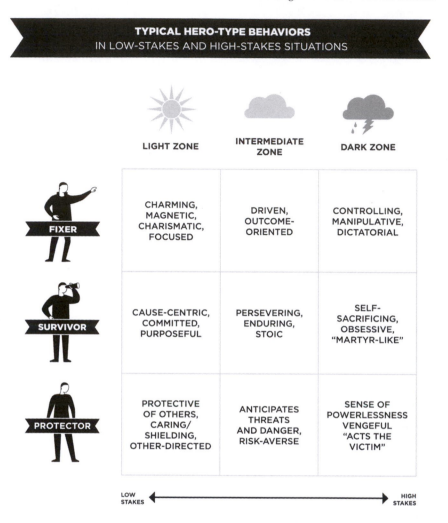

Figure 3.2 Mood swings in clients. Understanding changes in hero-type behavior as circumstances move from low to high stakes.

affect and will display great care and compassion for others, even under situations of high stress.[9]

I'll have much more to say about each of the hero types in future chapters. For now, what is important to know is that as a client's hero type begins to emerge (typically, in high-stakes situations) you need to be prepared. You need to remain grounded and self-aware. You need to carefully observe what's going on, discern what pressures the client is under, and decide how best to engage that person in conversation at that moment. You need to calmly and confidently read the situation for what it is, and adjust your own action stances in response to the client's presenting behavior at that time. This requires not only strong interpersonal confidence, but also sharp emotional intelligence, social agility, and the ability to stay very much in the moment with the client.

Understanding Yourself as a System

Up to this point in this chapter I have been talking about your clients—be they individuals, couples, or families—as human *systems* who tend to display different types of behavior under different life circumstances. I've also talked extensively about how an understanding of structural dynamics can provide a robust and flexible framework for dealing with clients under a variety of low-risk and high-risk circumstances.

So now, let's apply the principles of system dynamics to the conversations you have with *yourself*—specifically about money and investing. For like your clients, you too are a human *system* with a unique set of variables and life experiences that inform how you "show up" in the world around you, and how you respond to others in moments of both low and high stress. Like your clients, you too have feelings, emotions, and stories that derive from your childhood, and that have sprung from your life experiences of challenge, adversity, pain, and loss.

Getting in touch with these emotions and stories is critical to do, in order to be optimally effective in eliciting similar life experiences from your clients.

So, let me ask you some questions:

1. Were you raised in a wealthy family where money was no object? If that's the case, your emotions and attitudes about investing are likely to be quite different from those of someone who was raised in more modest circumstances and who worked his or her way up the economic and professional ladder.
2. What were the messages you got about money when you were growing up? From parents, grandparents, and other significant others?
3. Were you imbued with a scarcity mentality as the result of adults telling you that "money doesn't grow on trees so don't waste it!"? Or, did you get the message that though your family might be wealthy or at least "well-off," learning how to use money wisely, grow it, and be a conscientious steward of wealth were nonetheless expectations that authority figures in your life (parents, teachers, ministers, etc.) had of you?
4. Were you raised in a larger family where, as an older sibling, you were required to work for your allowance and perform many household chores while your younger siblings got a pass? If so, how did this make you feel?

You can see, just from these brief examples, that as a wealth advisor you potentially bring any number of perspectives (a.k.a. "personal stories") about money and wealth to your role as a counselor to others in managing their own assets.

Advisor Know Thyself!

Quite often, our personal stories about money are inextricably interwoven with other things such as our thoughts about personal security, self-concept, worthiness, success, intelligence, and especially emotional hurt and loss. For example, if, as a child, your family went from living comfortably to living on the economic margin, there are undoubtedly a lot of emotions that you may associate with discussions of money. Conversely, if your family was once of modest means but became wealthy in your childhood, you, your siblings, and your parents all had to "immigrate" to the "land of wealth," a trip that sounds glamorous, but that, as James Grubman describes in his book, *Strangers in Paradise*, can be fraught with stress, confusion, family conflict, and loss of identity.[10]

Your Views about Money and Investing: A Personal Inventory

Given that almost any discussion of money and how a person feels about it can be freighted with emotions and meaning, here are some questions that I invite you to take time to answer. Doing so will help you articulate your emotions and feelings around issues of money, wealth, and investing, and help you come up with an overall philosophy (*point of view*) about wealth and investment planning. Doing so then provides you with a baseline for working with clients, and helping them to articulate *their* values and priorities around wealth as well. So, take out a pad of paper and answer these questions:

1. Growing up, what were the messages you were given about money in your family?
2. What positive messages did you receive?
3. What potentially negative messages (if any) did you receive?
4. Growing up, what expectations do you think people had of you relative to money?
5. Did having money carry with it explicit (or implicit) expectations and responsibilities?
6. What values or opinions about money did you derive from your parents or other significant people in your life?

7. Do you, in any way, associate discussions of money with issues of personal security, loss, or other emotions? (Please specify.)
8. How have these experiences affected how you think about money and wealth *today* as an adult?
9. How do early childhood experiences or messages you got about money affect how you undertake investment planning for yourself and your family today?
10. How have these experiences become "stories" about money that you carry around with you every day of your life?
11. How do they impact how you think about investing and risk-taking today?
12. How would you describe your own risk tolerance when it comes to investment planning and wealth management? For example, what's your risk tolerance in a rising market (low-stakes situation)? In a falling market (high-stakes situation)? If different, how do you reconcile this?

After you answer the above questions about the past, answer the following as they relate to how you approach your role as a wealth advisor *today*:

13. As a wealth management professional, what conversation "stances" do you tend to use most often in conversations with others, and in particular clients and prospects?
14. What would you describe your own "hero" type to be in high-stakes situations? Would you say you are a Fixer, a Survivor, or a Protector?
15. What are the values you consider personally important to adhere to in working with clients?
16. What is your "vision" of the wealth management advisory process? How do you think it should work?
17. As a wealth management professional, what are you passionate about? How does this inform your work with clients?
18. What ethical commitments have you made to yourself, as a wealth management professional?
19. How do you currently articulate your advisory approach to clients?
20. How do you build partnerships with clients? What approaches/techniques do you find most effective?

Preparing to Meet the Client

Answering all 20 questions in detail is very good preparatory work for future work with clients. Why? Because if you're able to excavate the emotions, feelings, experiences and "stories" that you hold inside yourself relative to money and wealth, the easier it will be for you to inquire about and recognize similar or different feelings, emotions, and stories in your clients as part of the investment planning process.

As a wealth advisor, it may be necessary for you to do significant work to help clients unpack all the emotions and feelings they have about money as part of the wealth management and investment planning process. Doing so is critical pre-work for being able to then engage them in thoughtful discussions about their investment goals and wealth management plans.

Conclusions

In this chapter I've talked extensively about interpersonal (group) dynamics, and how it provides a model and framework for understanding the nature and texture of the human relationships you have with clients. Mastering the basics of interpersonal dynamics and behavioral profiling can be of tremendous value to you in your work with individuals, couples, and families, and is key to understanding how your clients think, deliberate, and make decisions (either personally or collectively) around wealth management and investment planning matters.

We've also discussed the various "action stances" clients typically take in their relationships with you as their advisor—specifically the *Mover,* the *Follower*, the *Opposer*, and the *Bystander*. And we've noted that everybody—both you and your clients—has an "action propensity." In other words, everyone tends to act in one of the four ways outlined in the model.[11]

Under pressure or changing market and financial circumstances however, other client propensities can surface in the personalities of the Fixer, the Survivor, and the Protector. As future chapters will show, each brings a different set of issues, expectations, and behaviors to the wealth management process, and each poses unique challenges to you, as the wealth advisor, to deal with.

PART II

Client Relationship Management

CHAPTER FOUR

Understanding Your Client's Engagement Style

A system is a set of things—people, cells, molecules, or whatever—interconnected in such a way that they produce their own pattern of behavior over time. The system may be buffeted, constricted, triggered, or driven by outside forces. But the system's response to these forces is characteristic of itself, and that response is seldom simple in the real world.
— Thinking in Systems: A Primer *by Donella H. Meadows*

Thus far in this book, I've talked extensively about clients as psychological "systems" and about how to build strong relationships with them, based on understanding their "stories" and emotional templates. I've introduced you to the Four-Player model and the ways you can use it to engage clients, interact with them, and create collaborative working relationships with them. We've talked about people's "hero types" and how a person's personality traits become pronounced in situations of high stress and high stakes. And I've described how different people communicate with different purposes and intents. The client who speaks in the language of *power* is a person of action who likes to set goals and accomplish things. The client who speaks in the language of *affect* is focused on feelings and relationships. The client who speaks in the language of *meaning* is concerned with their life purpose and is oriented toward thinking, logic, and ideas to support their mission in life.

Appreciating all of these things is important in navigating the nuances of client relationships and understanding what makes our clients tick, but it isn't all you need to build strong and lasting client relationships. You also need to create strong rapport and chemistry with clients by meeting them where they are, understanding their preferred style of social engagement, and adjusting your own style of engagement accordingly. This is essential in building long-lasting client relationships, based on deep trust and mutual understanding.

Every new client relationship begins with the advisor acting as the formal host and convener of that relationship, setting the table for discussion and creating a "safe container" in which conversation occurs, information is shared, opinions are voiced, options are discussed, and decisions are made. To handle this role effectively an advisor must be a deft conversationalist, able to manage conversations with people of widely differing personalities and interpersonal styles.

In my experience, clients generally display one of three possible "engagement styles" when interacting with an advisor.[1] These include:

- An Open style
- A Closed style
- A Random style[2]

Three Styles of Engagement with Individual Clients[3]

Open Style. People who prefer an Open style of social engagement typically put a high value on back-and-forth interaction and discussion. They make decisions about things by gathering, discussing, and vetting ideas from different sources, weighing options, and arriving at decisions through careful deliberation and reflection. As an advisor, you've undoubtedly had clients who bring this style of engagement to their investment discussions with you. As you work together to define investment goals and implement wealth management plans, such individuals display great openness to new ideas. They're willing (often eager) to weigh many options, to discuss choices exhaustively, and to make investment decisions in close partnership with you, as their advisor. You often hear such clients talk about the importance of "process" to the decision-making they undertake with you.

Closed Style. People who prefer a Closed style of engagement are less focused on process and inputs and more focused on efficiency, planning, results, and the bottom line. Of the three styles, this style is the most traditional, hierarchical, formal, and structured in its approach to decision-making. This transactional style can be very "black and white" when considering options. You'll likely recognize clients who operate using this style. They are data-driven, closure-oriented, and like to "cut to the chase" and "bottom-line things" when talking with you and making decisions about investments. Such individuals often come across as all business and are sometimes time-sensitive in their dealings with you. They want to use their time with you efficiently. Professional credibility is very important to such individuals, and they tend to look to you to provide specific subject matter expertise. At the same time, these clients often like to drive conversations and place more importance on completing tasks and identifying/reaching objectives than on the actual process used to make decisions.

Random Style. Individuals with a Random engagement style value creativity, individuality, and spontaneity of expression above all else. In contrast to others, they can come across as having all the time in the world to talk with you. To the untrained eye, Randoms can appear unfocused, disorganized, or distracted when talking with you about investment goals, personal values, and long-term wealth management and estate plans because their interests and priorities can be all over the place. They may have trouble making decisions, given multiple possibilities and choices, and you may be challenged in bringing conversations with them to a close for the purpose of deciding on definitive courses of action. That's because individuals who operate with a random style have no hard and fast ideas on how to make decisions or review options. As an advisor, you need to bring structure and organization to your discussions with Randoms to facilitate individual, joint, or collaborative decision-making.

Clearly, each of the aforementioned engagement styles requires you to interact with the client in different ways. With the client whose interpersonal style is Open, it's important to take sufficient time to discuss goals, priorities, and options—"to process"—before the two of you make investment decisions together. With the client whose interpersonal style is Closed, you need to be respectful of time and the client's desire for "efficient" conversation with you. With the client whose interpersonal style is Random, it's vital to keep client conversations on topic, to avoid tangents, and to periodically summarize and reframe the goals and objectives of a particular conversation. (For more on the characteristics of clients with each of the three aforementioned engagement styles, see Table 4.1.)

Adapting Your Engagement Style to Your Client's Personality

It's critical that you identify the engagement style of your client to ensure a successful working relationship with that person. Once you do, it will provide you with clues about how to adjust your own style to work with them in the most effective way.

Let's say your own engagement style with others is Open, and you find it relatively easy to work with clients who share this same engagement style. But if your client's engagement style is Closed, what then? In that case, it may be harder to exert influence, introduce new ideas, build client trust, generate enthusiasm for new investment products, or get the client's agreement to consider new investment choices, until you first build credibility and establish a track record of success that the client respects.

CLOSED	OPEN	RANDOM

CHARACTERISTICS

CLOSED	OPEN	RANDOM
• Efficient communication • Results-focused • Task-oriented in decision-making	• Deliberative and process-oriented • Open to input from numerous sources	• Creative thinking • Spontaneity • Finds it hard to narrow options as part of decision-making

ORIENTATION

CLOSED	OPEN	RANDOM
• May operate in the domain of "power" • Focused on action, planning, and completing tasks • Favors organization and structure in decision-making • Often formal and traditional in personal demeanor	• May operate in the domain of "affect" or "meaning" • Focused on connection with and care for others, or, on the search for answers • Favors vigorous discussion of different ideas, options, and viewpoints • Often warm and/or expressive in personal demeanor	• May operate in the domain of "affect" or "meaning" • Focused on individual expression of ideas • May appear disorganized or unfocused since there is no clear path to (or preference for) how decisions are made • Highly individualistic in self- presentation

VALUES

CLOSED	OPEN	RANDOM
• Disciplined, structured, and organized approach to planning and decision-making	• Open-ended discussion of ideas and options • Welcomes alternative perspectives when making choices	• Creativity, innovation, and brainstorming • Expression of views can be more important than narrowing choices and making decisions

OPERATING PREFERENCES

CLOSED	OPEN	RANDOM
• Business-like in his/her approach to making decisions • Looks for evidence of your credibility and credentials as an advisor	• Makes decisions through discussion, and "processing" of input from different sources • Values engagement with others in making decisions	• Originality and individuality of expression are primary • Innovative thinkers who favor exploration of ideas and options over other considerations, including decision-making

POTENTIAL BENEFITS

CLOSED	OPEN	RANDOM
• Clarity and efficiency of goal-setting and decision-making • Strong vision of what's right • Disciplined approach to thinking and planning	• Intellectually inclusive approach to decision-making that encourages full exploration and discussion of options • New learning achieved through vetting new ideas and approaches	• Innovative thinking style that invites consideration of novel opportunities and options • Can generate new ideas for consideration

POTENTIAL LIMITS

CLOSED	OPEN	RANDOM
• Focus on efficiency may limit opportunities for full exploration and discussion of ideas and options • Possibility of closing down discussions too early	• Too much focus on conversational process may prevent reasonable and timely decision-making on ideas and options discussed	• Lack of discipline, structure and organization in thinking can sometimes make decision-making difficult • Can lead to chaos or indecision if not monitored

Table 4.1   Characteristics of the Three Engagement Styles.

If your engagement style is Open, and your client's Random, you potentially have different challenges. How do you keep the client focused on the investment planning process? How do you partner with a client who may have a million ideas about what to invest in but finds it hard to prioritize options and make actual decisions about investments and estate planning? Because Randoms don't generally have set ideas about how to make decisions, it's important for you, as the advisor, to bring sufficient structure and process (including milestones and timeframes) to the work you do with such clients, to facilitate disciplined and effective decision-making.

As noted in Chapter One, an individual's preferred style of social engagement is formed early in childhood, impacted profoundly by a person's relationships with parents, family, teachers, religious figures, other authority figures, siblings, and peers. For decades to come, it becomes an integral part of a person's psyche and emotional template, shaped by specific life experiences of pain and loss and based on response patterns to the external world that were blueprinted at a very early age.[4] None of the three styles of engagement—Open, Closed, or Random—is inherently best. It's important for the adviser to remain nonjudgmental about this. The styles simply offer a predictive model for how an individual is likely to present themselves in conversation with you.

Understanding Your Own Engagement Style

Identifying the engagement style of your clients is one thing; identifying your own preferred engagement style is another. How do you determine yours? For starters, listen to yourself talk at your next client meeting. Does the structure of your sentences and style of engagement show the characteristics of an Open, Closed, or Random style? (See Table 4.1.)

To gain personal insight into your own engagement style with others, think back to your family of origin. What was the culture of your family system like? Was it

- Autocratic: Regimented, controlling, and highly organized?
- Patriarchal: A traditional family where "Father Knew Best"?
- Egalitarian: Where informality between adults and kids was the norm?
- Free-Wheeling: Spontaneous, creative, and even chaotic with few limits or rules?
- Tight and Secretive: Where loyalty and "family membership" were highly valued and outsiders weren't always welcomed?
- Missional: Where hard work and sacrifice for the greater good (perhaps the good of the parents?) was emphasized?

My Own Style of Engagement

My own family system was characterized by a Closed communications style. It was hierarchical and highly organized. Perhaps my parents saw no other way to run their household, given that they had five rambunctious boys to raise, whose birth years spanned almost 15 years!

In any case, my preference for operating using an Open communications style was in direct reaction (and rebellion) to having grown up in a regimented environment. As a young adult, I made a very conscious decision to adopt a different engagement style and also developed Protector tendencies (more about these later) in response to the arbitrary and often ruthless behavior of my parents, especially my father.

The Role of Engagement Style in Building Successful Client-Advisor Relationships

Harmonizing your style with that of your clients calls for careful observation and determination of *their* style, as well as social and interpersonal agility on your part, using appropriate language, vocal tone, action stances, and communications intent (*power, affect,* or *meaning*) to establish rapport, build trust and understanding, and forge the foundation of a strong mutually respectful working relationship. Doing this is both a science and an art. Kantor's systems dynamics model may be research-based, wonderfully nuanced, and shed light on the multiple dimensions involved in any functional human relationship. But building real connections with others is also creative work, requiring you to act on intuition, take risks, read social cues and clues, and improvise and experiment, all in the service of working through the kinks that are inevitably involved in establishing close working relationships with others.

Form, Storm, Norm, and Perform

Did you know? When groups first start working together they must go through a process of forming and storming before they can effectively norm (work together) and then perform as a group.[5] The same holds true for the relationships you have with your clients—whether that client is just one other person, a couple, or a family. The early stages of establishing a relationship involve a sifting and sorting process, as personalities interact, roles are defined, trust and rapport are created, and norms of communication and behavior are established between the parties. Sometimes elements of "struggle," ego, and the quest for dominance are also involved. Be mindful of all these dynamics as you begin new relationships with clients, because the relationship-building process should not be rushed. Indeed, you owe it to yourself, to your client, and to the professional relationship the two of you are building to establish that relationship based on mutual respect and strong professional and ethical understandings.

When Building Client Relationships Is Difficult

While building strong and healthy working relationships with clients is essential to your professional success (and that of your client), it isn't always easy to achieve. For example, it's very difficult to establish strong and healthy working relationships with clients (individuals, couples, or families) where there is a history of long-term family dysfunction, hostile co-dependency between parties (e.g., between spouses/partners), or in situations where individuals display symptoms of mental illness, traumatic brain injury, pathological distrust of outsiders, physical or emotional abuse, substance abuse, or other psychodynamic factors. If you perceive such dynamics at play in dealing with particular clients, proceed cautiously and carefully. In some cases, it may be critical to involve other family members to provide a psychological support system to the client whom you are advising.

Getting an early read on the psychological healthiness of your client, be it an individual, couple, or family, should always be a top priority. After all, you and the client will be working on issues with tremendous implications for the client's welfare, and his or her judgment and decision-making abilities will be key to a successful working relationship with you.

So, how do you gauge the psychological healthiness of your clients and your ability to connect with them? While doing this is critical when working with individuals, it becomes even more important when dealing with couples and families where system dynamics are more complex.

The pioneering family therapist Carl Whitaker, in his early research and observation of individuals, couples, and groups with whom he worked, found that healthy, functional human "systems" (be they individuals, couples, families) are those in which the possibility and potentiality of change and growth exists for the individuals involved in that system.[6] Functional systems can thus be defined as healthy (my word) if and when they support an individual's personal growth, development, and self-direction. The possibility of individuation (again, my word) exists when an individual (or individuals) within a system has or develops the capacity to act independently of past history and action, to transcend past roles in a family system, to display independence of thought, and to assert personal agency (i.e., act for themselves).

Conversely, Whitaker would likely describe as unhealthy an individual, couple, or family system where an individual (or individuals) seems incapable of personal growth, development, and change. Examples of such arrested development include a grown adult in a dysfunctional family system who is unable to assert independence of thought or action, because of his/her decades of enmeshment in the culture of that family system; an abused or battered spouse who is unable to leave a toxic relationship; or the wife in a traditional marriage who is unable to grow personally and psychologically into the role of financial steward on the occasion of her husband's death or deteriorating mental and physical condition because she never learned to be an independent actor in her decades-long marriage.

In my experience, Whitaker's early work with systems (functional and otherwise) has tremendous implications for our advisory work with individuals, couples, and families because assessing the psychological health of a client system is critical to our ability, as advisors, to work with such clients.

Meet the Schibasky Family

Consider the case of the Schibasky family of Aurora, Colorado, with whom I worked about 15 years ago. Stuart Schibasky (the family patriarch), age 62, had always been the chief financial officer of the family assets. It made sense, as he'd been head of a highly respected trust company in Denver. His wife, Alissa, also age 62, happily complied with this arrangement, feeling that she was well taken care of financially and emotionally by her husband. The couple's five children also felt secure in this arrangement, even after they left home, finished college, and started their own careers and families. Indeed, they felt safe knowing Dad was in charge.

Stuart wound up taking early retirement. Alissa was initially pleased with this decision because it afforded them the opportunity to travel. But shortly after Stuart retired, some red flags appeared. The couple's spending habits, always a bit on the extravagant side, became over-the-top outrageous. Ultra-luxury items began appearing in the home, the garage, and as accessories on Alissa's arms. Gambling excursions, several ultra-exclusive vacations, expensive artwork—even money transfers to foreign banks following receipt of Russian and Nigerian emails pleading for help—ensued. Stuart seemed happy-go-lucky, almost oblivious to the reality that he was no longer working and needed to budget the couple's spending because of their reduced income. Finally, the truth came out when Stuart's annual physical revealed that he had early onset dementia, which had adversely impacted his executive functioning skills.

It was at this difficult, crucial time that I was retained by this concerned family to help it come to grips with the new realities now facing all of them. Suddenly, Alissa was thrust into a new role of handling the family's books and paying bills. She needed extensive help with these new responsibilities because she had never had to deal with these tasks before, and she found them quite daunting. The first priority was to get control of the couple's assets away from Stuart. This meant financial upheaval as accounts were closed and credit cards were taken away. At the same time, we needed to find in-home care for Stuart and employed home health care aides to eventually provide 24-hour care. (Eventually, Stuart's health declined so much that he was moved to a nearby assisted living facility.) Little by little, Alissa began to get control of and rein in the couple's expenses. She had to carry the entire burden herself, with my firm providing assistance in paying the larger bills. She showed incredible fortitude in taking on these duties, and she earned my great respect.

The children, interestingly, felt ambivalent. They were surprised at their mother's transformation but also concerned about her long-term ability to manage the couple's complex finances. Would their parents run out of money? Where finances most affected the five Schibasky children was in the decision Alissa made (with my assistance) to scale back gifting to each of them. This created a psychological shock wave in the family at first, as the children had to re-adjust their expectations regarding inheritances.[7]

As I worked with the Schibaskys, I found myself embroiled in a very tricky set of family dynamics. My job, as *Bystander*, was to explain to Alissa how protective her children felt toward her, while also telling the children how impressed I was with all that their mother was doing. Playing this mediating role proved crucial in this family's life at this moment, because it enabled each party to appreciate the other in new ways and kept family members from taking on hardened roles that would not have been useful to them or to the family system. However, I found it was easy to overstep my bounds, as I did once by telling one son that he needed to reduce his spending. This was not taken well. I was not his father, whom he missed deeply. There was no way I was going to fill his shoes.

To the extent I ultimately proved successful, my role with this family—whose culture generally reflected an Open engagement style—was to apply sufficient "grease" to the system so that the parts could work more easily than they might have otherwise. This involved facilitating communications among the five Schibasky siblings and also convening several sessions involving both Alissa and her children, so that "the kids," in Alissa's words, "would all be on the same page with regard to my wishes, needs and priorities."

Adjusting Your Style of Engagement, Based on the Client's Engagement Style

While the Schibasky family's engagement style was Open, it could just as easily have been Closed or Random. Had it been closed, it would have been much more complicated to engage family members about a discussion of Stuart's needs, because they might have initially taken the attitude that there was nothing they could do. Stuart would have resisted help and even refused to acknowledge his deteriorating health. And Alissa, confronted by her husband's deteriorating health, could have played the role of helpless wife and kept her children uninformed and of no help to her.

Conversely, had the engagement style of the family been Random, the children would have long since gone their own ways and distanced themselves years before, in pursuit of their own goals and lives. It's also likely that they would have failed to achieve any kind of sibling consensus or alignment around how best to deal with their aging parents.

Families, of course, can mean a couple and a child, or it can mean 30 or 40 people meeting in a room together. Group dynamics change as you add players to family wealth management discussions. Besides differing agendas, the more family members you have, the greater the diversity and complexity of engagement styles at play in that family system.

In such situations it falls to you, as the advisor, to facilitate and "broker" communications among parties. This is where your ability to stay emotionally detached, and to initially play a *Bystander* role—framing and reframing discussions and facilitating connections among people (perhaps across multiple generations or family branches)—becomes critical.

Because of all the psychodynamics involved in a family system, when you first begin working with a wealthy family, it's important to learn as much as you can about all of the family members and their relationships to one another. Each is a stakeholder in the family system, and it's important to understand the motivations and engagement styles of each to the fullest extent possible.

In-depth, one-on-one discussions before full family meetings can help you prepare to broker the perspectives of all family members. In family meetings, discussion of genealogy can stimulate discussion of a family's unique history, values, and goals and help align family members of different generations around common wealth management and investment objectives. This can be particularly important to do in a multigenerational situation, where members of the family's wealth creation generation seek to connect better with younger family members who may be Millennials, Gen-Xers, and Gen-Yers.

Large family meetings held to discuss investment and wealth management topics are quite stimulating and eye-opening for all the participants involved. They often reveal simmering intra-family jealousies, sibling rivalries, divergent family values, opposing financial objectives, and much more. Conversely, they can also help forge close relationships among family members of different generations. When I'm involved in facilitating such meetings, I often ponder how many people might actually be in the room if we included ancestors from all previous generations as well as the family's youngest members. The roles and accomplishments of ancestors figure prominently in the DNA of many modern wealthy families and, if adroitly invoked, can help multiple generations of a family to discover familial roots and values they share in common.

The Harrisons

Some years ago, I had occasion to work with the Harrisons, a multigenerational family based in California that was very much in disarray following the death of the family's patriarch and original wealth creator. The family governance system had fallen apart. This family included four generations of family members. As a controlling personality, the patriarch had been close to two of his children for many years before his death, but had nonexistent relationships with his two other children, one of whom was gay. As part of his final wishes, I was asked to become involved and help the family come back together after his death and forge common wealth management goals for the family's future.

I was approached by the two grown children closest to the patriarch and asked to convene and then facilitate a family meeting. Part of my mandate was to "set the table" for all the parties involved, and help them work through what, in some cases, were years of misunderstandings and feelings of hurt, exclusion, and estrangement. Over a period of 18 months, I worked closely with the four siblings of the patriarch and with their own families as well. The work consisted both of large group meetings and numerous small group and one-on-one meetings with the patriarch's four grown children and in some cases their grown children.

Ultimately, working together, we were able to chart a future direction for the family's investments. We also reviewed and revised inheritance plans and strategies for multiple generations of the family, worked to create better communication and transparency among the various branches of the family, and built a stronger climate of trust and alignment among the patriarch's four grown children. I'm pleased to say that the patriarch's four children ultimately were able to repair their broken relationships from years past. Two siblings who had not spoken in ten years put their past estrangement behind them, and the gay son, long a black sheep, was welcomed back into the family, along with his long-time partner and their two adopted kids. In addition, the patriarch's four children agreed to review the family's investment strategies and goals on a regular basis, and also agreed on communications plans for discussing these goals with each generation of children as they reached the age of majority.

The Harrison family ultimately was able to come together and work collectively to establish future family wealth management goals, in large measure, because the four siblings were able to put the family's unpleasant past behind them and rethink their relationships with one another. As siblings, they were willing to "rewrite their family's DNA" in order to forge new relationships and to intentionally and systemically transform how the family operated.

Unfortunately, not all families are as functional as the Harrisons. Sometimes wealthy families have internal feuds or become conversationally paralyzed when making investment and estate planning decisions after a major family patriarch or matriarch, who served as the family's emotional glue, has died. Consider a family in which a Random engagement style predominates. In such a family system, establishing a method of governance can be a big challenge. While family members may have robust discussions about disposition of the family's wealth, there may be such a divergence of views expressed that the family can't easily reach consensus about a course of action to take.

In such cases, the advisor must be careful not to become emotionally involved. Instead, he or she needs to remain as much of an objective observer and arbiter as possible, to assess the system dynamics at play in the family, and to develop strategies for dealing with a large family group.

I have found that, in situations like this, the Four-Player model again becomes a powerful tool that can be used to help shape a group's decision-making. By taking the *Bystander* role initially, an advisor can serve as the convener or "host" of family discussions. At some point in that process, it then becomes possible for him or her to assume a *Mover* stance, introducing aspects of more Closed systems such as goal setting, option reviews, and milestones for completing specific work tasks. Advisors can supplement these efforts with the use of meeting agendas, performance reviews, visioning exercises, and asset allocation discussions, all of which anchor family meetings in discussion of practical, concrete wealth management priorities.

See how complex and multifaceted the dynamics in family systems can be?

Working with Couples

Although advising families is complex work, so too is working with couples. Often a husband and wife (or the two partners in a same-sex relationship) will display different engagement styles. One partner might prefer a Closed engagement style, and the other an Open style. These differences might have attracted the two individuals to one another when they first met, but now these differences may be a source of stress within the relationship. A wife might have loved how competent and in charge her husband was when they first met. But, today she may resent his controlling nature. Meanwhile, the husband may have enjoyed having his wife be so dependent on him during his working years, but now that he's retired he may resent her for relying on him so completely—financially and emotionally. Understanding such dynamics when working with couples is crucial if you are to serve effectively their common financial interests.

When I first begin working with a couple, I pay close attention not only to the ways in which each half of the couple talks to me but also to how they talk to one another. I can discern a great deal about a couple's relationship by observing their body language, their vocal inflection and tone, the way they sit in each other's presence, and the distance or closeness between them when I meet with them. At times, a couple's relationship almost becomes another party to the discussions. Do the two members of the couple use the same engagement style in talking with each other? Or do they seem to clash in this area? A husband perhaps is exhibiting a Closed style, while the wife shows an Open or Random style, or vice-versa.

As an advisor, I often become a mediator when working with couples and families in which the clash of engagement styles has the potential to generate conflicts, create misunderstandings, or cause communications breakdowns. In such instances, an advisor sometimes must step in to "referee" discussions so that sound financial decisions about retirement, investment planning, and estate management are possible.

Bringing Self-Reflection and Mindfulness to Your Work with Clients

Regardless of who your client is, know that you are part of the client, couple, or family system with whom you work. Many advisors would take issue with this, but I would argue that simply by being in the room with your client you inevitably become part of the conversational system. So, what can you do optimize your working relationships with clients?

Here's a checklist of items to attend to:

1. At the beginning of a new client relationship, take time over two or three meetings to assess the nature of your client's engagement style with you. What do you notice about the way your client communicates? What kind of language structure/pace/tone does he or she use?
2. Of the three engagement styles I've discussed in this chapter, which style does your client display? Open? Closed? Random? What prompts you to say this? What have you observed?
3. What is *your* own engagement style? What do you discern as the key strengths and weaknesses of this style?
4. Does your style seem to click naturally with your client or not? If it does, why do you say this? If not, why do you think it does not?
5. Learning to navigate and negotiate relationships with clients is an ongoing task for a wealth advisor. What can you do to better manage your one-on-one communications with clients?
6. What kind of feedback, if any, have clients given you about your engagement style in years past?
7. What steps or actions will you take, after reading this chapter, to help you build stronger working relationships with your clients?

Become Fluent in All Three Communications Styles

As you grow increasingly familiar and comfortable with your own engagement style, understand its strengths and weaknesses. Commit yourself to becoming a student of human nature when you work with clients and to developing a facility with all three of the engagement styles I've discussed in this chapter, based on the style that the client displays to you. You may also want to familiarize yourself with other tools and models for understanding social styles, including the Social Styles matrix developed by Wilson Learning of Eden Prairie, Minnesota.[8] As an advisor, I have found that the more I'm able to operate using all three engagement styles, as situationally appropriate, the more easily I'm able to connect with different client types and with a larger variety of clients. I will provide more insights on dealing with different client types when we get to the next chapter of this book, which deals with Fixers, Protectors, and Survivors.

Heroes Rising: The Different Types of Clients That Emerge in High-Stakes Situations

Tell me what you pay attention to and I will tell you who you are.
—Jose Ortega y Gasset

By now you know that there are three classic hero types that typically emerge in client situations, especially in circumstances of high stress and high stakes. Based on the work of psychologist David Kantor, these personality types include the Fixer, the Protector, and the Survivor.[1] Each type displays unique behaviors and motivations, requiring you to adopt a customized strategy to counsel them effectively and build strong working relationships. In this chapter, I talk more about each personality type and how to effectively work with each.

Looking at Hero Types in More Depth

The Fixer. Fixers have a very strong sense of self, and their orientation toward others and the world is often one of *power.* They typically use a closed engagement style with others, like to be in control, and are often perceived as driven individuals who are determined to overcome whatever obstacles stand in their way. Under everyday circumstances, Fixers often dominate social situations. They can be charming, charismatic, seductive, and great self-presenters. Fixers appeal to your ego and possess an edge that, under normal circumstances, many people find alluring. Not surprisingly, a lot of CEOs are Fixers because of their ability to get things done. They display energy—at times outsized—that's hard to resist. These are the characteristics one would ascribe to a Fixer under everyday circumstances (what Kantor calls the light zone).

But watch out. As circumstances change, Fixers can morph rapidly. If put under moderate pressure, a Fixer can become aggressive, grandiose, and inflexible. When the circumstances become truly high stakes, and the Fixer feels under tremendous pressure, he/she is said to have entered the dark or shadow zone and can become implacable, arrogant, and even abusive. They're likely to lash out at you, demean you, question your competence and professional judgment—even ridicule you. "What!?! You lost my money? How the hell are you going to ever recoup that for me?" Be prepared! If a Fixer speaks this way to you, stay calm and don't be intimidated by the words and tone of voice that are directed at you.

A Well-Known Fixer Personality from History: General George Patton

Patton quote: "A good plan violently executed right now is far better than a perfect plan executed next week."

The Survivor. Whereas the Fixer often uses the language of *power* in relationships with others, the Survivor frequently employs the language of *meaning* in their communications and interactions with others. Often displaying a Random engagement style with others, Survivors are dedicated to valiant, sometimes lost causes—and to causes above and beyond themselves. They are idealistic, moralistic, and sometimes unrealistic because of their allegiance to values or goals that others have abandoned or never thought attainable. They are highly resilient and have a tremendous ability to persevere even in the face of daunting challenges. Much of this ability is due to their faith in themselves and in the merits for which they struggle.

Survivors make great leaders of worthy causes and often excel as leaders in dangerous situations. For example, after his ship became icebound in the Antarctic in the early 1900s, polar explorer Sir Ernest Shackleton led a small group of survivors in a lifeboat in a perilous 800-mile journey across Antarctic ice. Though doomed to fail in this venture, Shackleton and his crew members somehow survived.

Under normal circumstances (the light zone), Survivors are shrewd and highly discerning leaders. They are good at assessing situations, determining their odds of success, staying cool, and taking action based on reason and information. As stakes rise, however, they become stubborn, unmovable, and can lash out at others. As circumstances move toward high stakes (the dark or shadow zone), Survivors will sacrifice themselves as martyrs to higher causes. Ever heard something like this from a client?: "Well, market losses are to be expected, I guess. The markets are really risky places." That's a Survivor. When things go well, a Survivor is likely to be muted in their response. "The stock went up? Amazing. Well, that'll help offset losses elsewhere." Very philosophical!

Even in high-stakes situations Survivor clients have a propensity to act out of *meaning*, as opposed to out of selfishness, self-concern, or even love for those closest to them. A Survivor's value system is the driver of their behavior in making investment decisions. They may stick with a bad investment, for example, because it is morally or ethically important to them. Their motives, wishes, and goals can be tough to comprehend, because at times their value system seems to ignore easy answers or common sense and straightforward solutions.

A Well-Known Survivor Personality from History: Sir Ernest Shackleton

Shackleton quote: "I . . . vow[ed] to myself that someday I would go to the region of ice and snow and go on and on till I came to one of the poles of the earth, the end of the axis upon which this great round ball turns."

The Protector. The Protector personality is different from both the Survivor and Fixer. Whereas the Fixer may communicate in the language of *power*, and the Survivor in the language of *meaning*, the Protector tends to use the language of *affect*. More than either of the other two types, the Protector is a steward and guardian of others. They have the ability to feel great empathy for others and often employ an Open engagement style with others. They tend to have deep personal relationships and to display care and concern not only for those closest to them but also for those with whom they work or interact outside the family. In a wealth advisory context, you'll recognize a Protector client because they will be overwhelmingly concerned with the welfare of others—a spouse, partner, children, and others. Their mantra is to take care of others, and this will figure prominently in conversations you have with them about investments, wealth management, and estate planning.

Under normal circumstances (in the light zone), Protectors tend to battle injustice, act as passionate (and compassionate) fighters for the rights of others, or to sound alarms of concern before others do. Many therapists, clergy, and other helping professionals are Protector personalities, such as Mother Teresa, who worked in the slums of Calcutta. Protectors are also very vigilant about what's happening in the wider world. They often perceive risks and dangers as being widely present and thus, from an investment standpoint, are the most risk-averse of the three hero types.

As Protectors are forced to deal with higher-stakes situations, they will express feelings of vulnerability, which the other two types do not. They can become fatalistic and pessimistic. "As my advisor, you've taken away my ability to care and give to others. I live my life to care for others. Now, I'm less able to do that because of the losses I've experienced." Under situations of high stress, when Protectors are deep in the dark zone they become "victim avengers." They're likely to strike out—at you or anyone else in their midst—if the pain of setbacks becomes too much.

While Fixers and Survivors see themselves as being able to exert power in many situations (the Fixer through indomitable will, the Survivor through mission zeal), the Protector tends to believe that the source of power lies *outside* themselves. Rather than trying to control the environment, they are likely to shield others and themselves from the outer world—the environment, the market, bad decisions, callous or uncaring people, insensitive family members, and so on—and not believe they have power to change or alter circumstances.

A Well-Known Protector Personality from History: Mother Teresa

Mother Teresa quote: "Let us touch the dying, the poor, the lonely, and the unwanted according to the graces we have received and let us not be ashamed or slow to do the humble work."

Origins of an Individual's "Shadow Side"

I've been alluding in recent pages to a person's dark or shadow side. Where does a person's shadow side come from? How is it formed, and what causes its appearance? The emergence of a person's shadow self is typically triggered by something in the present—an *event, situation, person,* or

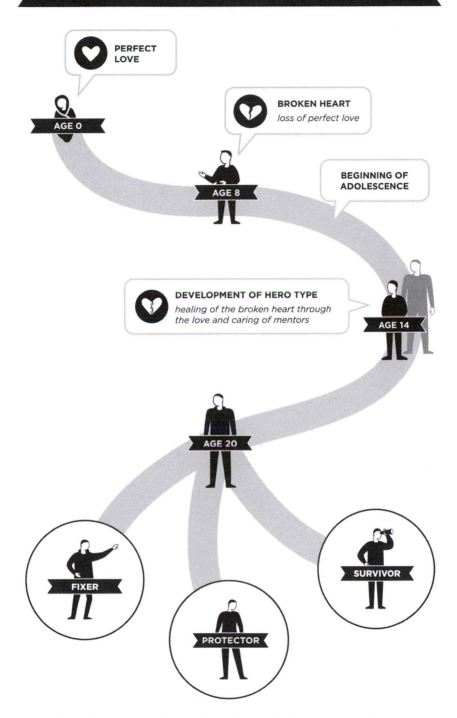

Figure 5.1 Journey to Selfhood: Formative early life experiences lay the foundation for an individual's hero type.

interaction—that sparks a flashback, reminding that individual of an event from their distant, childhood past that threatened or hurt them deeply, according to psychologist David Kantor.[2] Kantor says there are ten key psychological triggers of the shadow, including a person's fear of

- Failure
- Being unjustly seen as lacking character
- Radical change
- Poverty or loss of livelihood
- Having one's basic identity questioned
- Being unjustly accused of wrongdoing
- Being publicly humiliated
- Being denied fundamental rights and liberties
- Dying before one's time
- Being discovered as inauthentic—a fraud

It's easy to see how marketplace volatility, financial uncertainties, or the threatened or anticipated loss or depletion of one's financial assets could cause any (or many) of the above fears on the part of a client. In my experience, the specific kind of emotion (fear) that a client feels (and its degree) is determined principally by a person's unique hero type, as is the intensity of loss or gain he or she feels based on market performance.

For example, while Kahneman and Tversky determined that, in general, peoples' experience of loss is twice as intense (painful) as their experience of gain is pleasurable, I estimate that for Fixers the intensity of pain from loss is far greater than that of the general population. Why? Because Fixers have iron wills and believe strongly in themselves and their view of the world. They ascribe great power to themselves to shape and influence events in their lives by virtue of their own individual efforts. Consequently, loss, when it occurs, is offensive to them. To the Fixer, life is a battle to be won. Thus, it's very hard for Fixers to accept defeat.

For their part, Protectors, who in high-stakes circumstances believe themselves to be morally in the right, also hate to lose, but for them the intensity of financial losses is mitigated because they believe that the actual power to affect events lies mostly outside themselves—with others, market forces, and so on. Further, a Protector's experience of pleasure at financial gains (when they occur) is dampened by his or her general sense of anxiety about dangers and threats that lurk about them. Because they anticipate that danger and threats will surround them as they ponder financial and investment decisions, they are less emotionally invested in securing big gains at any cost. They are better able than Fixers to "bystand" market situ-

Figure 5.2   The behaviors and personality characteristics of all hero types change as circumstances move from low stakes to high stakes.

ations and keep both losses and gains in reasonable perspective.[3] As clients, you'll find Protectors to be less demanding of big returns than a Fixer client will be. Even so, when Protectors do experience loss, they're likely to think of it as a diminished capacity to care for and love those close to them.

Survivors are another case again. Survivors expect their lives to be difficult and, from an investor's standpoint, expect losses to occur. In preparation,

Understanding the Hero Type That *You* Bring to Client Discussions

So what about you? What hero type are you? Understanding your own hero type is critical to being an effective advisor to others. So, before we move forward, take a moment now to reflect on and to write down your answers to the following questions based on the descriptions of hero types provided in this and previous chapters:

1. What "hero type" do you think you are? (Fixer, Survivor, Protector)
2. Why do you say this?
3. What formative experiences from childhood do you believe helped shape the hero type that you are today? Examples:
4. Can you think of instances in which your hero type played itself out as the market was selling off? Or in an interaction with a client? Examples:
5. Based on the descriptions of the hero types provided in this chapter, what challenges do you think you face in dealing with clients (or other people) whose hero types are different from your own? Give examples.

they willingly "salt away gains" (hedge their bets with investments) in anticipation of losses, feeling such experiences are inevitable. Consequently, their experience of both loss and gain tends to be more muted than it is for either Fixers or Protectors. If the market goes up, they're pleased, of course, but always anticipate that a loss is not far behind. If losses occur, it simply validates the Survivor's belief that losses are to be expected. Based on these mindsets, my experience has been that while Survivors don't enjoy losses any more than other hero types do, they bear them better and with greater resilience than do Protectors and much better than do Fixers. And when financial gains do result from investments, Survivors are likely to experience less pleasure (about half as much) as the average Protector investor does. (Note: I'll have much more to say about each of the hero types in Chapters Six, Seven, and Eight.)

Dealing with Different Hero Types in Client-Advisor Meetings

You won't likely identify a person's hero type the very first time you meet them as a prospect or client. Hero types are rarely so obvious. Moreover, as noted, a person's hero type typically doesn't become evident until the stakes become high. Initially, however, you can look for clues and listen for traits that will enable you to begin developing a profile of what that person's hero type is likely to be, as stakes grow higher. Remember, for example, that Fixers are often charming and charismatic self-presenters in low-stakes situations and frequently "Movers" in conversation who communicate "in power" with others. In contrast, Survivors often display strong missionary or idealistic zeal, appear fatalistic at times (presenting as Bystanders), and communicate "in meaning," whereas Protectors talk animatedly about those whom they love, communicating "in affect" about those whom they want to protect and nurture. (See also Table 4.1.)

There's an infinite variety of personality combinations you can encounter as an advisor, based on the diversity of human nature in general. Richard Davidson, PhD, professor of psychology and psychiatry at the University of Wisconsin-Madison and author of *The Emotional Life of Your Brain*, has written extensively on emotional style and how this manifests itself in the ways an individual expresses him or herself to others. "[D]ifferent people have different Emotional Styles," he notes.[4] A person's emotional style consists of "constellations of emotional reactions and coping mechanisms that differ in kind, intensity, and duration."[5] Davidson points out that "Just as each person has a unique fingerprint and a unique face, each of us has a unique emotional profile, one that is so much a part of who we are that those who know us well can often predict how we will respond to an emotional challenge."[6]

Surveying the Emotional Landscape: Eight Key Questions to Ask New or Current Clients

To help me construct and maintain accurate emotional profiles of clients I may ask them certain framing questions to guide our work going forward.[7] The questions may include the following:

1. What, from your perspective, is the purpose of your money?
2. What is the source of your money? How was it earned? How was it accumulated?
3. What is your relationship to the person who earned the money? How would you characterize the nature of that relationship? (Close or distant? Loving or cold?)
4. What messages about money did you get when you were growing up? Were there specific values that were communicated to you about money and its use?
5. Was "wealth" defined as consisting of different forms of capital (e.g., human, social, and intellectual as well as financial)?
6. To what extent does your family abide by those same values today? How might it be different?

7. What feelings do you have about the money you possess? For example, is there a sense of sacrifice associated with the money? If inherited, do you feel there is a "cold hand from the grave" controlling the money? Is the money in any way tainted? Is it an expression of love and caring from an ancestor or spouse?

8. What messages do you want to convey with the money if you pass it on to others: a spouse, children, grandchildren, a charity, etc.?

You can draw a lot of inferences about a client's hero type based on how they answer these questions. Ask two different people what purpose they see their wealth serving and one person might respond, "That's simple. I want to grow it. There's nothing more satisfying than to win at your own stock market game. Just don't lose it or, I'll be really pissed!" This person is likely a fixer. They're using a Closed engagement style with you and communicating "in power."

Another client might say to you, "Wow, well, obviously I want this money to be used to take care of my husband and me, first and foremost, then my children. Did I tell you about my children? The youngest one has a traumatic brain injury (TBI) and needs me to take care of her. Her condition is very upsetting. So, that's the purpose of this money." This person is probably a Protector. They're displaying an Open engagement style with you and communicating "in affect."

Yet another client might say to you, "Well, I'm really glad you asked me about the purpose. I've never really thought that through with any advisor in the past. Yet, it has so much bearing on whether I'm able to still work as an artist for the rest of my career, and supplement my small artist's income with what this account can produce. I hope we can continue to discuss this as we get to know each other better." This person could well be a Survivor. They clearly have a Random engagement style and are communicating "in meaning" with you.

A Road Map for Working with Different Types of Clients

Now, obviously there are many permutations of client responses to all the questions you ask of clients. Space precludes me from detailing every potential conversation path here, but in chapters to come I detail how to use the eight aforementioned questions to help you develop a nuanced and definitive picture of the client you're dealing with at any particular time.

Dealing with many different hero types (under both low-stakes and high-stakes circumstances) can present a proverbial minefield of challenges to navigate in wealth management discussions. With that in mind, the remaining material in this chapter presumes that you know which hero type you have sitting across the table from you as a client. It also assumes that you know what hero type you are.[8] So, let's start at the top.

If You Think Your Client Is a Fixer:

- Prepare a formal agenda for your meetings.
- Be prepared to provide a crisp overview of your credentials, your investment philosophy, and the track record of results you have generated for other clients.
- Stress your business training and background and your investment planning expertise and approach (just as the advisor does with clients James and Serena in Chapter Nine).
- Ask leading questions of the client, as they will enjoy talking about themselves.
- Ask how the client achieved success (built a career/business, amassed a fortune, pursued a dream, achieved professional stature/recognition, etc.). Doing so will give you a treasure trove of insights into how this client thinks—both about themselves and others.
- Ask assertive questions about the client's investment or estate planning goals and objectives.
- Be brief and concise in your exchanges. Fixers often prefer a Closed communications style that's more focused on results and outcomes than conversational "process."
- Wrap up the meeting on time, as agreed to at its start.
- Offer to provide independent or external proof/validation of your wealth management credentials (e.g., references, summary spreadsheets of past portfolio performance for your clients, etc.).
- Provide timely follow-up to your meetings. Summarize key points of discussion and next steps, based on the meeting.

If You Think Your Client Is a Survivor:

- Ask questions aimed at getting the client to share his or her value system with you. To that end, ask him/her about their family background, key individuals in their lives, early (and formative) stories from childhood, and their philosophy about money today. Also, ask about the client's intentions regarding bequests, multi-generational wealth transfer arrangements, and so on.
- Listen with interest, curiosity, and empathy to the stories the Survivor client shares with you—about family, parents, loved ones, and others. What clues do you gain from listening?
- Move thoughtfully to ask questions. Reflect back your understanding of what the client shares with you.
- What messages about wealth did the client get from his/her family, loved ones, grandparents, teachers, clergypersons, or others? How do these inform the kind of person the client is today?

- Work collaboratively with the client to prepare wealth management plans, paying special attention to investments and goals that reflect the client's value system and his/her specific goals and priorities today.
- In some cases, you will need to actively steer wealth management discussions, as they sometimes display a random engagement style.

If You Think Your Client Is a Protector:

- Take time to listen to the client's personal story. For what purposes does he or she want to use their wealth?
- Who are the significant people in the client's life? How do these people factor in the client's wealth management and estate plans?
- Feel free to ask lots of questions, as Protectors tend to display an open engagement style.
- Ask questions about the client's value system and how they want these values to shape the work you do with them.
- Express empathy, appreciation, and understanding for what the client shares with you.
- Gather detailed information about the client's intended heirs and beneficiaries, as providing for them will likely be a top concern. (Beneficiaries can include individuals, organizations, causes, and so forth.)
- Assess the client's previous experience with wealth advisors.
- Evaluate the client's level of risk tolerance.

Nine Potential Hero Type Pairings in Advisor-Client Relationships

Generally speaking, there are nine potential pairings of hero types that can occur in advisor-client engagements:

- Fixer Advisor-Fixer Client
- Fixer Advisor-Survivor Client*
- Fixer Advisor-Protector Client*
- Survivor Advisor-Fixer Client
- Survivor Advisor-Survivor Client
- Survivor Advisor-Protector Client*
- Protector Advisor-Fixer Client
- Protector Advisor-Survivor Client
- Protector Advisor-Protector Client

The asterisks represent pairings that are potentially problematic or very productive, as discussed in the sidebar, Special Hero Pairings.

You will most readily identify with clients whose hero type is similar to your own. Conversely, you will be challenged in dealing with personality types unlike your own. To help you navigate these and other relationships,

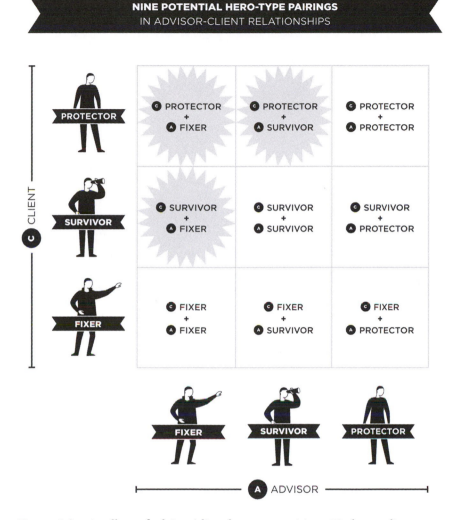

Figure 5.3 A gallery of advisor/client hero-type pairings. Understanding your own hero type and that of your client can help you to build, nurture, and sustain strong client relationships based on understanding the interpersonal dynamics at play. Those with a starburst have special characteristics that advisors should be aware of. (See sidebar, Special Hero Pairings.)

here are general rules of thumb in dealing with different advisor/client personality pairings:[9]

■ Pairing 1: FIXER/FIXER

If you are a Fixer advisor dealing with a Fixer client, you both tend to communicate in the language of power, and both of you have a closed engagement style:

- The client will most likely feel like the boss, be directive, and want to be in control.
- Initially, you need to suppress your natural tendency to talk and take control of the conversation.
- You need to be ready to follow the client or practice being a Bystander who can then shift to either move or oppose stances, as required.
- You *do* need to assert appropriate control in setting the table for discussion and preparing an agenda for the meeting.
- Briefly and concisely outline to the client the economic outlook, investment options, and financial choices.
- Be prepared to readily answer questions asked of you by the client.
- Resist leaping to conclusions or making assumptions about the client, because your styles are similar.
- Summarize decisions made in all advisor-client meetings with a prompt email to the client after meetings.

■ Pairing 2: FIXER/SURVIVOR

If you are a Fixer advisor dealing with a Survivor client, you speak "in power" and the client speaks "in meaning."

- Take sufficient time to get to know and understand the Survivor client's value system and how their personal life stories impact their view of investing and wealth management.
- Remember that as a Fixer, you will want to run the meeting rather than being of service to the client. As the client is not a Fixer, you will need to be aware if you start to dominate the conversation too much.
- Prepare open-ended questions to ask the Survivor at the start of the client engagement process.
- Take care to ensure the client feels heard and understood by you. This will require you to play the Bystander role, in many cases, to give the client room to discuss his/her priorities, goals, and concerns.
- Exercise patience in listening to the client discuss issues of meaning to them.

- Remember the Survivor's interest in meaning as you recommend investment options (even specific stocks/companies in which to invest).
- Understand the Survivor's willingness to "go down for the cause," or to stick with a course of action (e.g., hold onto a sinking stock or stick with an unproductive investment strategy) long after you, as their advisor, have determined that they need to change course (e.g., sell that stock).
- Find opportunities to balance the Survivor client's point of view about investments by introducing other perspectives.
- Avoid judgments of the Survivor client as uninformed, unrealistic, or naïve.
- Be ready to gently move conversations along if the Survivor client gets "stuck" in meaning.
- Use the Bystander stance periodically to summarize points discussed and to move conversations forward in a systematic and organized manner—from discussion, to goal-setting, to action planning, to decision-making on critical topics.

■ Pairing 3: FIXER/PROTECTOR

If you are a Fixer advisor dealing with a Protector client, you speak "in power" and the client speaks "in affect."

- Protectors are relationship-oriented. So, adjust your default engagement style to build a strong level of trust and rapport with the client. This will be critical to any subsequent work that the two of you do together.
- Remember that as a Fixer, you will want to run the meeting rather than be in service to the client. As the client is not a Fixer, you will need to be aware if you start to dominate the conversation too much.
- Be very aware of the risks you face if the stakes become high and your shadow and that of the client's both come into play.
- Appreciate, more than you're used to, the psychological factors (care and compassion) that motivate Protectors.
- Understand that Protectors need to explore and process their feelings about wealth management and investment planning.
- Don't judge Protectors as ill-equipped to make hard-nosed business-oriented decisions about investing and estate planning. They may surprise you with their ability!
- Conversations with Protectors may feel inefficient, or too process-oriented for your liking, but extensive, open-ended discussion is critical to how Protectors make decisions.
- Be mindful that the Protector is the most risk-averse of any of the hero types. This is important to keep in mind in providing wealth management advice, ideas, and investment options.
- Appreciate that the Protector client will be motivated as much (if not more) by care and love for others as by profit and portfolio performance.

Special Hero Pairings

In the pantheon of hero pairings, three specific pairings deserve special mention:

Fixer-Protector pairings are problematic to navigate because the Fixer often has no tolerance for affect in others. The shadow side of the Fixer (who is an abuser) and the shadow side of the Protector (who is a victim/accuser) mix like oil and water.

Survivor-Protector pairings can be a mixed blessing. The Protector deeply values the constancy and stability of the Survivor, as we will see in Chapter Nine. But, if a Survivor advisor is to guide the Protector client, he or she will need to pay extra attention to the tendency of the Protector to simply give up when situations become high stakes. The Survivor's shadow is the martyr who endures while the Protector is the sufferer who accuses. Both parties in such a pairing need to be mindful of the potential pitfalls of their respective shadow selves and appreciate the ability of the Survivor (advisor) to provide stability and constancy to the Protector (client).

Fixer-Survivor pairings, if managed well, can be powerful and extremely productive. In such pairings, if the advisor is a Fixer and the client a Survivor, then the Fixer can lead the charge while Survivor is the fighter, ready to invest along the lines that the Fixer recommends. In such instances, the dynamics of the Four-Player model come synergistically into play with the Fixer playing the role of Mover-Opposer and the Survivor playing the role of Follower.[10]

Each of these unique pairings is highlighted with a starburst in Figure 5.3.

■ Pairing 4: SURVIVOR/FIXER

If you are a Survivor adviser dealing with a Fixer client, you speak "in meaning" while your client speaks "in power."

- Take a businesslike approach in advising your client, focusing initially on establishing your credentials with this individual and crisply articulating your firm's wealth management philosophy.
- Convey credibility and gravitas to Fixer clients. They will form perceptions about you based on your composure, clarity of expression, self-confidence, body language, wardrobe, word choices, and how you hold yourself physically when interacting with them.
- After introductions, get right to the business at hand. Focus on discussion of the client's goals and objectives. For example, ask the client what his or her

wealth management or estate planning objectives are, what he/or she is looking for in a wealth advisor, and ask how you can be of most service.

- Prepare an agenda for the meeting, and when you first meet, highlight all the points that you want to cover with the client in that session.
- Be highly transactional and outcome-oriented in working with Fixers.
- Be cautious in your use of affective language ("I understand how you feel . . .") because Fixers often dislike such language. Instead, keep your communication with Fixers crisp and to the point.

■ Pairing 5: SURVIVOR/SURVIVOR

If you are a Survivor Advisor working with a Survivor client, both of you communicate "in meaning."

- Begin your conversations by ascertaining what purpose the client sees their wealth serving, what causes or individuals are important to them, and what kind of legacy (individual, family or professional) they want to help perpetuate with the use of their wealth.
- Because both of you are Survivors, and tend to use Random or possibly Open communications styles, prepare an agenda to keep your conversations on track.
- Take time at the beginning of a new client relationship to do a deep drill down into the client's background and family history. For example, in talking about the value system of the client's family of origin, try to surface stories that were formative for the client as a young person, and ask him or her to describe how those experiences influence their approach to investing and wealth management today.
- Inform the Survivor that, as their advisor, there may be occasions when you will give them advice that clashes with their deeply held opinions and views. This is likely in situations of high stakes, when you may recommend courses of action that run counter to the Survivor's instincts and past experience.[11]
- Remain objective when working with a Survivor client. You may feel a strong personal identification with this individual, but don't become emotionally enmeshed.

■ Pairing 6: SURVIVOR/PROTECTOR

If you are a Survivor advisor working with a Protector client, you speak in the languages of "meaning" and "affect," respectively.

- Remember that for your client, care and compassion for others may supersede any other considerations, including portfolio performance.
- Realize that a Survivor advisor can provide tremendous comfort for the Protector as client. This is because of the comfort and stability that a Survivor often brings to a relationship.[12]

- Be aware of whom the Protector wants to protect, by virtue of undertaking investment and estate planning.
- Emphasize discussion of long-term or multigenerational wealth management planning with Protector clients. You and your client are likely to be closely aligned in such discussions, with you resonating with the dimensions of "meaning" associated with this exercise and the client resonating with their interest in the stewardship or guardianship of others' interests.
- Listen carefully to the Protector's life narrative, to understand how their own world view differs from your own. Remember, Survivors tend to persevere and endure in the face of challenge. They feel the resolve and power to do so, but Protectors often "feel" danger, and believe they aren't in control of circumstances. Remind your Protector client that there are steps they can take to safeguard their assets and, in so doing, protect their loved ones as well.
- Remember that the Protector is the most risk-averse of all the hero types. As such, help them to expand their comfort zone in order to achieve wealth management goals they establish for themselves.
- Develop patience in addressing the Protector's risk-averse nature. Because of their propensity to shield others, they may be loath to take risks, consider new investment options, or make any major investment decisions until they have fully satisfied themselves that danger is not involved.
- Consider conservative investment options for Protectors, given their tendency to anticipate danger and fear of financial loss.[13]

■ Pairing 7: PROTECTOR/FIXER

If you are a Protector advisor counseling a Fixer client, you communicate "in affect" and your client communicates "in power."

- Prepare thoroughly for meetings with Fixers, and be ready to show evidence of your past track record of success with clients.
- Be very businesslike and goals-oriented in your conversations.
- Project poise and self-confidence. This will garner the respect of Fixers, who respect power and presence in others.
- Establish your professionalism and credibility early on, as the Fixer tends to look for weaknesses in others and for ways to exploit them.
- Be ready to clearly and crisply state you and your firm's wealth management philosophy.
- Be cautious about using the language of affect with your client, as they may not respond positively to it.
- Develop social nimbleness when dealing with Fixers. Speak in the language of power, and be results- and outcome-oriented. As conditions move from low stakes to high stakes, stay psychologically, emotionally, and professionally grounded, no matter what the Fixer might say to you or your colleagues in these

circumstances. (Note: As a Protector, I have personally experienced Fixers as charming on the one hand and abusive and accusatory on the other.)

- The Bystander role can be a very powerful tool for Protectors to use in navigating client situations with Fixers. By mastering the various roles embedded in the Four-Player model, you can navigate even the most challenging of interpersonal situations with Fixers, based on your ability to "sense the wind" in conversation, and pivot back and forth among the roles of Bystander, Mover, Opposer, and Follower.
- The case study in Chapter Nine provides a good illustration of how Protectors typically interact with Fixers in client situations: The Protector advisor, upon realizing he was dealing with a Fixer, quickly shifted his conversational approach after reading his client's body language. This case study is based on my own experiences as a Protector, working with a Fixer.

■ Pairing 8: PROTECTOR/SURVIVOR

If you are a Protector advisor counseling a Survivor client, you communicate "in affect" and your client communicates "in meaning."

- As a Protector advisor, it'll be quite natural for you to want to nurture the dreams, goals, and causes of the Survivor.
- Ask questions to identify the client's value system. Take time and listen to the client articulate their values, and link them to wealth management and investment goals.
- Focus on establishing strong rapport with the client. Your natural tendency to build relationships based on care and stewardship will sync up nicely with the Survivor's pursuit of noble causes, missions, and goals.
- Use an Open or Random engagement style with your client. You tend to speak in the language of "affect" while the Survivor speaks in the language of "meaning." Consequently, there are lots of opportunities here for cross-connections.
- Align yourself with the Survivor's sense of stewardship and pursuit of things noble. You will no doubt be able to have significant conversation around topics that interest and speak to you both.
- Be prepared for the Survivor's pursuit of lost causes.
- In times of a market meltdown, the Survivor's tendency to stay with even bad investments may leave you with a sense of frustration. Further, the Survivor's tendency toward martyrdom will tend to clash strongly with your impulse to protect and to shield them and their assets from dangerous market conditions. Such dynamics could potentially play themselves out in a turbulent market when you advise a Survivor to bail from owning a particular stock, but they feel emotionally attached to it and are determined to prevail and retain the stock under any circumstances.
- Establish strong relationships with Survivors in low-stakes circumstances. This will enable you to play an important advisory and even interventionist role in

high-stakes situations, offering advice, counsel, and options that may run counter to the Survivor's beliefs and instincts.

- Recognize that the Survivor's risk tolerance may be higher than yours. Notwithstanding this, there's still room for you to advise them on how to exercise caution and reasonable prudence in a turbulent or uncertain market.

▪ Pairing 9: PROTECTOR/PROTECTOR

If you are a Protector advisor counseling a Protector client, you both tend to communicate in the language of "affect."

- You're likely to feel protective toward this client but will need to temper that empathy with your professional judgment as to what kinds of investments will be best for them from a financial standpoint.
- Keep a degree of professional distance from this kind of client, as you tend to be a steward, and the client will feel that same way toward family, loved ones, and beneficiaries.
- Be aware of the Protector's risk-averse nature. Keep this in mind as you make investment suggestions, but also look for opportunities to educate your client about reasonable investment options that may carry a modicum of risk beyond their normal risk tolerance.
- Protectors tend to feel that the power to impact events lies outside of them. Consequently, they're sensitive to changes in the market and may display anxiety or even despair in moments of market turbulence. Temper your own Protector tendencies with sound financial advice that carefully weighs potential investment choices and their attendant risks.[14]

Chapter Conclusions

In this chapter I've talked about how to approach working relationships with Fixers, Survivors, and Protectors. I've provided guidelines you can use for this purpose and offered suggestions and advice on how to keep from becoming emotionally enmeshed or entangled with clients.

As you can see, learning to navigate the emotional and psychological shoals of client relationships is something of an art form. Concern with the social and interpersonal dynamics of client-advisor relationships was scarcely mentioned in the business literature as recently as 20 years ago. However, as knowledge of human psychology has grown, and as the principles of process consulting, counseling, and coaching have increasingly been embraced by the investment services industry, the benefits of doing so have become increasingly clear: The better we understand our clients and *ourselves* the more effectively we can understand, anticipate, and serve our clients' needs. Understanding the complexities of human nature, and the dynamism of human relationships is not only an exciting and rewarding undertaking in its own right, but also a valuable point of view to embrace as part of maximizing your effectiveness as a wealth management professional.

There's clearly much more to say about navigating the complexities of client relationships, which is why the next three chapters deal in depth with how to work effectively with Fixers, Survivors, and Protectors.

CHAPTER SIX

Advising Clients Who Are Fixers

If you operate by consensus, you're not making hard decisions.

—Al Dunlap

Willingness to change is a strength, even if it means plunging part of the company into total confusion for a while.

—Jack Welch

As you know by now, Fixers tend to display *power* when interacting with others. They like to be in control, have a strong sense of purpose, and are highly concerned with overcoming obstacles and odds and winning in everything they do. In normal everyday situations, Fixers win the admiration and respect of other people because of their high energy, proactive approach to problem-solving, and their commitment to goals. They come across as having charming, charismatic, and magnetic personalities and often win followers to the causes they embrace. Many high-level business leaders are Fixers because of their ability to focus, get things done, overcome obstacles, and "move the ball forward" regardless of what area of human endeavor they operate in.

In the light zone, Fixers give off great energy and can be inspiring to be around. But the qualities of a Fixer, when taken to an extreme, can manifest themselves in other ways. The goal-oriented individual can, in extreme circumstances, come across as edgy, argumentative, obsessive, and aggressive. The person who's effective at getting things done and achieving goals most of the time, can, when put under pressure, become almost fanatical about achieving their objectives and winning at any cost. In essence, they can go to the dark side and go there fast! This is because aggression is at the heart of the Fixer's personality.

If you're an advisor dealing with a Fixer in high-stakes situations (a roiling stock market, a significant life or professional transition) it's important

Figure 6.1   The Fixer.

to be prepared for changes in personality and behavior, be it in client meetings or even in phone conversations.

Meet Walter and Nancy Ossenfeldt

Take a recent experience I had with a couple I have worked with for many years.

Walter and Nancy Ossenfeldt are a wealthy German couple I've worked with for over 20 years. I meet regularly with them to assess the financial performance of their portfolio and quite often to do asset rebalancing. Walter, who retired as a partner from a major engineering firm at a relatively early age, is an aggressive investor who, in recent years, has pushed his wife Nancy to agree to investing greater and greater portions of their assets in equities. They raised their percentage of equities from 65% to 70% in 2010, then moved to 75% in 2012 and then to 80% in 2013, which is where their portfolio stands today.

Their portfolio is currently valued at about $12 million. Walter contributed perhaps $2,000,000 of that amount, half of which was in his company's stock. The rest came from Nancy's family through multiple trusts and gifts. In a recent conversation, Walter told me that with a pending inheritance of money from Nancy's elderly and very ill aunt, the total value of their estate will likely reach about $15 million in the near future.

This has emboldened Walter to believe that, with this anticipated near-term addition of assets to their portfolio, he and his wife can afford to become even more aggressive with their asset allocation. He wants to go to 90% equities, reasoning that had they been more aggressive in the recent past, their assets today would be worth $14 million instead of a "paltry" (his word) $12 million! The perceived "loss" of this $2 million annoys him intensely.

Moreover, Walter believes that any sort of volatility that the markets might display in the near term would be tolerable, even if he and Nancy were 90% invested in equities. Why? Because, he says, at the pit of the 2008 market downturn, the S&P 500 only lost 40% of its value. Thus, if their $15 million were invested 90% in stocks and the market lost 40% of its value, they would still have more than enough to meet their daily needs.

One of my challenges in dealing with this couple is that Nancy is not nearly as aggressive in her investment thinking and philosophy as Walter. She tends to be much more reserved as an investor. Her perspective is one of "patient" capital borne of growing up in a multigenerational family where wealth grew steadily *but* slowly, and family members did not live beyond their means. This drives Walter crazy and tends to trigger exasperation in him.

"Nancy always drags her feet when the two of us talk about increasing our weight in equities," he has complained to me on several occasions. Not surprisingly, Walter works hard in every client meeting we have to get Nancy to come over to his way of thinking about their investment portfolio. He is a Fixer (and *Mover*) with a Closed power engagement style, while she is a Protector (and *Follower*) with an Open affect engagement style.

As I prepare for my meeting with the Ossenfeldts this day, I can almost hear Walter railing that if they don't seize the moment and go to 90% equities *now* they'll lose out big-time on future gains. His rationale: As we prepare for today's meeting, the market is experiencing a protracted run up of value in small cap stocks, which has generated lots of street talk on Wall Street and become the topic de jour among financial journalists and financial pundits and prognosticators at Bloomberg and CNBC. Walter and scores of other investors like him have taken this bait, smell easy profits in this kind of run-up, and thus want to "chase the hot dot," as we wealth advisors call it.

And it's true. At this moment in time, small caps *have* significantly out-performed the larger cap S&P 500. But Walter's behavior today (and every day) isn't driven just by stock market speculation (though he may believe it is.) I also believe other forces are at work. As I reflect on Walter's approach to investing—"going for broke"—I'm reminded that he grew up with two siblings, both of whom had very successful careers and both of whom are life-long strivers in their own right. One became a world-renowned inventor of micro-surgical devices, the other a highly successful California real estate developer who's done very well with investments in real estate and bio-tech stocks. While Walter has never spoken to me directly about his siblings, I have surmised that he grew up in a household where there was a lot of focus on winning at any cost; a household, in fact, where winning was everything, and love was likely doled out based on achievement and success.

Even at the age of 67, Walter remains a competitive guy, concerned with looking good and having around him all the trappings of success. He and Nancy live in an affluent retirement community. They have a world-class wine cellar (9,000 bottles), travel frequently and lavishly, and run in a status-conscious social circle. Keeping up with their neighbors continues to be a concern to both of them, especially Walter. In my view, this fuels his obsessive need to coax ever larger profits out of their investments, even when with a $12 million nest egg they can well support their current life-style at a lower, less risky equity weight.

As I mull over how to manage today's meeting with the Ossenfeldts, I'm struck with the fact that any discussion of asset rebalancing will require bringing Nancy out of her role as *Follower*. But do I really want to do that? Is it advisable? (I think not.) Given the personalities and temperaments of these two individuals, it's not surprising that I feel a bit like a marriage counselor about to broach a very difficult topic with my clients!

Taking the Bystander Role Early in the Conversation

Given everything I've shared with you about the Ossenfeldts up to this point, what conversational stance would you suggest I take with them on this particular occasion? At least at the beginning of our meeting?

If you said *Bystander*, you'd be right!

On this particular day, Walter is clearly ready to take even greater risks with the couple's portfolio, while Nancy is hesitant to change the current asset allocation. For that reason, I decide that taking the *Bystander* stance early in the conversation is advisable. Initially, this simply means setting the table for conversation, outlining an agenda for discussion, and creating space for each of them to express their views, listen to one another, and hopefully, with my assistance, come to common agreement about the future course of their investments.

First, I review the couple's portfolio with them and highlight their allocation history over the past several years. I note that they've had a nice run-up in the value of their portfolio, but that bull markets don't last forever.

Then, I detail current market conditions of valuation and performance and note that while small caps have been roaring of late they are, in my opinion, now highly overvalued and ripe for a market correction. By doing this, I set the stage for gently *opposing* Walter's desire to invest in small cap stocks at that moment. I say: "Walter, are you willing to hear something about this subject that you may disagree with?"

Asking Fixers a question like this tends to disarm them because it questions their thinking and challenges them to either rebuff you or to hear you out.

In fact, when I say this to Walter he quickly replies (sort of harrumphs), *"Of course I want to hear what you have to say!"*

Presto! The door is now open for a broader conversation among the three of us about the Ossenfeldts' portfolio and the couple's future financial plans for it.

So what about increasing the portfolio's equity weight from 80% to 90%?

This is the second part of the conversation I have with Walter and Nancy this day, and it proves a little tricky to navigate because, as we meet, the overall market (other than small caps) *is* reasonably valued.

Acknowledging this, I decide to discuss price-earnings ratios, price-to-book, and dividend yield matters, all the while watching Walter's and Nancy's body language, how they engage with me, and also with each other. Nancy listens intently and seems to hang on every word I say. Meanwhile, I sense Walter's continuing desire to increase the portfolio's equity weight to 90%—even if it's to be in large cap stocks. I sense the need to tamp down his "emotional exuberance" at this moment and give him a firm dose of reality. But how should I do it?

Walter asks me for a 12-month economic forecast, which I'd anticipated and had prepared. I present it with the following caveats:

- First, I tell him, "12-month forecasts are usually incorrect and full of assumptions that rarely work out." I go on to say that "While I might be bullish about equities over a 10-year period, I wouldn't dare forecast with certainty where they're going to be over a 12-month period."

- Second, I tell him that the market usually makes a 10% to 20% correction once every year or so. "Every investor needs to be aware of this," I remind him. "Even though the low-interest rate environment induced by the Federal Reserve's quantitative easing program has made such corrections increasingly rare in recent memory."
- Finally, I note that as equity markets run up in value, investors often gravitate to them because of all the attention they get from financial journalists, TV commentators, and business analysts. I caution Walter and Nancy to avoid this "herding instinct" and to be careful about gravitating toward "hot dots" and "pretty girl" stocks, even if they're the momentary darlings of Wall Street analysts.

By offering up these qualifying comments to Walter and Nancy in our conversation, it puts the brakes on Walter's enthusiasm to increase their weight in equities at that moment. And, by gently cautioning Walter and Nancy about the dynamics—sometimes the histrionics—of the market I also position myself to gently *oppose* Walter's desire to increase their weight in equities.

"In light of everything I've just outlined to you," I note, "I recommend that you keep the equity weight at 80% right now. Walter, if you absolutely must add equities I suggest you use lower beta names to control the portfolio's volatility."

Nancy is visibly relieved when I suggest this, and after hearing my caveats about the market Walter also agrees that talk about revisiting the equity weight of their portfolio "can wait for another day."

I wrap up my meeting with the Ossenfeldts on this particular day by telling them, with a chuckle, "I know the matter of equities will always be an important part of future agendas for the three of us, and that's a *good* thing!"

This vignette shows you just one potential strategy to use in navigating financial conversations with a Fixer, doing so in a way that leaves both you and the client feeling that the client conversation has been worthwhile.

Even though I'd thought before the meeting that increasing the couple's equity weight was ill-advised, I probably would have gotten a lot of resistance from Walter had I said this at the start of our conversation. In fact, had I challenged Walter about this, Nancy might well have felt the need to spring to his defense and agree with him (as *Followers* sometimes do in such situations).

My strategy for engaging with the Ossenfeldts on this particular occasion was based not only on what I thought was in the couple's best financial interests but also on my understanding of the dynamics of their marriage, and of the dynamics the three of us had forged over the course of many years of working together. I'd long since learned that in dealing with the two of them it was always best to let Walter assert his opinion about a course of action first (even if I disagreed with it) and then only challenge (*oppose*) it after he had fully expressed his point of view to both Nancy and myself. Operating this way allows a Fixer, like Walter, to be in control for a good portion of the conversation (which Fixers like).

At the same time, by taking a *Bystander* stance initially, I, as the advisor/observer of the conversation, had a chance to read the room (in this case, the dynamics between Walter and Nancy) and to make determinations as to how best to intercede or intervene at the opportune time with my own point of view about their investments—a point of view buttressed with well-thought out reasoning and specific data points.

Believe me, playing the *Bystander* in any conversation can be challenging, especially when you enter a conversation already possessing a strong point of view about the subject being discussed. But with Fixers, being deliberate about how you engage them in conversation is critical, given their need for control. If you challenge them too early, you risk damaging your credibility and having them dismiss you altogether. In other cases, they will simply shut down or walk out of the room! Neither of which serves your client's financial needs or supports your service objectives!

Too often, I think, wealth advisors (especially young and inexperienced ones) try to operate primarily as subject matter experts in dealing with clients or as pushers of specific financial products. They have a tendency to push their views and agendas on clients without really listening to them, and often without adjusting their own engagement style based on the personality of the person with whom they're talking. In my experience, however, adjusting my approach, and being deliberate about it, makes all the difference in managing successful client interactions—be it with Fixers or any other client hero type. It's also more likely to generate outcomes that will, in the end, benefit both you and your client.

When Fixers Dig in Their Heels and Won't Sell

As noted earlier, Fixers often display a number of discernible characteristics in high-stakes or high-stress situations. Control, for example, is so important to Fixers that it often crowds out other considerations, including facing reality and making decisions based on sound financial reasoning! When caught in the throes of a plunging stock market, for example, I've seen more than a few Fixers take a haircut financially because they often refuse to sell a poor performing stock to buy one of higher quality. Why? Because they can't bear the idea of taking a loss (or even acknowledging it to themselves). Because they must win at all costs, the idea of cutting losses—even to improve the portfolio—isn't an option!

Seeing the Glass as Half Empty (the Case of Joseph)

Take Joseph, for example.

"I don't like to take losses! What part of that statement don't you understand?" he groused to me, exasperated and sarcastic, at the beginning of 2009 when I suggested he sell his falling Proctor and Gamble (P&G) stock and buy shares of Church & Dwight, a successful developer and manufacturer of household and personal care products in the United States and abroad with growth prospects far better than those of P&G.

At the time, Joseph was clearly operating from the Fixer's dark zone!

Ultimately, we sold P&G and bought Church & Dwight, which proved to be the right thing to do, because P&G has since struggled and now labors in its turnaround, while Church & Dwight has done relatively well, even during subsequent turbulent markets. Still, for a long time afterwards, Joseph complained about "selling out" his P&G stock. Why? Because the idea of a loss was so repugnant to him. And somehow he couldn't let go of this feeling.

Anchoring

What accounts for Joseph's behavior?

It's known as anchoring. People who display anchoring characteristics base their business decisions and estimates not on facts or data but on emotions, perceptions, feelings, and experiences that have no direct bearing on the actual situation at hand. It is instinctual, anal-retentive reasoning rather than intellectually based reasoning. In my opinion, because the emotions seem so deep, I suspect they are rooted in unresolved hurt or pain from childhood.

For Fixers, feelings about gain and loss are particularly powerful as motivators of their behavior. Thus, anchoring is hard to overcome as a predisposition. Fixers always need to win, so they will hold on to things (e.g., a bad stock) even when the opportunity costs of doing so *should* motivate them to reinvest their capital elsewhere.

As a wealth advisor, observing such behavior can drive me nuts. It's ludicrous to hold on to an investment that's going over a cliff. Still, for Fixers the downside of acknowledging a loss can be more compelling than any other consideration, including investing in something more promising and profitable!

Don't Confuse Me with the Facts (the Case of Stanley)

Here's another example of client anchoring. Stanley, another client of mine, bought PetSmart at $58/share, but soon thereafter the stock lost value, dipping to $52 a share. Stanley had a minor meltdown when this happened and got quite upset with me about why we'd bought the stock in the first place. "What were you thinking?" he said to me. To this, I coolly replied (playing the *Opposer*) that PetSmart had been a good value at $58 and was an even better value at $52/share, because at that price we were broadly adding to client portfolios across the firm. (In fact, market forecasts at the time we bought the stock showed it had potential to go to the high $60s or even $70 a share!)

Temporarily mollified on hearing this, I thought Stanley's concerns had been put to rest. But then, rumors began to circulate that at $52/share, activist investors were targeting PetSmart with the goal of getting seats on its board and forcing management to pursue a more aggressive growth strategy. Now normally, when activist investors get involved, a company's stock price begins to climb. Investors typically get excited about this. But not my Stanley. Instead, he remained concerned that the stock not lose any further value. The prospect of the stock actually rising in value almost didn't register with him!

So what accounts for this?

Because Stanley's fear of further losses was greater than his desire to realize profits, he wound up selling his PetSmart shares prematurely—at just $60/share ($2 above the original purchase price). This, even though valuation models had shown its potential to go far higher!

Ironically, a few weeks after Stanley sold his PetSmart shares, and after activist investors got deeply involved in the company and put it on the auction block, the stock price soared—to the low $80s!

A couple of days later, Stanley called me and said he wasn't really upset about bailing out before the stock rose in share price. Instead, he said, "I'm glad we held on to the stock long enough to avoid taking a loss on it. I don't mind that we sold when we did."

I know, it's hard to understand.

So, what do I make of Stanley's behavior?

To me it reflects an unconscious confirmation bias. In other words, it reflects Stanley's belief that the market, in general, is more likely to lose value than to gain value, even if this is not supported by fact. Stanley's thinking obviously limits his ability to take investment risk and to entertain the possibilities of large-scale positive returns from such investments. But the effects of confirmation bias can be very strong, especially when it comes to emotionally charged subjects (e.g., money) and deeply held beliefs about loss.

Objectively speaking, if Stanley were to look at Figure 6.2 he would understand what he missed out on by selling his PetSmart shares when he did—before the original target price of the stock had been realized. But I doubt that his *Fixer* tendencies would have enabled him to embrace such empirical data and use it to change his investment thinking.

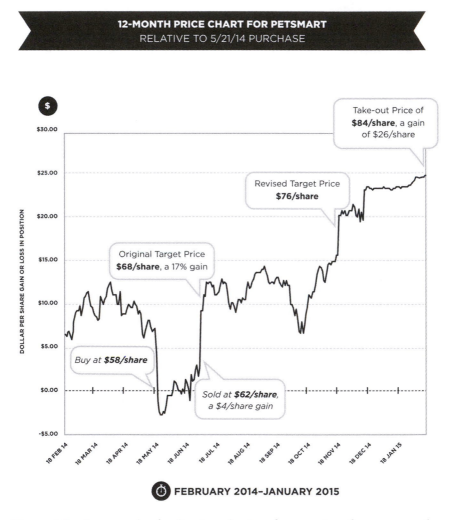

Figure 6.2   An example of a client's anchoring of expectations for returns to the purchase price of a stock; in this case, PetSmart, Inc. The anchoring behavior is made all the stronger due to the Fixer hero type.
Source: FactSet.

In for a Penny, in for a Pound (Jessica)

Here's yet another example of how a Fixer client tends to display anchoring. A client of mine whom I will call Jessica decided to buy Staples at $18/share after it had dropped dramatically in price. After she bought it, the stock dropped further to $14/share and then to $11/share.

At some point, most rational investors would take a second look at a holding that had dropped 20% below its purchase price to see if they'd missed something in their initial assessment of the stock's long-term attractiveness. But not Jessica! A Fixer like Jessica is likely to dig in her heels and determine that a stock can't be sold for *any* reason, because doing so means acknowledging a loss—even in a tax-exempt account! It took me several client meetings with Jessica to get her to finally reconsider her ownership of Staples stock.

Ironically, Jessica only agreed to sell her Staples stock once it finally recovered from its loss. But she didn't give it any opportunity to actually rise in price above that. To avoid the potential of any future loss, she, like Stanley, sold the stock prematurely. Again, the possibility of future loss was a stronger consideration in Jessica's thinking than was the idea of reaping profits from holding on to a stock as it began to rise in share price.

An interesting side note about Jessica: She is an attractive, single woman, now in her late 40s, who has had many potential suitors in her life. In our sidebar discussions over the years, she's often shared with me that being independent has always held more appeal to her than taking a risk on investing in a relationship that might not work out in the long term. Do you see a connection here? I don't want to overgeneralize, but I always remember these conversations with Jessica when it has come to assessing her tolerance for taking risks—financial or otherwise.

To be sure, Fixers come in many shapes and shades. They can be very tough to deal with, partly because they seem to operate using counterintuitive reasoning. Advising them takes patience, careful calculation, and artful conversation management! It also requires good timing, good listening, and a great deal of social agility.

You may be inclined to throw your hands up with Fixer clients because they sometimes refuse to acknowledge reality, deal in facts, or take your advice—even when you offer it in a straightforward fashion. And when you see anchoring behavior at play, things can become truly exasperating and stressful for you, as the wealth advisor!

Fixers and Anchoring Behavior

All three hero types (Fixers, Protectors, and Survivors) show anchoring behavior in high-stakes situations, but for Fixers it is acute. When dealing with Fixers who are displaying anchoring behavior, it's important to stay grounded and not react emotionally, even if you feel strongly that the commonsense solution is right in front of you both.

As noted, *Bystander* behavior has some influence on a Fixer's thinking, but even this does not always work. Sometimes the best tack to take when a Fixer refuses to sell a badly performing stock is to suggest that they sell it and buy the stock of a high-quality company with superior management that's more likely to grow consistently in value over time, and less likely to experience wild vicissitudes in share price.

But sometimes not even that works!

Sometimes all you can do is keeping talking to the Fixer client. In many cases, such clients, though they can be "high overhead" for you, stick around and surprise you by actually taking your advice when you least expect it. Moreover, a Fixer client may add assets to their portfolios and thereby build assets under management as well.

Over time, you can often build trust with Fixers and issues can be revisited. This is my ongoing strategy with the Ossenfeldts and with Joseph, Stanley, and Jessica. I've found that by repeatedly revisiting investment strategies with Fixers, and reminding them of the flaws, shortcomings, and opportunity costs of anchoring and other biases, I've helped them to adjust their thinking about investments. It's not unlike being an advertiser who realizes that a message has to be repeated many, many times (at least seven) for its impact and implications to finally sink in with the audience!!

Managing Conversations with a Highly Narcissistic Client

Up to now I've shared some of the ways that wealth advisors can experience a Fixer up close, especially in situations where things become financially stressful or high stakes for the investor. Being able to read the room at such moments is critical if the advisor is to be effective and avoid getting caught up in the drama of the situation.

But getting caught up in the drama isn't always easy to avoid. There are times, in fact, when we, as wealth advisors, get intimately tied up in the dynamics of client situations—in the relationship between two members of a couple or in the highly complex dynamics at play in many family situations.

In our work with clients, we're not acting as psychotherapists or psychologists, of course. But, in many cases, it's still important to bring sensitivity, keen observational skills, and even intervention-style expertise to our work, because in some cases there are "elephants in the room."

Take the case of a couple I'll refer to as Alan and Suzanne. Alan recently retired as VP of Human Resources for a regional insurance company.

Suzanne, his wife of 40 years, recently retired after 30 years as a middle school principal. Both of them now have a lot of time on their hands, and in meeting with them recently I noticed that they didn't look at one another much during our meeting. Alan was very quiet while Suzanne seemed withdrawn, even a little sad. Sensing that they might be in the midst of adjusting to their new found retired status, I gently inquired what was going on.

"What's wrong, Suzanne? You seem a bit down today."

"I *am* feeling down," she said. "I just don't feel as if I matter very much anymore. I feel that I worked hard all my life and have a nice retirement income, but Alan says it isn't enough."

"Suzanne, what precisely do you get from your retirement fund?" I asked.

"Oh, I don't know . . . maybe $4000 a month."

"That's nothing to sneeze at," I said. "It means you are getting $48,000 a year. Let's look at how much money you would have to have in a portfolio to generate that sort of income." I took out my calculator and crunched numbers for a few moments.

"Suzanne, you'd have to have several million dollars, which is close to what Alan has in his portfolio."

Suddenly, Suzanne perked up and looked brighter. She sat up and, for the first time in the meeting, looked at Alan with a sense of pride.

Alan was not happy with this turn of events.

"Now, Chris, you're comparing apples and oranges. Suzanne doesn't actually own that several million dollars. You're just feeding her a line."

"Well actually, Alan, she does control those assets indirectly because she's legally entitled to that income as part of her educator's pension," I responded. I wasn't about to acquiesce to Alan at that moment. His Fixer side (need for control) was coming out and he was moving to the dark side. Here he was, sitting with me and his wife of 40 years, trying to parse her financial worth, at a moment when she wasn't feeling very good about herself.

Often, Fixers behave this way in situations like this because of deep-seated insecurities. It comes across as narcissism or even abuse of others. Why was Alan so threatened by Suzanne having any financial wherewithal of her own? Perhaps he didn't want Suzanne to get any ideas of self-worth or independence. They'd had a very traditional, long-term marriage where he was clearly the principal breadwinner. But why make a big deal out of this at this point in their lives? When they had more than enough financial resources to clearly enjoy themselves and one another?

Perhaps because Alan didn't want to acknowledge his transition to another stage of life (retirement) or give up his role as principal breadwinner in the relationship.

Fast forward: It's three months later and the three of us are again together for our regular quarterly review meeting. I greet Alan and Suzanne and soon learn of their plans to go on a cruise. They both remind me that I'd suggested they find ways to reconnect with one another, now that they are both retired. So, they'd decided to go on a cruise through the Mediterranean.

"How did you decide on the Mediterranean?" I ask.

"Well actually, Alan just presented the idea to me one day," says Suzanne. "I don't think we ever really discussed it. But Alan has always been in charge, so this is nothing really new."

"I see," I reply, trying to read the body language Alan and Suzanne are expressing to each other and to me at that moment.

"Well, let's look at your finances and maybe we can now treat them as a shared project where the three of us work together to help them deliver the results you want them to." I pause, then add, "I'm not sure we have ever really looked at the need for a budget for the two of you, have we?"

Alan squirms.

"Alan, I know this may seem painful, and I also know your salary used to easily cover whatever you and Suzanne needed or wanted to do. But now you're retired and so is Suzanne. We need to work together to adjust your spending so that you both can live comfortably and within your means."

"Look, Chris," Alan says to me. "I've always controlled the checkbook in our house and have made the decisions on what we did and what we spent money on," he says. "Besides, I don't think Suzanne has a very good financial sense anyway, so these things are best left to me."

I am stunned by the bluntness of his words.

"I disagree," I say, actively taking on the *Opposer* role. "I think Suzanne has a good sense of proportion, and I also think the two of you working together can come up with better decisions for the two of you than if you just do it on your own. Let's try to work on a budget together and see where it takes us." (See me moving to the *Mover* stance here?)

Suzanne warms to this idea. "This sounds like a great thing to do. Alan, what do you think?"

"This is really unnecessary," he says. "I've got things under control. There's no need to spend a lot of time talking about this stuff. Besides, Chris, all you need to do is make the portfolio grow a little faster and then we'll be all set."

"Okay," I said. "Let's look at the portfolios and see what that can tell us about your budgets."

After about a half hour, I happen to notice something.

"Alan, am I mistaken or are you coloring your hair? I always thought your sideburns and hair color matched my own gray!"

Alan is taken aback by being asked about this. Clearly grappling for words he blurts out, "Well actually, Suzanne made me do it."

Suzanne was having none of it. "No, I didn't, Alan. I don't know why you'd say that. I've always thought you looked just fine the way you are. Chris, I don't know why he's saying that. Maybe he's trying to impress someone?"

Our meeting that day ends on an awkward note. We decide to keep the portfolio where it is. I encourage them to continue the conversation of how to work together on their retirement plans moving forward, and then I wished them a great time on their cruise.

But somehow I couldn't shake the feeling that this relationship was in for some rocky waters ahead.

And sure enough, about two weeks after the couple returned from their cruise, Suzanne called me to say that Alan had left her for another woman.

I was saddened but not that surprised, given the way Alan had acted in our last meeting together.

Alan had displayed classic Fixer behavior (tending toward the dark side) in my last conversation with him and Suzanne. His patronizing behavior toward Suzanne, his insistence that she didn't have good financial sense, and his insistence that he'd always been the manager of their assets (and had made most of their financial decisions) only reinforced for me the grandiosity that Fixers can display in high-stakes situations. Or, in situations of high stress.

At the time of our conversation, it seems likely that Alan was already deep into an affair with the woman for whom he would soon leave his wife of 40 years. The insensitivity of his words in our last meeting, and the narcissism of his actions, only reinforced in my mind the profile of a Fixer in a high-stakes/high-stress situation.

As noted earlier, Alan had been the VP of a regional insurance company and clearly had been accustomed to making many major decisions on his own for much of his life. In the last conversation I had with him and Suzanne, he treated her almost as if she hadn't been in the room. While one could argue that at times a business executive might make decisions on his or her own, the truth is that in dealing with a couple's financial circumstances, it's seldom advisable for only one party in the relationship to be in total control or to make all the decisions regarding that couple's finances. The fact that Alan was so blatant in his desire and urge to control his and his wife's financial planning was a red flag to me; one that was difficult to address directly, except by encouraging both parties in the relationship to work together for the sake of their collective financial security.

Ten Suggestions for Dealing with Fixers

As the case studies in this chapter have shown, Fixers can be tough for wealth advisors to deal with. With strong personalities, and often the ability to dominate and manipulate others, it's important that you be prepared to deal with them. This requires that you do your homework on their accounts, study their portfolios, and most important, get to know them as individuals. By doing so, you can then employ the Four-Player model as a tool through which to manage even difficult client meetings and conversations.

To help you successfully navigate client relationships with Fixers here are ten suggestions.

Suggestion 1: Building good relationships with clients is key, but always do it initially in low-stakes circumstances. This is especially important when working with Fixers, who, under stress or pressure, can be very difficult personalities to work with. They can undergo true Jekyll-Hyde transformations. Once they do they're often not in a good place to make intelligent or rational decisions about their investments. This is truly tough ground for any wealth advisor to navigate. On the one hand, you'll be tempted to do as the client asks (even if he/she is acting unreasonably or rashly in your view). On the other hand, becoming rigid or reactionary yourself doesn't help, as it will tend to fuel tensions. My advice: Stay as calm as possible, and leverage the *Bystander* stance until you can insert undeniable logic into whatever argument you ultimately make to the Fixer to solve a problem, help them make an investment decision, or simply conclude a conversation.

Suggestion 2: Once you establish trust with a Fixer client (which can take some time) and have learned their personality type and traits, try using humor to shine a light on the Fixer's unhelpful or counterproductive traits. If you do this with a Fixer in low-stakes circumstances, he or she can step back and take a clear and honest look at themselves. They may even be able to laugh at themselves!

Suggestion 3: If you must confront a Fixer, do so only after assuming the Bystander stance first, from which you can observe the behavior of all parties to a conversation, assess the dynamics at play, and decide what kind of Oppose or Move stance is most appropriate to take. When to shift from *Bystander* to either *Opposer* or *Mover* is very much a judgment call. The Fixer may see little value in your *Bystander* stance, since the *Fixer* loves confrontation and may try to draw you out. "C'mon Chris, that's just B.S. Tell me what you really think!" In any case, avoid reacting emotionally to what the Fixer may say to you. Instead, calibrate your *Oppose* or *Move* stance as seems appropriate to the situation. The precise way you do this will depend on several things: the depth/length of your relationship with the client, your knowledge of the client's personality, and your self-confidence. If being direct feels right, then maybe it is. Perhaps the Fixer needs somebody to tell them something that no one else has dared say. In my own experience, I've had Fixers compliment me when I confronted them. In fact, the sincerest compliment any Fixer can offer an advisor is to tell you, when you challenge them, "Hey, you're freaking right!" But take care, using Mover or Opposer stances too early in a conversation may trigger an escalation in the conversation that won't be helpful.

Suggestion 4: Know yourself! If you are a Fixer yourself, you may have an easier time dealing with a Fixer client than other advisors would, although there's no guarantee here. If you are a *Protector* and are likely to use the language of affect in conversations, the Fixer may well despise you. He/she will see you as weak. If you are a Survivor and employ the language of meaning when you speak, the Fixer will likely see you as weak and easily manipulated as well. You may have to modify your style to be effective in communicating with a Fixer. To fully understand the dynamics (social styles) that are at play in client situations, refer back to Chapter Four and especially Table 4.1. Also, I recommend you read *The Social Styles Handbook*, published by Wilson Learning. The concept of social styles is used by salespeople in many different industries to understand and effectively navigate conversations and interactions with others (primarily clients) who are unlike themselves in personality and temperament. Over the years I've found that a knowledge of social styles (coupled with an understanding of a client's hero type) can go a long way toward navigating often difficult or tricky client interactions.

Suggestion 5: Be ready to take tough stands with a Fixer, if and when it seems called for. Sometimes Fixers need a show of strength from you, to put their own sense of self in perspective at that moment. That said, experiment with different ways of "opposing" or "moving" conversations along. If your client has a highly expressive personality, try being expressive in the questions you ask, or the comments you make to your client. If your client speaks very analytically, use data and logic in what you say back to him or her. Sometimes just speaking with firm intention is best. For example, by saying things like this: "You might want to consider using a total return approach averaged over the last 12 quarters rather than just looking at the account value at the end of last year."

Suggestion 6: If you must deliver a difficult message, start with a question. Say something like this: "Are you open to hearing something from me that you don't want to hear?" Or, "May I give you some feedback right now on what I see going on here? I think it will be helpful to moving this conversation along." Such questions create a challenge for the Fixer, and usually he/she will accept the challenge. Fixers don't like the idea that they can't handle a challenge—even a conversational challenge!

Suggestion 7: Fixers like things simple. Keep in mind that their preferred engagement style is Closed power. As I've noted, control is very important to Fixers. Proposals need to be tightly presented with clear logic and supporting data. Objectives and goals need to be spelled out, as in this example: "Your heavy weight in bonds in this portfolio has really hurt the overall performance since interest rates have recently risen. I suggest you consider reducing the bond weight and increase equities. Over the long term, equities are a better hedge against inflation and will help the portfolio to grow."

Suggestion 8: Cultivate good conversational timing! Because Fixers like control and power, this can easily set you up for early confrontations with them, when the two of you are focused on conversations about money, loss, or gain. In such situations it's easy to "lose" the conversation if you take an Opposer or Mover stance too early. Why? Because Fixers like confrontation and even conflict. In fact, they thrive on it. If you take an Oppose or Move stance too early in interaction with them, you risk generating resistance to your ideas/advice (often displayed with great energy on the *Fixer's* part). Wait for just the right moment to intercede with the Fixer, using facts and logic. The Fixer *will* respect your opposing views, but you need to express yourself in a logical, constructive, and well-timed way.

Suggestion 9: If in doubt how to best engage with a Fixer, begin by taking a Bystander stance. By taking the Bystander stance initially, you retain maximum flexibility to assume other stances, as the conversation calls for. From a *Bystander* stance you can shift to *Oppose*: "I think we're on the wrong track!" Or, you can assume a *Mover* stance: "Given what I've just observed, I think we should go in this new direction by considering this stock for an investment." Or, you can *Follow*: "We saw the direction in which we were going and now, after some discussion and thought, I agree that we should adopt what you proposed." Finally:

Suggestion 10: Developing interpersonal sensitivity and strong listening skills is essential if you are to leverage the Four-Player model with maximum effectiveness in client situations. In this chapter, I've shown that it often behooves you, as an advisor, to begin client conversations in a *Bystander* stance. Certainly this is the case with Fixers. But as you have seen, it will be important for you to be able to toggle among stances, as conversations proceed, and to shift to *Oppose*, *Move* and *Follow* stances, based on the circumstances and needs of the situation. The point here is to begin developing an internal mastery of the Four-Player model and how to leverage it for maximum effectiveness in *any* client situation. Using it effectively requires an awareness and sensitivity to interpersonal dynamics, of course. But it also requires that you bring other skills and personal traits to client interactions as well, including shrewdness, instinct, tact, a sense of timing, and the ability to be both a participant and observer in each interaction you have with clients.

Chapter Wrap-Up

This chapter has dealt in depth with how you, as a wealth advisor, can effectively manage client conversations with Fixers. I've shared with you a few fictionalized case studies drawn from my professional background. You no doubt will be able to relate to these stories and may have had similar experiences with your own clients in the course of your career. I concluded the chapter by offering up ten practical suggestions of how to conduct yourself with *Fixers* in the context of client meetings and conversations.

Let's go on now to Chapter Seven, where we will spend time understanding the mindset and developing strategies to deal with yet another client hero type—the Survivor.

Advising Clients Who Are Survivors

Do not judge me by my successes, judge me by how many times I fell down and got back up again.

—*Nelson Mandela*

When working with clients who are Survivors, the most important thing an advisor can do is to value and acknowledge the client's wisdom, life experience, and personal values. That's because Survivor clients dwell deeply in the world of meaning and causes. Though stoic in disposition, they know very well the challenges and obstacles the world can put in front of them, and they frequently experience pain and hardship for the beliefs, decisions, and causes they embrace—the "crosses they bear." It's no wonder that famous Survivor personalities from history include Nelson Mandela, Mahatma Gandhi, and concentration camp survivor Victor Frankl. Mandela spent 27 years in prison in South Africa during the years of Apartheid. Gandhi faced violence, injustice, and arrest as a proponent of Indian sovereignty from the British Empire in the early 1900s. And Frankl endured years of suffering at Auschwitz during World War II.

Reflecting on his release from prison in 1990, Mandela said, "As I walked out the door toward the gate that would lead to my freedom, I knew if I didn't leave my bitterness and hatred behind, I'd still be in prison." Gandhi, reflecting on his life as a leader of social change in India noted, "You can chain me, you can torture me, you can even destroy this body, but you will never imprison my mind." And Frankl, on reflecting on his personal suffering and search for meaning even in the squalid confines of Auschwitz, observed, "Everyone has his own specific vocation or mission in life; everyone must carry out a concrete assignment that demands fulfillment."

Many of the core traits of Survivors (in *any* walk of life) are reflected in the quotes of these famous historical figures. Like Mandela, Survivors in other walks of life often put up with tremendous pain and suffering for

Figure 7.1   The Survivor.

causes bigger than themselves, and do so through stubborn perseverance. Like Gandhi, they rely heavily on their intellectual systems of belief to fortify them in times of stress, challenge, and hardship. And, like Frankl, they often feel a messianic call and purpose in their lives, a purpose that transcends consideration of their own interests, to the point that they may sacrifice themselves to a cause, no matter how challenging or futile.

Quentin, the Good Steward

Take my client, Quentin, whom I've known and worked with for over 15 years. Quentin is a single man, now in his late 60s, who never married, and whose life has been filled with loneliness. A successful businessperson, he has traveled the world for decades working in the import-export business. Because he never married, Quentin has spent much of his life committing himself to worthwhile international causes, such as the preservation of United Nations World Heritage Sites and restoration of the Amazon Basin.

As the oldest of four children, Quentin has always tried to be a good steward of the money he and his three siblings inherited, in the form of family trusts from their parents, in the late 1950s. Though financially comfortable by most standards, Quentin has always taken a highly conscientious, even parsimonious view about the conservation of the wealth he inherited and has always assumed that his siblings did as well. Consequently, though he can certainly afford to upgrade, Quentin's rambling home in suburban Chicago is in disrepair, and he lives well below his means, seldom buying new clothes and driving a 12-year-old car. His "tightwad" approach to money management was forged largely by listening to the experiences of his father, whose professional fortunes in manufacturing rose, fell, and rose again during the decades of the Depression and World War II. It was during World War II that Quentin's father made a large fortune in manufacturing by supplying aircraft parts to the U.S. military. A series of family trusts was later set up, just before the death of Quentin's parents, to provide for Quentin, his twin brothers, and his sister—all of whom are much younger than he. "Always watch your money like a hawk," his father frequently told him when he was a boy. "Once you get it, you can lose it again very fast."

Watch Your Money Like a Hawk

Learning, as a child, that wealth can be lost far more easily than it can be amassed, Quentin made a commitment to himself very early to avoid dipping into the family trusts to support himself or to give himself a posh lifestyle. Instead, he has worked hard all his life to fund his own retirement through his career, taking comfort in the fact that there was always a "rainy day" fund that he could have access to, at some point, should he want or need to tap that money.

Not long ago however, Quentin sat in my office, shaking his head. He was angry at what he had just discovered.

"I recently found out that my siblings have been raiding our family trusts like a goddamn cookie jar," he exclaimed to me. "Two of my siblings don't even work, and yet they've been making big draw downs on the Trusts now for several years—both for themselves and their kids. These people all live very showy and conspicuous lifestyles too and it really annoys the hell out of me."

Quentin went on to tell me that he'd become suspicious about 18 months before, when he noticed that quarterly balance statements from the Trusts had shown some large and unexplained withdrawals. He hadn't noticed this before because he spent so much time out of the country and therefore wasn't regularly reviewing the mailed statements. But, on this occasion, while at home, he did a little detective work by rustling through past bank statements and then contacting the corporate trustee who oversaw the Trusts.

Preserving Family Assets

After initially getting the runaround from this trustee (a lawyer-accountant), Quentin was able to determine that regular, under-the-radar withdrawals by his siblings had been occurring for at least four years. Quentin did the math and determined that the rates of withdrawal were not sustainable for the long term, and that they collectively threatened the 25% of the overall family inheritance that was rightfully his and his alone.

When Quentin discovered this, he lashed out in anger at the trustee and also got on the horn with his three siblings to excoriate them for raiding the family's trusts. His anger was intense. He demanded that the family trusts now be formally split up in four equal ways. He also demanded that those siblings who had taken more than their fair annual share over a multiyear period repay the trusts. This, in turn, caused outrage on the part of his siblings, who, never before having seen him get angry about anything, were totally unprepared to deal with his intense emotional display.

"This whole thing caused deep fractures in my family to reopen in ways that I haven't seen in decades, and that our family has never really dealt with," Quentin said. "Most of my family turn passive-aggressive in the face of any kind of conflict."

Growing up, Quentin had always felt responsible for his siblings and their livelihood but never felt they learned financial responsibility at the hands of their parents. "My parents never did a very good job at educating my siblings about our assets and how to preserve them," he said. "My dad took time to educate me about money, but he didn't school any of my brothers and sisters."

Now, decades later, his resentment and even hatred over his siblings' behavior was boiling over in my office.

When finding themselves in high-stress or high-stakes situations, Survivors often explode with anger, followed by a period of smoldering frustration and distress that simmers under the surface and causes them great pain and anguish.

Displaying a Tendency Toward Self-Sacrifice

But even as Quentin festered with resentment over what he'd discovered, he fretted about further depleting the family trusts with the legal fees that his investigation and demands for reimbursement would now require. So, as we sat there together that day, he mused about whether he alone should pay for the legal costs that would be incurred from pressing his siblings as he was doing.

"Maybe I should pay this bill because I'm the one who's making a stink," he said.

"That's unnecessary," I told him. "The fees in question are reasonably assumed by the family trusts as a whole, as they relate to the family as an entire group." As I said this, I was amazed that even as Quentin struggled to stay focused on his mission (the preservation of his family's trusts) a part of him was also willing to take the fall in the process.

His despair at the situation was further accentuated by the fact that, over the years, he had tried to keep an eye out for his siblings and their kids, as he has no immediate family of his own. Thus, his pain at dealing with his siblings' profligacy was a double-edged sword. Yes, he felt they had violated a family pact (to preserve the family's assets). But, by calling them out on it, he was also jeopardizing his relationships with his siblings—the only family he'd ever had.

Looking at Quentin that day, I saw a man caught in a painful emotional and psychological double-bind, feeling the need to be the adult in the room when no one else was acting like one but also willing to sacrifice himself to bring greater order and sanity to his family's finances.

I worked to assure Quentin that his anger at his siblings was justified. He seemed only nominally assuaged by this, concerned that he'd probably made a "bigger fuss over the whole damn thing than I should have."

As I write this, Quentin is currently in negotiation with his siblings and the new corporate trustee to split the family trusts into four equal parts. Whether those siblings who took more than they should have from the family trusts will ever repay that money has yet to be determined. And my guess is that Quentin may well forgive them for their selfishness.

Fretting about the Financial Future

His siblings' bad behavior isn't the only topic on Quentin's mind as he meets with me this particular day. He's also fretting over his own, independent portfolio. As a Survivor, Quentin is a very cautious investor and finds it very hard to see his portfolio drop beneath a certain level. In the months just preceding this office visit, his personal portfolio has dropped significantly in value, and it's causing him alarm. Quentin relies on this money, separate from his family trusts, to live on. Characteristic of a Survivor, he views these funds as his storehouse of sustenance to get him through hard times. But, just as an Arctic explorer might view his long-term food stores and sled dogs as resources, he doesn't want to think of tapping these resources (eating the seed corn or the dogs) unless he absolutely has to. I assure him that I don't think this eventuality will ever arise.

Comforting a Survivor in such situations can be challenging. With Survivors, there is no use strategizing with them on how to increase their nest egg with more aggressive investments, as you'd do with a Fixer. Instead, with a client like Quentin, it's important to help the Survivor keep things in perspective, to look not just at a single stock's performance but at the overall relative performance of the portfolio through a rough market period.

Quentin is a conservative investor. He pinches pennies to build his retirement accounts, funding them from his modest corporate salary. He also forbids himself to carry any consumer debt and takes great comfort in the fact that his credit scores are outstanding. This is a badge of honor for Quentin and proof to him that he is living a just and good life, even though he makes sacrifices for others and doesn't live as lavishly as he certainly could afford to do.

Crafting a Financial Legacy for Himself

As a Survivor, "meaning" is highly important to Quentin, and because Survivors have Open or Random communications styles, our conversations are typically quite free-wheeling. I encourage him to keep a "realistic" view of his financial portfolio, not to worry about it, and to consider how and where he wants to continue to honor the financial legacy of his parents and eventually use his own share of his family inheritance for purposes after his death. To that end, he and I have begun to talk about eventually making large financial bequests to the World Heritage Fund and to several museums and nonprofits he is particularly fond of. These are very much in keeping with the goals and objectives of Survivors, who, in low-stakes moments, are able to view clearly the long term and to see uses of their wealth beyond themselves.

As I work with Quentin, I continue to ponder the apparent loneliness in his life and its origins. For me, as a Protector, my resolve is to help Survivor clients find meaning in their lives, and in the uses to which they put their wealth, be it for others or, for worthy causes in which they believe. It's not my role to help Quentin fill the personal void that exists in his life, but as his advisor I can help him move forward with important decisions to ensure his financial well-being since he lives a reclusive life that does not lend itself to expansive thinking about investing or wealth management. In Quentin's case, I've encouraged him to be a little more aggressive with his retirement planning efforts, in an attempt to balance his highly conservative and risk-averse nature.

I have found, with Survivor clients like Quentin, that frequent phone and email contact from multiple advisors in the firm is critical to letting clients know that I'm paying close attention to their portfolios. In Quentin's case, our attorneys are counseling him as he negotiates with his siblings and the corporate trustee who now oversees the family's trusts. This gives Quentin an additional touchpoint to assure him he is not alone. I also work closely with Quentin's accountant, communicating the status of capital gains taken periodically throughout the year so he knows whether to adjust Quentin's quarterly payments to the government. Quentin has a team to support him that I sense he values tremendously, since his family of origin is so dysfunctional.

Dreamy David

Sometimes a Survivor's dreams are highly idealistic—even romantic in nature, and can be quite costly to pursue, especially if they entail a change of one's current career and a complete change in life direction and lifestyle. At age 37, and well ensconced in a business career, David had a dream of going back to school to get his doctorate in archeology with the goal of becoming a full-time archeologist. Archeology had always been a passion of his, and he confided to me, when we first began working together, that he felt it was the career he should always have pursued, especially after he had a chance to visit Cairo, Luxor, and the Valley of the Kings in Egypt (where King Tutankhamun's tomb is located) as a high school student.

Yet, growing up, his family offered him no emotional or psychological support to pursue a profession that his father always described as "very romantic in nature but also very poor paying." His mother had only compounded his hurt when she told him as a teenager that "I know you love Indiana Jones, but he's just a movie character, not a real-life person. You need to focus on making a real living when you grow up."

Nurturing a Long-term Dream

Instead, David's father, a Harvard MBA and highly driven businessman who had started a successful small manufacturing business, pushed David to pursue an MBA, and, with a natural gift for numbers, even David himself momentarily thought a career in business would be a good choice for him. He took the GMAT and entered business school. But, after completing his MBA he found that "the urge to dig in the sands of Egypt and discover Cleopatra's tomb," as he put it, was still with him.

This admission came one day as we were meeting to discuss his finances and how he could potentially pursue this midlife dream, even with some significant new and existing constraints in his life. David was in the midst of his second divorce. He was also the father of three kids, one with special needs, and faced some significant logistical challenges in being able to carve out time to pursue his studies while also sharing custody and parenting responsibilities with now two ex-wives who lived in different cities. We were discussing how to structure payouts to his second wife as part of a divorce settlement when I assured David that he could move forward to pursue his doctorate in archeology.

Fortunately, his finances were in better shape than he realized. He had inherited a sizeable amount of money (approximately $11 million) from the sale of his father's business when his father died some years earlier. At the time of his first marriage, he'd had the good sense to sign a prenuptial agreement with his first wife, which limited a cash payout to her when they divorced. Unfortunately, he had *not* signed a prenup with his second wife, whom he married on the rebound "because she seemed like my perfect love."

So, now we needed to think through how to limit David's financial responsibilities to the second wife while also putting provisions in place to ensure a pass-through trust was established for two of his children and a custodial trust was put in place to care for the child with special needs who would need intensive medical treatments all his life. I told him that if we could do that, we could then address his educational interests.

Refocusing David

I have always enjoyed working with David because he is a creative spirit, a gentle soul, and a dreamer. But "dreamy David," as I sometimes call him to myself, seldom thought through the long-term consequences of any life decisions he made, which is partly why he was in the position he was now, trying to re-invent himself while standing on the ashes of a previous life and identity that now lay in disarray.

It is at times like this, when working with Survivor clients, that an advisor can be of tremendous help in getting a client to focus on key financial priorities while not losing sight of their long-term personal or professional goals and passions. "Getting things done" is often a challenge for Survivors because of their "random" engagement style, their diverse interests, their often relaxed attitude about planning and business matters, and their frequent dislike for convention and conformity.

Determined to Make Informed Choices

David was at a point in his life though, where he felt it was really decision time. He'd come to realize that if he didn't do *now* what his heart had always beckoned to him to pursue, he'd never do it and would regret it for the rest of his life. So our conversation went something like this.

"Chris, my personal and professional life is a mess, and has been for two decades. Now, I'm a twice-divorced father of three. I feel like a real F-up." From expressing these thoughts, I knew David was in the dark zone, seething with anger, as much at himself as with others in his life, including his now two ex-wives.

"I feel I really need to get a grip, get organized, and live my life the way *I* want. All my life I've tried to please other people and it's never been enough. And it's never been very satisfying to me. I really feel called to a career in archeology at this point in my life, and I'm determined to have that career no matter what. Please help me to do this."

"David, the good news here is that there's enough money in your portfolio to do what you want, though the divorce payments to your second wife will be painful. We need to reinvest some assets to generate additional income that will enable you to live and meet monthly expenses. You also have to go on a budget, get some structure and organization into your life, and make a strong personal commitment to your goals in order to achieve what you want."

"I feel guilty though, about wanting a career. I have three kids to raise. I feel obligated to parent them."

"Of course you do, but these two things you're talking about aren't mutually exclusive," I said. "If you commit yourself to getting organized, and to working closely with me, we can put a plan in place that will enable you to live comfortably off of the interest and dividend income and long-term growth generated by your various accounts. But, even as we do that, we need to put other mechanisms in place, such as trusts for Kim and Molly (David's kids from his first marriage) and a custodial trust in place for Simon (his special needs son and David's child by his second marriage). Are you with me?"

"Yes, I am," David said. "I've got to get my ass in gear."

"Yes, I agree," I added with a knowing smile.

David got it. He then turned philosophical on me. "You know, sometimes I dream of being the next Howard Carter" (the archeologist who discovered King Tut's tomb in the early 1920s).

"Yes, I know," I said. "You've said that to me a number of times. You've told me that he was perhaps the most prominent and famous archeologist of his time."

Though I thought the world of David, he sounded, at times, like an aging graduate student, still trying to figure out what to do with his life. In those instances, my role seemed to be as much that of therapist and confidant, as wealth advisor.

Taking a Structured and Organized Approach to Investment Planning

That day, David and I continued with our discussions over coffee for a good two hours. I knew we had to have very structured conversations about the steps he was going to take in coming months. So, by the end of that day we had agreed that David would do the following:

1. Commit himself to a monthly budget (which we would develop together) that took into account his living expenses, alimony payments to the second wife, private school tuition for Kim and Molly, and special needs expenses for Simon. Indulgences like paying full price for first-class air travel, private car service, and other frills had to go.
2. Begin investigating various graduate programs in archeology in the Greater Boston Metropolitan Area. He decided that several months of research were required before he could choose a program that best served his needs, including his financial needs. We agreed that after six months, he would choose the programs that most interested him and he would begin the graduate school application process.
3. Continue (for now) in his current job as a corporate executive with a leading bank in the Boston area, but would begin making plans, privately and discretely, to leave that job within 12 months.
4. Approach both his ex-wives to work out arrangements for sharing joint custody, with the goal that within a year's time, agreements would have been struck allowing him sufficient free time during the week to pursue doctoral studies. (Fortunately, both ex-wives lived in the Greater Boston Area.)

Meanwhile:

• My firm's attorneys worked with the second ex-wife's lawyer to work out an alimony plan. Fortunately, David was on relatively good terms with the second wife, which expedited planning and agreements in this area.

- Our accounting team worked with David and me to develop a complete, up-to-date snapshot of his portfolio, and how we could potentially change the asset allocation to generate more income.
- David and I agreed to meet or talk every two months to review his finances and to tweak financial plans, based on changing circumstances. He also agreed to keep me abreast of his progress in reviewing graduate school programs and update me periodically. Finally:
- I formalized the agreements, which David and I discussed, by sending him a detailed follow-up letter after our in-depth meeting that day.

I bulleted out many of the specific items that David and I covered in this meeting, because with a Survivor client like David, who is a Random, having systematic discussions is key to covering multiple topics of conversation, making decisions, and articulating and finalizing financial plans. It's also a highly useful way to keep both the advisor and client aligned around common understandings and agreements, especially when follow-through on such matters is essential to achieving desired, long-term outcomes.

As I have worked with David over time, I've had to balance my Protector tendencies with my training as a wealth advisor to keep us focused on his long-term goals and dreams. With Survivor clients, this often requires micro-managing the relationship at times, sending emails, calling, and scheduling regular appointments to be certain the client is staying on task. David's plans had multiple moving parts, and neither of us could afford to let plans slide or get delayed. David has now firmly committed himself to new professional goals, and I have committed myself to doing everything I can, as his advisor, to help him reinvent himself and take his life in a totally new direction.

Malcolm and Deborah, Philanthropists

While some Survivors are wedded to extremely personal or professional goals and pursuits, others are dedicated to great charitable and philanthropic causes. Deborah and Malcolm, a couple I've worked with now for five years, are the creators of an innovative school-to-work training initiative targeted at disadvantaged, inner-city minority youth in major metropolitan areas across the United States. The couple met while serving as Peace Corps volunteers in Zambia. While there, they tutored African students in English and fell in love with teaching (and each other!). Later, back in the United States, they went to business school together and, upon graduation, decided to dedicate their lives to working with disadvantaged minority kids who wash out of traditional public school systems, and who may have had minor brushes with the law. Today, the training initiative they founded in the Pacific Northwest—originally known as The Inner City Frontier Academy, has affiliates in 25 major U.S. cities and has garnered numerous media and community service awards for its social and economic justice impact on minority youth.

Partners in Love, Business, and Service to Their Community

Counseling Deborah and Malcolm is a joy because they are partners in every sense of the word: partners in love, partners in business, and partners in service to their community. I have seldom met a more community-minded couple or one more dedicated to giving their talents and their wealth (approximately $95 million inherited from Malcolm's wealthy parents) to service.

Despite their great personal, professional, and financial assets, couples like Deborah and Malcolm need an advisor to help them manage their business and estate affairs. That's because like many Survivors (and entrepreneurs, for that matter) they have engagement styles that tend to be Open or Random (the randomness contributes to their creativity), and because their life focus is on "meaning" (e.g., worthy missions and causes), rather than on management of their considerable wealth. Deborah and Malcolm's dreams about what to do next with their wealth can be all over the map. They've talked about expanding their network of affiliates to other cities, and even to other countries. They're also interested in forming partnerships with corporations to further advance their educational goals for inner-city minority youth. And both of them have talked about taking on roles as goodwill ambassadors to developing countries and getting involved on the boards of international relief organizations.

Bringing Order to the Management, Conservation, and Growth of Their Wealth

Survivors like Deborah and Malcolm need expert advice to manage their complex affairs, ensuring discipline, organization, and structure in the management, conservation, and growth of their wealth. The educational enterprise that Deborah and Malcolm founded is not a cash-generating business. Rather, it is an expression of their joint dreams and identities and will continue to rely on funding from Malcolm's family fortune for the foreseeable future. Moreover, because they are so invested in meaning and in the mission of education to others, Deborah and Malcolm don't think about budgets, long-term wealth conservation and growth, taxes, and other administrative matters that are critical to wealth formation and conservation. As their advisor, I've spent countless hours with them, emphasizing the need to build infrastructure to support the administration of their inner-city educational academies. As Survivors, they appreciate that we spend time talking not just about their dreams for the future but how, through savvy business planning, they can potentially expand their educational academies to other cities, recruit a top-flight oversight board, and take advantage of tax laws to maximize their status as a nonprofit educational enterprise.

In our discussions we have also begun to talk about the long-term future, about how they might want to bring their own children into the family business at some future point, and about what messages around wealth and its uses they would want to inculcate in the next generation.

Defining Wealth in Multiple Ways

In working with Survivors, advisors must never lose sight of the Survivor's calling to a mission that is often "beyond financial capital." Financial capital provides the means for supporting a mission or cause, but the accumulation of wealth, in and of itself, may not be a goal or personal priority of the Survivor client. In such instances, it's important that the advisor be able to engage the client in conversations about the other kinds of capital (human, intellectual, social) that exist in a couple or family to ensure a sound and sustainable wealth legacy.

With this in mind, I've started to work with Deborah and Malcom to help them assess their goals and dreams for the future, based on a framework developed by Lee Hauser and Douglas Freeman and outlined in their seminal book, *The Legacy Family: The Definitive Guide to Creating a Successful Multigenerational Family*. The framework consists of assessing the four types of capital (financial, human, intellectual, and social) that exist in any couple or family and exploring how these can be effectively leveraged to ensure a strong and sustainable wealth, family, and/or business legacy.[1]

Planning for a Life Legacy

For example, if a couple (like Deborah and Malcolm) is truly interested in sustaining their educational enterprise beyond their own lifetimes and wants to consider bringing their own children into the family business at some point, it's important to plan for that contingency. For Deborah and Malcolm, this involves focusing on human capital priorities such as effective parenting and grand parenting, family communication about wealth, and passing along of key values, morals, and ethics around wealth to their own children.

Deborah and Malcolm also need to attend to issues of intellectual capital development, including the education of their children, and encouragement of them to follow in their parents' footsteps, if they so choose. Development of a social conscience in one's children (social capital that includes a focus on philanthropy, community service, etc.) is also important. Finally, of course, no discussion of wealth management is complete without substantive discussion and planning relative to wealth creation and conservation, wealth transfer, family business administration, and what Hausner and Freeman call "financial parenting" (preparing the next generation to be responsible stewards of wealth).

Addressing all of these issues is key to creating a successful legacy family; note Hausner and Freeman, "[I]f you regard wealth in terms of numbers only, you will be doomed to failure, as you will not have directed sufficient energy into building the three other critical capital accounts, those of Intellectual Capital, Human Capital, and Social Capital."[2]

Obviously, Hausner and Freeman's framework can be applied with any type of investor whom you may be advising, but it is particularly vital to use with Survivor clients, as their Random and Open engagement styles will be more focused on dreams, causes, and missions and probably less on the nuts and bolts of managing businesses and growing wealth over time.

Ten Suggestions for Working with Survivors

As you can see in this chapter, Survivor clients come in a variety of forms, but dealing with them effectively requires different approaches than working with either Fixers (Chapter Six) or Protectors (Chapter Eight). To help you successfully navigate client relationships with Survivors here are ten suggestions:

1: Survivors tend to get "stuck" in the meaning domain. They love to talk about issues, especially the markets, and why they should or should not be invested in particular stocks. So, share with them your *own* investment ideas to give them alternative perspectives.

2: Survivors get quite wedded to their investment positions, especially if those positions are borne from their assessment of market risks. In low-stakes situations, Survivors are very good at data-gathering and fact analysis, which helps them assess and manage risks effectively. However, when market conditions change, they may have a hard time abandoning earlier thinking and choices to meet new challenges. You might need to be assertive at times, telling the Survivor client, "I know that stock has been a long-time favorite of yours but here's some new information that you may not be aware of regarding that stock's new market valuation." This will likely give you an entrée to revisit the mix of the Survivor's stock portfolio.

3: Survivors often have Random engagement styles. As such, they need active direction and guidance in making financial decisions. Depending on their family background, it may prove helpful to focus on budgets with Survivors, to help them organize and focus their thinking around investments and estate planning. Some Survivors are so challenged by budgets that the advisor needs to start with the very basics, or encourage the Survivor's spouse/partner to help with the project, if the spouse is a Fixer or Protector.

4: Survivors sometimes see themselves as lacking the ability to affect outcomes but will stick with a course of action nonetheless. Advisors need to be attuned to the tendencies of Survivors to persevere at all costs, when, in fact, it may be advisable for the Survivor to change tactics and course.

5: As with the other hero types, the advisor needs to build bridges to the Survivor in low-stakes circumstances so that good communications and rapport are established. Informing the Survivor that you are aware of their tendency to abandon or martyr themselves in high-stakes situations enables you to work with them in such cases, and for the Survivor to develop trust in your independent and objective perspective in such instances.

6: Survivors believe strongly in causes and thus are very charitably and even selflessly inclined. If operating budgets are an area that need attention, it's likely that honest talk about "a budget for giving" is appropriate. Be certain to tie the Survivor's charitable tendencies to causes and goals he/she believes in and that are aligned with their personal values. Is it education? The environment? The arts? A religious institution? All of these are appropriate areas for discussion with Survivors.

7: Be organized and structured when holding discussions with Survivors. Prepare a meeting agenda each time you meet. Give the client gentle deadlines by which to follow-up with you on topics you and they discuss. In some cases, you may need to take on housekeeping issues for Survivor clients (e.g., talking to their lawyer or accountant), but be careful about adding too much to your workload and offloading such responsibilities from the client.

8: Survivors tend to be loyal clients and will stay in situations that are not financially productive or useful to them longer than they should. You, as the advisor, will need to be proactive in selling stocks with poor prospects rather than sticking in nonproductive investments. If you have full discretion in managing the account, you need to counsel the client about such situations when they arise. You may also need to weigh in on situations where you see a Survivor client being mistreated by a lawyer, accountant, family member, or spouse. (Remember, Survivors tend toward self-sacrifice even when it can be readily avoided.)

9: Survivors tend to be very even-keeled. They can be the bedrock in a relationship and tend to have a very long-term investment focus. They are predisposed to long holding periods for investments, so private equity or venture capital options may be very appealing as long as the funds are not overly risky. Highly volatile investments, such as some hedge funds or small cap stocks, can be inappropriate even if the investment might seem attractive, based on a long-time horizon.

10: Listen carefully to Survivors who seem willing to sacrifice it all—or too much. For example, when they are willing to leave money on the table or don't act to avoid losing money. An advisor needs to be ready to confront the Survivor in such instances and to inform them that they are not safeguarding their assets as they should.

Chapter Wrap-Up

This chapter has dealt with the client who is a Survivor, and what you need to know about the Survivor hero type and personality to effectively advise such individuals about their investments. I've shared a number of fictionalized case studies that illustrate some of the ways Survivors may present themselves to you in client situations, and I concluded the chapter by offering ten specific suggestions for how to deal with Survivors, be it in low-stakes or high-stakes situations.

Let's go on now to Chapter Eight, where I will discuss how best to deal with Protector clients, who are substantially different from either Fixers or Survivors. Here again you will learn how to adjust your own engagement style to deal with yet another kind of client, one whose psychological and emotional needs are quite different from the two hero types I've already discussed.

Advising Clients Who Are Protectors

It is with the heart that one sees rightly; what is essential is invisible to the eye.
—*Antoine de Saint-Exupery,* The Little Prince

The best way to describe Protectors is to think of them as guardians and caretakers of others. Many Protectors choose careers that focus on the needs of the sick, the poor, and the marginalized. They often become therapists, social workers, civil rights advocates, and environmental activists because of their dedication to protecting and advocating for others, safeguarding natural resources, and being stewards of the global environment. Protectors are highly vigilant to potential dangers that they see—or anticipate could be—around them. They're not hesitant to speak up about such threats, even when they are not seen by others. And, in moments of high stakes they often take the high moral ground, even to the point of appearing self-righteous and emotional.

Protectors also tend to assume guardian and caretaker roles as investors. As an advisor, you'll know you're dealing with a Protector because he or she often operates in "affect" and may display a very Open engagement style. They'll talk expansively about how they want to use their wealth to benefit others (spouses, children, and loved ones) or to benefit specific missions or causes (e.g., the environment, the whales, the rainforests, the arts, etc.). Bottom line: they're very generous. Think of John Beresford Tipton, the fictional benefactor in the 1960s TV Show, *The Millionaire*, who gave out $1 million checks each week to people he had never even met. Or of that indulgent aunt or generous uncle of yours. Or, the doting father or cheek-squeezing grandmother you had as a child. All of these are stereotypes of individuals who are Protectors.

Figure 8.1   The Protector.

Despite their generosity, Protectors are the most risk-averse of all the hero types, even in low-stakes situations. As situations become more high stakes, Protectors display emotions of vulnerability. In the dark zone, Protectors can become victims of what they perceive to be happening around them, and in contrast to Fixers and Survivors, they don't believe they have any power to control events or to take action to lessen those dangers. So, the time to talk with Protectors about being assertive with their investment and estate planning efforts is in low-stakes settings, when they aren't feeling that the world is a dangerous place. Take advantage of this window of opportunity to move them beyond their normal comfort zone.

Conversely, in high-stakes situations, it's important to be able to "talk Protectors down" from the intensity of threats they may feel around them at that moment (e.g., a plunging stock market) to help them take charge of their situation, explore options, and plot courses of action to help them ride out circumstances of extreme market volatility.

Caretaker Jill

Jill is an unmarried, 57-year-old woman who lives with her wealthy 88-year-old father who is in deteriorating health. Laid off from her job over a decade ago, and with no urgency to make a living of her own, she moved in with her father and, through the years, increasingly has played the role of nurse and housekeeper as her father ages and experiences a gradual physical decline. One of four grown children, Jill one day stands to inherit approximately $11 million, her share of her father's fortune, which he built as an early pioneer in the field of genomics.

A Risk-averse Client

For several years now, I have been working with Jill's three siblings and their dad to help the family make collective and systematic decisions regarding the transfer of his wealth to his four children and 12 grandchildren upon his death. We've been endeavoring to involve Jill in this process as well, although it has been difficult, to say the least. Highly risk-averse, and somewhat childlike in outlook, especially about money, Jill has been unwilling to discuss estate matters, feeling it is "inappropriate and unseemly" given that her father is still alive. She has actually said this to her father, even though he has been pushing her to become involved in the family's estate planning process.

Jill's hesitancy to discuss estate matters is rooted in a troubled childhood, a deep-seated distrust of her siblings, a generalized anxiety about change in general, and an inability to make adult decisions in most aspects of her life. For Jill, even the purchase of a car is an anxiety-producing experience. Consequently, her 1999 Saturn no longer works and sits unused in the driveway of her father's home. Some years ago, when she was still working, she was in the process of buying a home of her own for the first time (at age 42) but backed out at the last minute, feeling to do so was too risky. This, despite the fact that Jill was worth at least $7 million at the time, had a steady job, no consumer debt, and the purchase price of the house was under $800,000.

Jill displays many classic signs of a Protector. Though she grew up in a wealthy family, she has always viewed the world with a large dose of generalized anxiety. As I've gotten to know her, I've learned that her parents were emotionally distant; didn't encourage her to be independent or to have a career; and didn't display much parental warmth, love, and support of her as a child. All these decades later, she still feels aggrieved about this and complains to anyone who will listen that, growing up, her parents loved her three siblings more than they loved her. Jill's feeling of being alone is only compounded today by the fact that she is single "with no one to look after me," even though she bowed out of two engagements when she was in her 20s.

The Classic Indicators of a Protector

Though her relationships with her siblings are frosty, connections with other family members are important to Jill. She grouses about having to take care of her aging father—a "terrible patient," according to her—though she tends to his every need. She also adores her niece, 24-year-old Shelby, a college dropout, aspiring punk rocker, and mother of two little girls, ages 2 and 4. Jill showers all three of them with gifts on their birthdays and at many other times throughout the year. Jill even displays a very loving attitude toward her siblings from time to time, sending them newspaper clippings about hometown events, baking brownies, and sending them gift packages at holiday time, but always "shutting down" as one of her brothers puts it, "whenever anybody ever tries to engage her in 'an adult conversation' about money."

"My sister Jill hides behind a pretense of formality, pleasantries, and 1950s-era nostalgia," notes her younger brother David. "She's pleasant enough to everybody, but none of us in the family can reach her and have a serious estate planning conversation with her. And she won't talk about herself either, in terms of what she's going to do after our father is gone."

Meanwhile, Jill stays busy being the housekeeper and in-house nurse to her father, spending her days grocery shopping, cleaning, cooking, and making occasional forays to a local Starbucks to read the paper and drink her beloved hazelnut lattes, one of the few indulgences she permits herself.

I became involved as an advisor to this family through one of the father's sons, Matthew. For the last year and a half, I have been spending time with Jill to help educate her about the family's fortune and why it is important that she play a proactive part with her siblings and dad in planning for the future. I have been striving to act as a mediator, helping Jill connect with her siblings and dad around a discussion of estate plans, especially as it concerns bequests and multigenerational gifting. But, as I noted earlier, suspicions about her siblings run deep, and Jill carries around a lot of unpacked psychological baggage from childhood that has kept her from growing up and becoming a fully self-actualized and empowered human being.

Dealing with the Client's Anxieties

One of Jill's fears is that once her father dies, her siblings are going to force her to move out of her father's house. On the surface, such fears appear to be frivolous, as Jill has more than enough money to buy the house outright from her siblings, if she wishes, or to purchase a brand-new house of her own. However, if you scratch the surface of this story, you soon recognize that Jill's loyalty to her father, to the house in which she and her siblings grew up, and even to the town in which she once again now lives with her dad, are all efforts, on her part, to "shield" herself from contemporary reality and to live in the past; a past that ironically wasn't that happy, but which is, at least, well known to her.

Like many Protectors, Jill does not feel that she possesses power to proactively direct and affect the direction of her life, which is why Protectors can become victims when they enter the "dark zone." This is part of the reason it's so difficult to talk with Jill about money, and about making proactive estate plans. She doesn't feel in control of her own life, but at the mercy of forces "out there"—other people, circumstances, bad luck, a stock market that might "go south" at any moment, and so forth. This orientation is also why Jill is often unable to make any decisions relative to other issues in her life: getting a job, getting her own apartment or house, buying a new car, pursuing a relationship. The list goes on and on.

Building Bridges to Jill

Recently, I have been making progress in my efforts to build a closer relationship with Jill. Over time, I've found that by getting her to talk about her family upbringing and her relationships with her parents, she has been willing to open up emotionally, at least a little bit. As she has an Open communications style, she's inclined to talk about these matters endlessly, once she has established a trust level with a conversation partner (outside the family) such as myself.

I have listened to, and resonate a great deal with, many of the experiences Jill has shared with me about her painful childhood years, and my patience and protective tendencies toward her have helped to build trust. She, like so many others, has her own story of "imperfect" childhood love. It turns out that, as a very young girl, Jill was deeply hurt by a female friend of hers—someone she considered her best friend—who eventually told her she never wanted to see her again. As Jill recounted this story to me, she reflected that this might have been the point in her life at which she began to shield herself from the world around her, to detach from her own feelings, and to avoid getting too close to other people, for fear of being hurt. She readily acknowledged to me that "my fear of being hurt" was a key reason that she walked out on two engagements when she was in her 20s. Though she hasn't said it, I believe the reason Jill isn't closer to her siblings today is that she also fears being emotionally hurt by them.

Interestingly, though Jill finds it hard to trust other adults, she displays a strong love and attachment to children. As noted, she showers her niece and her niece's daughters with gifts every chance she gets. She also (I discovered) enjoys occasionally babysitting for the children of her siblings, and for neighbors in her father's old neighborhood.

Find a Way to Your Client's Heart

When I realized this, I immediately saw an opening to Jill's heart, a way to finally engage her in an adult discussion about estate planning and wealth management matters: by talking about children and how, with her existing and future wealth, she was in a great position to be of service to children both now and in the future.

So, one day I broached this topic with her.

"Jill, over time, as we've talked, it's become very clear to me that you have a great love of and commitment to children. Where do you think that comes from?"

"I think it's born out of my own early life experiences of not feeling loved by my parents, and also feeling estranged from my siblings," she offered. "I see my niece Shelby now, at 24, trying to raise two kids and my heart goes out to these little girls because they need so much, and their own mother is not really equipped to be a mother as she should be. So, I see myself wanting to play a big role in their lives—if not as a mother then as a loving aunt."

Empowering the Client

"I think that's wonderful," I said. "I know you're also very involved in running the nursery school program at your church. You've said that working with little children is a thrill and delight for you. I'm curious, have you ever thought about applying this interest in other ways? For example, by becoming supportive of child charities or child welfare groups? With your existing and future wealth, you're in an excellent position to be supportive of child charities and child-related causes. They need all the help they can get from devoted donors. What's your thought about that?"

"Hmmm, I've thought about that on occasion, but haven't really investigated it. In what ways could I potentially become involved, do you think?

"There are so many charities and programs devoted to saving children and educating youth, both in this country and overseas," I noted. "If you're interested, you could give some thought as to how charitable giving could become a part of your own wealth management plans for the future. There are some candidate organizations that I and some of my colleagues have worked with in the past that you could at least become familiar with as a way to test your interest further."

"I really do care about kids," she said. "They're my passion, especially since I don't have a family of my own. I think, in some ways, I see my own childhood as having been the catalyst for my love of children today. Every time I see a child, on TV, on the street, in a grocery store or, at a bus stop, I wonder how much they are loved, how much they are cared for. Do they have a warm home? Enough to eat? Do they have loving parents? I hope so. I want every child to know they are loved and cared about," she said, choking up as she spoke. "I didn't have that kind of love as a child, and I think it's absolutely essential for any child today to feel loved and cared for."

As our conversation concluded that day, I knew that I had struck a chord with Jill. I had identified something that meant a great deal to her, which could be the impetus for her taking a more active role in the management of her current and future wealth.

A couple of weeks later, Jill got back to me to tell me she'd done some online research and also talked with a few close friends.

"I really took to heart what you said to me a few weeks ago, Chris. Children mean so much to me, and I'm now finally ready to give thought to ways I can be of service to them financially."

Since that conversation, Jill has had an awakening. She's becoming actively involved with several children's charities and causes, including the Children's Defense Fund, the Make-A-Wish Foundation, and one overseas religious organization that provides meals and medical care to children in East Africa.

In supporting these causes, and acknowledging an interest in doing so over the long term, Jill has finally begun to realize the importance of thinking about and undertaking financial/estate planning for the future. I'm delighted to say she's rising to the occasion well, and has in the last year become much more hands-on in the management of her current and anticipated future wealth in coming years. Happily, she's also been able to reconnect with her siblings. Though the relationships aren't perfect, there's a lot more conversation going on now than ever before in the family's history.

Ashley and Leonard's Imperfect Love

Ashley is another Protector client with whom I've worked, but her issues as a client are far different from those of Jill. Twice married, she met her second husband, Leonard, an early venture capitalist in the computer industry, shortly after her first husband, David, left her for another woman. Though she didn't exactly marry Leonard on the rebound, his rugged good looks, sophistication, social graces, and evident financial success at an early age (they met in their early 30s) seemed like "a gift from heaven," Ashley later told me. Her first marriage had ended abruptly and without closure. Making matters worse, David had left her just weeks before Ashley was due to give birth to a son, whom she would name David.

Soon after they met, Ashley and Leonard married, and Leonard soon adopted David. All of a sudden, Ashley felt she had an ideal life. By her own admission she was a "traditional girl" and Leonard was a "traditional, 'small town Midwest' kind of guy." He'd received his MBA at the University of Chicago and came from a family whose historical forebears included one of the signers of the Declaration of Independence.

Their marriage "contract" was clear from the outset, if not explicitly stated: Leonard would work hard to build his business and support the family, while she would be active in the community representing their social interests. She, of course, was open to having other children, and within five years they'd had two more, a boy, Tommy, and a girl, Jessica.

A Fairy Tale—for a While

After her experience with her first husband, Ashley had developed a tendency to distrust most men on sight, doubting their character and assuming them to be selfish and narcissistic. But Leonard, she decided, was different. He was a great provider, and thanks to his professional success, they lived in a beautiful, leafy suburb of Chicago, were members of a local country club, and traveled extensively. Though clearly successful, and knowledgeable about money and power, he wasn't "dictatorial" with her. He didn't try to run her life, or expect that she would be a trophy on his arm at business events. Nor did he ever talk down to her, or try to psychologically conscript her to his way of thinking about everything, the way she saw the husbands in many other corporate couples do with their wives.

Instead he was a thoughtful, kind, and considerate companion.

Their first few years together were blissful, but for entrepreneurs, like Leonard, building a business can be all consuming. Over time, Leonard spent less and less time with Ashley and the kids. He often worked late, on weekends, and over holidays, sometimes heading into the office unexpect-edly on Sunday afternoons after church, or even on Christmas day one year. Eventually Ashley began to wonder if he were having an affair. She knew that he hired new secretaries as often as other people get new cellphones. Why did they come and go so fast? Was he a terrible boss, or an office predator who couldn't keep his hands off bubbly, blond 25-year-olds?

Trouble in Paradise

A number of years passed. The marriage waxed and waned. There were times, when the kids were young, when Ashley felt emotionally abandoned by Leonard, and she knew her kids felt abandoned too. Tommy, the first child they'd had as a couple, was particularly affected. In high school he struggled academically and was angry a lot of the time. He had few friends, and the friends he did have Ashley didn't like. He also disdained interest in any extracurricular activities, a warning sign to Ashley that Tommy was on a potentially destructive path. Eventually he started dressing goth, smok-ing weed, cutting classes, and spending way too much time online. Leon-ard seemed not to notice. He was too busy at work.

One day, Ashley confronted Tommy and asked him what was going on. After initially trying to avoid her, Tommy exploded, letting loose a torrent of emotions at her. "I hate Dad," he told her, to Ashley's dismay. "He's never around. All he does is work. He doesn't care about me. Or you! I can't wait to get out of this house and away from both of you. I hate this house!"

Ashley was crushed. Her cherished dream of having "a perfect family" as a mother and wife was going up in smoke—literally! It wasn't enough that her husband had gradually grown distant and indifferent to her and the kids. Now, Tommy was stripping away any remaining veneer of domes-tic tranquility in her life. She felt guilty but also like a victim herself.

Tommy moved out on his 18th birthday. Several more years passed. During this time, Leonard's business grew and flourished. He became a wealthy man but grew increasingly distant from Ashley and all three of his kids. Ashley grew lonely, isolated, and despondent. During this same period, Tommy's anger at his father smoldered, but he also discovered that he'd inherited his father's aptitude for mathematics and computers. So much so, that by the time he was in his mid-20s, he had become a highly successful software programmer, commanding top rates from clients for his consult-ing work. By the time he turned 30, he'd become a highly sought-after "hired gun" in Silicon Valley, working for the biggest names in the com-puter business.

A Dark Secret

But beneath Tommy's apparent professional success—his effort to "beat" his father at his own game—lay a deep secret. Tommy had become a $2000 a week coke addict, stoking his capacity to meet crushing software release schedules in Silicon Valley with a destructive drug habit that was likely to cause his death by age 35 if he didn't get control of things.

When Ashley learned about this from one of Tommy's boyhood friends, she was distraught. She tried to talk with Leonard about it, and together they consulted a psychologist to see if he could intervene on their behalf with their son. Then to Ashley's dismay, Leonard directed his focus back to work. He was in the midst of selling his computer business to a foreign investor, so, as always, he was ceding most of the parenting to Ashley. Ashley felt a wave of resentment and victimhood come over her. She was furious at Leonard.

She also realized what her life had become. Not only had her marriage languished as Leonard built his business, but now she was in danger of losing her son as well, if not to his work, then to his drug habit. Her life was a mess. She and Leonard were materially very comfortable, but their relationship was strained, and their son was estranged from both of them. The financial success they enjoyed seemed like cold comfort in the face of the challenges she faced in her marriage, and with her son who had gone off the tracks.

All this made Ashley yearn for a time in her childhood when "everything seemed simpler" and "families were tightly knit." She realized how loving and involved her parents had been in *her* life and wondered, had she been as good a parent as she could have been to Tommy? She began to blame herself for the family's unraveling. If only she'd been a better and more attentive mother, a more understanding and supportive wife to her husband!

A Complex Estate Situation

Complicating the family's emotional and psychological challenges were the complex financial and estate issues involved. For tax reasons, Leonard's three children were co-owners (nonactive partners) in his business with him and his wife. Upon the deaths of Leonard and Ashley, the three children were to each be equal beneficiaries of Leonard and Ashley's estate, once the business was sold. Estimates of its eventual value were in excess of $250 million. But Tommy's problems with drugs were complicating this estate scenario, and the estrangement of Ashley's two other children from their father was prompting Leonard to rethink whether his children should be beneficiaries from the sale of the business at all!

The Advisor as Mediator

I was referred into this family by a good friend of Leonard's, with whom I had worked as an advisor in previous years. It became clear to me, on hearing the details of the family's story, first from Leonard, then from Ashley, and then from both of them sitting with me together, that Ashley and Leonard needed to come together at this critical point to help resolve the issues at hand. In observing this couple, it became readily clear to me that Leonard was a Fixer and his wife Ashley a Protector—a potentially combustible combination in high-stakes situations. Under normal circumstances—as in a day-to-day marriage—many Fixers choose Protectors as partners, and vice-versa. Each type is attracted by the other's characteristics, giving credence to the idea that when it comes to matters of love, opposites attract. But under stress or in high-stakes situations, this hero-pairing can bring out the worst in both parties. (See Chapter Five.) The Fixer can become an abuser and the Protector a victim/accuser.

And that's exactly what I witnessed when I met with Ashley and Leonard on one very stressful occasion. Signs that their marriage and family life had entered into the dark zone were clearly evident. From observing the couple's body language, it was clear that Leonard held himself at an emotional distance from Ashley and from the distressing situation of Tommy's drug abuse. At one point in the conversation, when Ashley tried to engage Leonard in conversation about how to deal with these issues, he pushed back from my office conference table, and lashed out at her, blaming her for not being a good enough wife and not seeing the signs of Tommy's drug abuse sooner. "This is your fault!" he said. In response, Ashley first grew quiet and then whirled at Leonard, calling him an "irresponsible and emotionally detached S.O.B."

For a moment, I thought I'd have to call building security. Really!

Setting the Table for Conversation

In working with this couple, I clearly had my work cut out for me. As Ashley and Leonard were clearly of very different types, it became necessary to act as the couple's mediator and to help each of them build bridges to the other. As usual, I began my engagement with them as a *Bystander*, inviting each party to express their point of view about the challenges they faced as a couple and a family, and how they felt these circumstances had arisen. Once they'd done this, I was then able to *Move* the two of them to agree that, as part of their existing estate plan arrangements, it was imperative that Tommy get drug counseling and treatment if he were to eventually inherit his share of his parents' fortune. I also encouraged the couple, as gently as I could, to seek some counseling to help them deal with their own interpersonal issues.

Ashley immediately saw the value of these suggestions, as she loved her son and wanted him to lead a healthy lifestyle and be a beneficiary worthy of their estate. It was clear to me that she also was still devoted to her husband but was exasperated about what had happened and wanted engagement from Leonard in trying to address the situation with Tommy.

For his part, Leonard looked down as I spoke with both of them, pondering what to say next. Clearly, he was a man of business, not of emotions, and I could tell that, at this particular moment, he felt way out of his emotional depth, both with his wife and his family situation.

I took a deep breath and hoped that my next words would be well received by both of them.

"If I may say so, I believe that, for the two of you to resolve this situation effectively, you have to do it in two parts," I said. "First, you must deal with the addiction issues that Tommy is struggling with. Then and only then should you decide what changes, if any, you want to make to the estate plans you've had in place for some time now."

I went on to urge caution and restraint, suggesting that they not let their emotions of the moment overrule their heads and cause them to immediately upend the carefully laid estate plans that they'd painstakingly put in place some years before.

"You might regret that," I cautioned.

I then went on to tell them that I thought it was important for each of them to bring respect for the other (e.g., appreciation of their respective roles as parents) to the discussions we were having. Otherwise, I believed that our conversations would go nowhere.

Moving Beyond Victimhood

At one point I expressed empathy to Ashley for a lot of the pain and grief she was carrying but also encouraged her not to let guilt or feelings of victimhood overcome her. "Those feelings will not serve you," I said. As for Leonard, I encouraged him to remember that yes, he had certainly built a very successful business, but as a father and husband, he also had created a wonderful family with Ashley. I encouraged him to accept the importance of conversation and discussion of problems as a way for the family to "process" its pain, and begin its journey to recovery.

To both of them I suggested that Tommy's drug addiction might, in fact, be "a wake-up call" that could be the basis "for the entire family aligning around supporting Tommy in his recovery, and bringing everyone closer together at a moment of great need."

"The two of you have a lot at stake, emotionally and financially," I said, adding, "I'm here to listen and to help in any way I can."

Navigating a Complex Emotional System

Navigating interpersonal dynamics like this with clients can be tough, and I don't always strike the perfect tone. But in this case, something happened. After I'd finished sharing my thoughts, Leonard turned to Ashley and apologized for not being more present as a parent, and for blaming her for Tommy's drug problems. "Both of us are his parents," he said. "I'm sorry for getting so angry. I think I'm mostly angry at myself for not being a better parent, and unfortunately I take that out on you."

"So, let's work together on resolving this mess," said Ashley, who, tearfully at that point, reaffirmed her loyalty to her husband, saying, "I'm very glad you are our kids' dad. You're a good man. Let's go forward together to bring this family together once again."

In this case study, Ashley clearly presented herself as a guardian and steward of others. Her primary concerns had to do with her family, her children, and her husband. Leonard, the Fixer, initially came into the joint conversations we had with a sense of arrogance and defiance, but he gradually softened as he realized that his absence as a father had caused estrangement with all three of his kids and was something he wanted to resolve, as he put it, "before my dying day."

As for my role in this situation, I began this tense conversation with Leonard and Ashley as a *Bystander*, so I could observe the dynamics at play between the two of them and understand the way in which they engaged each other. Remember, the *Bystander* stance can be a very valuable stance to take in such situations, as it gives you space to observe people, assess the dynamics at play in the situation, and to do other critical data-gathering before offering up advice, observations, or suggestions of action.

Jeremy and Ash: The Opportunities for Growth

As noted, interpersonal dynamics are always at play in client interactions, whether one is dealing with an individual, couple, or a family. Take Jeremy and Ash, a same-sex couple that I worked with for about eight years. My work with this couple was unique because it took place against the backdrop of changing marriage and estate laws affecting same-sex couples across the United States in the early 2000s, which culminated in the U.S. Supreme Court finally legalizing same-sex marriage in all 50 states in June 2015.

Jeremy was a classic Fixer. A highly successful land developer in the Miami Beach area, he had a hard-driving, hard-bargaining interpersonal style that tended to immediately charm you when you met him, while overwhelming you a bit at the same time. When I first met him, I realized why he'd been so successful in residential and commercial real estate. He had a charisma that was hard for customers to resist!

Ash, on the other hand, was a classic Protector, his introversion and quiet demeanor contrasted markedly with Jeremy's over-the top extroversion.

A Classic Fixer/Protector Pairing

Their investment styles were as different as their personalities. Jeremy had a high comfort level with risk-taking. When the three of us talked investments, Jeremy was always ready to go "all in." Forget about taking one-and-a-half-point percentage positions initially on a stock and working to build that up to 2 or 3%. Jeremy typically wanted 4% to start with! And, he hated small share positions. He disliked any purchases of under 100 shares and preferred a 500-share position if not a 1000-share position at the get-go. Translation: he went in with guns blazing. I imagine he figured that it had worked for him in real estate. So, why not in investing?

For his part, Ash was the polar opposite. Not only was he fundamentally non-conversant with investment matters, he was the kind of person who was more comfortable with checkbooks and passbook accounts than with high-rolling talk of alpha investing, hedge funds, and multigenerational wealth management. He and Jeremy would routinely banter about his preference for having a checking account with at least $100,000 in it, over any kind of investment that might outperform the S&P. When they talked, I always realized that Ash's risk-aversion drove Jeremy crazy. From Jeremy's perspective, it was a waste of liquidity. "Ash, that cash would be better invested in the markets!" But Ash always pushed back. A cautious investor, he'd grown up in the poor neighborhoods of Dallas, Texas, and was more focused on "hoarding cash and being able to pay the bills," as he put it, than speculating in "that big bad casino crapshoot in the sky" which was his term for the ethereal world of high net worth investing.

Over the course of several years, I got to know Jeremy and Ash quite well. When the three of us met, Ash would talk for long stretches in "affect," noting how fortunate he felt to have met Jeremy and to have enjoyed a "wonderful life" as a result of their relationship. He came from a large family, and always spoke of his interest in providing a financial safety net to his elderly mother, to his four siblings, none of whom had gone to college, and to ten nieces and nephews. "Jeremy has always been so supportive of this goal, for which I'm very grateful," he told me. He himself had had a career as a graphic artist before he and Jeremy met but did not possess wealth of his own before the two of them got married in Northampton, Massachusetts, when it became legal in 2004.

When the Fixer Departs a Relationship with a Protector

Sadly, Jeremy died quite suddenly in early 2014 at the age of 64. He and Ash had been legally married, at that point, for nearly ten years, even though they'd known each for ten years before that. Ash was devastated, of course, but soldiered on, despite the vast emptiness left by Jeremy's death. Jeremy had done well to provide for Ash. Once the estate settled it was worth approximately $70 million.

In the months following Jeremy's estate settlement, Ash decided that he wanted to make gifts to his mother, his four siblings, and his ten nieces and nephews. His requirement, as stated to me, was "that I can afford to make these gifts." It was my charge to then determine what amount such gifts should be. At age 52, Ash was younger than Jeremy. He presumably had many years, if not many decades, yet to live, so we needed to factor that into our calculations of gifts.

After researching the portfolio, running several analytical models, and considering the tax effects on the gift amounts, I determined, with Ash's cooperation, that he could make gifts of $3,000,000 to his mother; $1,000,000 to each of his four siblings, and then gifts of $750,000 to each of the ten nieces and nephews. I advised him to put these gifts in trust to protect them from careless spending or the corrosive effects of creditors or people wanting to take advantage of the family members. This was still a large amount of money for Ash to give away, but it gave him great pleasure to know that he could help his family with homes and educational opportunities that he had never enjoyed as a child or young adult himself. As a fellow Protector, I could understand.

Becoming Financially Empowered

About a year later, Ash called me one day to say he had decided to sell the condominium that he and Jeremy had owned in Naples, Florida, for ten years, and to move to Malibu, California. I have learned again and again that Protectors have a very keen "sense of nest" and that it's important to honor that trait when I see it. While ordinarily I would have counseled Ash to wait a bit longer after losing Jeremy to make such a big decision, I knew that the couple had talked for some time about "cashing out" and moving to California in a couple of years. So, the decision had been percolating for some time.

Protectors can be superb nest-builders, and Ash was no exception. With a bit of coaching from me, he negotiated the sale of the condo to friends who actually lived in an adjoining building. The buyer was a Fixer who, in my view, tried to pressure Ash on the issue of down payments and closing dates. He took this in stride, not rising to the Fixer's bait. He knew what he wanted, which was to sell the condo at a fair price, not to wring every last potential dollar out of his friends. That said, he did dictate the closing date for the condo sale, when construction of his new house in Malibu got delayed. When the buyer started to store furniture in the condo before the closing date took place, Ash chose to overlook what we both agreed was boorish behavior. We both agreed there were more important things to focus on. He held to his moral high ground, just as Protectors typically do, in response to the Fixer's inclination to cut corners and push others.

Taking Charge of the Wealth Management Process

A year later, Ash was in his new home in Malibu and called me yet again. He'd completed the purchase of the house, paying all cash for it, and wanted to consider making additional gifts to family members, "if I can afford it," he told me. We outlined another gifting schedule to provide further gifts to his mother, siblings, and grandchildren.

Ash's behavior here is typical of a Protector. Protectors put high value on relationships with others, and on protecting and supporting those to whom they feel close. I am proud of the fact that, after Jeremy's passing, Ash grew tremendously in his ability to embrace the wealth management process and to make well-informed, proactive decisions that would benefit not only himself but also those he loved for years to come. He overcame his former risk-adversity and his lack of familiarity with the markets to work closely with me, and to see his and Jeremy's portfolio continue to grow in value.

Today, Ash and I stay in close touch. It is very gratifying to see him take a keen and involved interest, both in his siblings and in their own children. Without a college degree of his own, it is no doubt tremendously satisfying to Ash that he is providing for numerous members of his family to attend college and to create strong springboards for rewarding lives and careers.

Madeleine and Lucas: Protecting the Assets

Ash's behavior clearly shows a Protector's behavior in the light zone, but what happens when a Protector moves into the dark zone? It happened with another client of mine, in this case a couple named Madeleine, 82 (a Protector) and her husband, Lucas, 87 (a Survivor).

Protectors like Madeleine can be very anxious about the preservation of wealth in the best of times and can become paranoid about it in the worst of times. They also strongly believe that they accurately perceive dangers outside themselves even when those around them don't see such threats. This can be crazy-making for Protectors when they share responsibility for loved ones whose hero types are different from their own, and who either handle threats differently or don't think they exist at all.

In Madeleine's case, her husband, Lucas, is a Survivor, who has little concept of outside threats as something to fear. He realizes that the world is challenging and difficult, but he believes that if he works hard, he will persevere and rise above any obstacles that may stand in his way. (Remember how Survivors tend to take on big causes with little thought of themselves?) As evidence of this, Lucas has run a successful business consultancy for many years and is world renowned in his field.

A Protector in the Dark Zone

Madeleine, however, is not convinced that her husband always sees reality for what it is, but instead for what he *sees* it as being. While Lucas believes he has the power and wherewithal within himself to overcome obstacles and challenges, often by just working a little harder, Madeleine is not convinced that she possesses that kind of quality in herself. When it comes to their finances, it drives her crazy that Lucas seems blind to the fact that they could fall into poverty before the end of their lives. This is especially worrisome for her because she is five years younger than her husband. He expects to live another three to five years, which means she's likely to be on her own for at least several additional years. Anxious about this endgame, she constantly asks him: "Will I have enough to live on after you're gone?"

Madeleine and Lucas have worked extensively with me on this issue. To help focus our conversations, I first ran Monte Carlo simulations[1] with assumptions about market returns, medical inflation, gifting to children, and Madeleine's and Lucas's lifespans. The simulation showed that they would live out their lives comfortably without having to sacrifice or limit their activities. This answered her questions for a while, but the results never really quieted her fears. So, a few years later, as she continued to fret about these issues, I offered to rerun the simulation with different assumptions. This time, I cut market returns by 2%, increased the inflation rate by 2%, and extended each of their lifespans by three years. Now the simulation showed that they would invade their savings more significantly, leaving them with less than $1,000,000 when she died.

At one point, Madeleine became so fearful about running out of money that she decided to take matters into her own hands. Protectors often take counsel of their fears, and when they become convinced that their fears are legitimate, they take very deliberate action believing themselves to be right. In Madeleine's case, she decided that Lucas's money would be better protected if it were in her account rather than in his. After all, he paid far less attention to how they invested their money than she did, and what they needed in this endgame was vigilance and diligence, not an attitude of "laid back and relaxed." Eventually, Lucas noticed the transfers being made. Fortunately, rather than seeing this as a violation of trust and evidence of stealing, he saw it as a statement on his wife's part of how fearful she was.

Dealing with the Protector's Anxiety

One positive result of Madeleine having done this is that it jolted Lucas to better appreciate the depth and intensity of her fears. Madeleine's fears about money had their roots in her childhood. Born in Oklahoma City, Oklahoma, and one of four children, her family had been poor, and her parents often struggled to make ends meet financially. They also were forced to move on numerous occasions when her father, an alcoholic housepainter, couldn't pay rent. These childhood memories of Madeleine's typically surfaced in times of high stakes or high stress, when she felt her financial security was at great risk. Fortunately, Lucas listened to her concerns. He recognized the need to become more attentive to the couple's investment portfolio, to ask more questions, and to pay more attention to what I advised them both to do!

For my part, I counseled Madeleine and Lucas that the assumptions I'd made in the second simulation were useful for framing our estate planning discussions. But, I noted, "They are simply projections into the future, not reality." As such, no one could know for certain what the future held. "We all have to live with uncertainty," I told them. "After all, none of us knows for sure what will happen."

Nonetheless, I counseled them that their portfolios could be tweaked to help improve returns over a market cycle by increasing the equity weight a bit. Not enough to vastly increase risk but enough to add perhaps a 1% increase in incremental return. They agreed to this approach and thereafter we arranged more frequent meetings to provide Madeline with greater assurances regarding their financial position. I also worked with the couple to help them more closely manage their household budget and to make sure expenses were kept in check.

11 Suggestions for Working with Protectors

As with the other hero types, Protector clients come in a wide variety of sizes, shapes, and styles. To help you successfully manage client relationships with Protectors, here are 11 specific tips:

1. Protectors are very anxious about the preservation of wealth. So, advisors must be sensitive to this and reassure them as needed. Protectors take immediate note when markets become volatile, when balances in a portfolio go below certain levels, when funds drop in checking and savings accounts, and when dividend checks don't arrive on time. In high-stakes situations, lower numbers cause Protectors to go toward the dark side and to blame others when they do. Conversely, higher account balances engender loyalty and trust—certainly in the light zone. In any case, it's critical to remember that the greatest desire of Protectors is to take care of and shield others including spouses, partners, children, grandchildren, and other loved ones. When market corrections occur, it can be a grievous experience for a Protector, who sees such losses as a diminished capacity to care for those they love.

2. The tendency of Protectors to shield and protect others can be a great asset when you're working with a client couple or family, where the other party (or parties) are Fixers or Survivors. In such cases, the Protector client helps temper the "full steam ahead" tendencies of Fixers, who may want to adopt high-risk investment approaches in designing wealth management plans. The Protector can also help his/her fellow family members who are Survivors adopt realistic and level-headed investment plans and approaches, rather than those which are impractical, unrealistic, or overly idealistic.

3. Because Protectors are highly risk-averse, they can be a challenge for advisors to deal with one-on-one. Protector clients can be overly sensitive to market risks and thus reluctant to embrace reasonable, moderate-risk options to grow a portfolio. In such cases, reassure them that you have completed due diligence efforts to ensure that the investment opinions and plans you are proposing are reasonable and well researched.

4. *Be sensitive to Protector anxieties.* If you are a Fixer, don't move too quickly to suggest or push specific investment options or courses of action. Instead, listen carefully to your client's concerns and reframe concerns as opportunities. If you're a Survivor, you may be inclined to take the Protector's anxiety at face value, not question it, and not offer *any* options to relieve the Protector's anxiety. Instead, offer your client reasonable, "middle way" investing and wealth management options.

5. *In working with Protector clients, use their commitment to others (spouses, partners, children, grandchildren, etc.) as a core premise in constructing investment or estate plans.* These commitments to others provide a natural framework for handling matters of asset allocation, risk tolerance, bequests, charitable contributions, and multigenerational wealth transfer.

6. *As the Protector's advisor you may need to call attention, at times, to the unhealthy dependence that a Protector's beneficiaries exert on him or her.* Relationships are of great importance to Protectors. But, at times such relationships can become a drain on the Protector's finances. Be prepared to step in to offer clear and direct advice regarding beneficiaries, if it seems appropriate to you.

7. *Look for opportunities to empower Protector clients.* As noted, Protectors tend to discount any personal power to direct their lives or to impact the success of their investment and wealth management efforts. Instead, they see themselves as vulnerable to forces "out there" in the markets. Be mindful of this and offer Protectors ways to take active control of the wealth management process by a) articulating a vision and mission for their wealth; b) committing to charitable giving; c) funding education for beneficiaries; d) starting a small business, or taking other proactive steps to avoid becoming a victim of circumstances.

8. *Remember, when circumstances become high stakes for the Protector, he or she can slip into the dark zone.* In such cases, the Protector can feel powerless, unable to control the situation, and resentful of those around them who seem to be adjusting better to the challenges at hand. If situations become very high stakes, the Protector will lash out and even seek revenge against you, as their advisor, or others close to them. In such situations it will be important to "talk the client down" as suggested by some of the actions shared in this chapter's case studies.

9. *Protectors typically display an Open engagement/communications style and will be inclined to "process" investment options with you in an open-ended way.* In such situations, discussion of estate planning and investment issues can

potentially take a long time, and reaching decisions can be difficult. So, when appropriate, take *Mover* stances to frame/summarize conversations, help the Protectors make decisions, and bring conversations to a logical and reasonable close.

10. *Some Protectors may present themselves to you as "spoiled," "elitist," or "entitled," especially if they long for further protection and for people to take care of them.* If they are wealthy already, they may also come across as self-indulgent and display irresponsible lifestyle habits including drug and alcohol abuse, promiscuity, and overspending. These tendencies can almost seem like forms of self-medicating. Establishing structure and budgets for Protectors in these cases is important.

11. *Because Protectors are known for taking the moral high ground in conversations, they can come across at times as self-righteous.* This can be problematic when it comes to discussing specific investment choices and options. Some Protectors, for example, may protest at investing in companies that do any military business, or not want to consider companies that have questionable environmental records. While bearing such concerns in mind is always important, it shouldn't shortchange consideration of investment opportunities that are otherwise reasonable, well considered, and highly attractive as stock picks.

Chapter Conclusions

This chapter has focused extensively on how best to work with clients who display the personality traits of Protectors. Regardless of what kind of hero type you are working with, being effective as an advisor requires you to build and nurture trust with clients. In the next chapter, I present yet another fictional case study, after which I outline the specific building blocks involved in building strong and resilient relationships with *any* kind of client—be they a Fixer, Survivor, or Protector.

PART III

Nurturing Client Relationships for the Long Term

CHAPTER NINE

Establishing Credibility and Building Trust with Clients of *Any* Type

Open Your Mouth and <u>You</u> Fall Out!

—Mary Rosenblum

James Cavanaugh, a new client prospect, and his wife, Serena, have arranged to meet you for a preliminary investment planning discussion at your office. At the age of 64, James is on the verge of retiring as CEO of one of the country's most successful national hotel chains and has been referred to you for investment planning advice by Lester, his accountant of 20 years.

Cavanaugh's golden parachute is worth about $75 million, based on the press reports you've read. You know, from your online research, that he's well regarded in the hospitality sector as a corporate turnaround artist (he took his current hotel chain to the upper tier of U.S. hotel chains over just an eight-year period), but that he's also regarded as a no-nonsense, somewhat quick-tempered guy who's been known to chew out even senior corporate executives in front of rank and file employees.

Cavanaugh and his wife live in one of the priciest suburbs of Boston, and based on what Lester told you, they own two other homes, including one in Southern France and another in Alaska. Cavanaugh's wife, Serena, is a bit of a question mark. The press hasn't said much about her. She's not active in the community, which is unusual. (This seems to contradict the old saw about there being a powerful and competent woman behind every successful man, a concept that still has resonance among some of your older clients, even though it's quickly vanishing as younger generations assume positions of leadership responsibility in business.) Thus, in this case you had thought she'd be connected to a charitable cause or two in the community, perhaps serving on a board or acting as a spokesperson for a charity, where she could serve as a social ambassador for her husband.

Now, they've come to meet you for advice about retirement. You're thinking that Cavanaugh may be feeling challenged, even insecure with his pending loss of role as a CEO. What's he going to do next in his life? And what about Serena? After years of being supported by a well-compensated, often out-of-town spouse, she's now facing the prospect of reimagining their lives together in retirement.

On the flip side of things, James and Serena are also wondering about you, their prospective advisor. You're somebody their accountant recommended. Will you be gracious, interested, and engaging? Will you have personality and warmth? Or will you simply be a transparently ambitious advisor interested in landing a big fish as a client?

James certainly hopes it's the former. He's dealt with the latter all his business life. Investment bankers are the worst, he feels. During one hellacious period in his career he dealt with them 24 hours a day, seven days a week, while he was trying to sell a hotel chain to a foreign buyer.

A Challenging Client Prospect

James knows a lot about the hospitality industry and creating a welcoming environment. After all, he's worked in the industry for nearly 45 years. As he prepares to meet you this day, he recalls a short vignette, a tiny, yet metaphorical little story involving, of all things, hangers from the days when he first took over the chain of hotels he's now selling. He used to spend a lot of time visiting all the properties in his chain, sometimes anonymously as an Undercover Boss, and sometimes with the full knowledge of the staff of the hotel he was "observing." In many hotels, he observed that the hangers in the closets were attached to the clothes rod. It used to drive him crazy because he felt it sent a message of hostility and mistrust to hotel guests. So, he had all the attached hangers replaced with high-quality and detachable wood hangers. And though the chain lost a number of hangers over the years, he never doubted the wisdom of his decision. It was his way of showing graciousness toward, and trust in, his hotel's guests. That's how focused James was on the most miniscule of customer service details!

So, now, he's wondering if he'll experience trust and graciousness when he and his wife meet you!

Cavanaugh and his wife arrive at your firm's tony, 20th floor cherry-wood-paneled, offices. They're greeted by Ashley, your receptionist, a polished and Prada-attired young woman who greets them by name. Cavanaugh suddenly thinks he might enjoy working with you, while his wife Serena is wondering what's going on. Her concerns are quickly mollified, though, when the couple is escorted to your firm's conference room with its tinted floor-to-ceiling windows exposing a breathtaking view of the city and harbor below. A silver tea service with English scones sits on the marble-topped conference table, which immediately gains a nod of approval from Serena.

You enter, right on schedule, to meet the Cavanaughs, dressed in a conservative blue suit, white shirt, red tie, and black shoes. You make immediate eye contact with Serena who seems to approve of your wardrobe, while Cavanaugh appears initially a little standoffish, thinking that you look too stereotypically the part of a stiff and waspy wealth advisor.

The three of you choose seats at the huge rectangular table, and immediately you begin to observe the human psychology and interpersonal dynamics on display in front of you. James and Serena sit three chairs apart from you at the table, which you find a bit odd. You make a mental note of it and then welcome them to the meeting and express appreciation that they've come. Serena beams as you speak, but James seems a bit uncomfortable, almost annoyed. You immediately realize that he doesn't like mention of emotions, and his response begins to suggest he feels that you're sucking up. You quickly change tactics to mirror his more analytical, no nonsense approach.

Breaking the Ice with the Prospect

"So, tell me about the hotel business and how you became so successful?"

Instantly, James seems more comfortable. You've given him the stage to talk at length about himself. It's a role he likes. He's in control, and launches into a lengthy verbal resume, highlighting his experiences in the hospitality industry over the last 40 years. As he talks, you look at Serena, who defers quietly while wearing a somewhat stoic face. She's heard all of this before, often at cocktail parties or country club functions, but is pleased that you've tapped into this part of her husband and seem to "get him" faster than most people, who are often intimidated by his business title and physical bearing.

You continue to engage James around his business background and finally ask about the structure of his pay-out. Will he receive stock from the acquiring company or mostly cash? Will he have any continued involvement and earn performance pay-outs? Are there options involved, and if so, are they ISOs or non-quals?[1]

Initially satisfied with the responses you get, you turn to Serena to ask her about her life. You learn she stays at home, enjoys knitting and sewing, and also serves on the board of a local art museum in their community. She has always fully supported her husband. They married early and were childhood sweethearts. They have three grown children, all boys, who now live abroad and have successful careers of their own.

You then pivot to pursue a new line of inquiry with both of them.

"So, tell me, at this point in your lives, what are your personal goals and aspirations? You've built a significant nest egg. What's in the future for the two of you? Are there new goals and dreams you want to pursue? Trusts for the grandchildren? New business opportunities? Additional property acquisitions? Travel perhaps, or involvement in philanthropic work?"

You probe further to learn a little about their families and childhoods. How did their early childhood experiences influence them and shape them into the adults they became? How did their early childhood and adolescent experiences with family, community, and schools inform their early adult years and their decision to get married and have a family?

James is getting fidgety. "This is all great, but what bearing does this have on our financial situation?" he asks you.

"Thanks for asking," you reply.

Understanding the Client's Personal Values

"In my experience, these types of questions get to the heart of my client's values, which are critical for me to understand because they should serve as the basis for retirement and investment planning discussions. Over the years I've had clients share very personal, decades-long wishes and goals when it comes to their retirement plans, wills, and preservation and management of their financial estate. I'm always amazed at the financial goals people share with me—goals that have often been passed down to them from a previous generation.

"Sometimes clients have personal passions or convictions—for example, a love of the arts or strong convictions about the environment—which they want reflected in any legacy gifting plans they eventually make. They may be interested in certain causes related to a sibling's childhood illness or a company or industry sector they want to target for future investment, using some of their financial assets. Other clients want to use their financial assets for the benefit of a dependent adult child or the community at large. There are literally hundreds of options a client might want to consider, depending on their personal values and financial situation.

"I've found that knowing the privately held thoughts of my clients can help me better serve their personal goals and interests. And, it can help them create a vision for what they want their wealth to accomplish."

James and Serena are quiet for a moment. They look at each other for cues about how to respond. Neither of them has ever thought about wealth management, investments, and estate planning in this way. Your calm demeanor is intended to assure them that the process of values identification and clarification is an ongoing process, but one that can be most helpful as wealth/estate planning conversations first get started.

Explaining Your Firm's Wealth Advisory Approach

You next go on to explain how your firm works. You talk about how you work with clients to build portfolios based on their ownership of individual companies, explaining that your firm's close relationship with the managements of many leading companies helps you to select those firms that can be entrusted with client capital, and that have a solid track record of financial performance.

This meets with ready approval from Serena, but James challenges you.

"Why don't you simply use mutual funds in building portfolios? That's what I've seen time and time again in other firms. What makes you think you can really understand a company when there are thousands of analysts out there who spend their entire day following a single company in greater detail than you can?"

"Excellent questions," you reply.

This tells you James is engaged, and you appreciate that he's sparring a bit with you. "My colleagues and I have worked in the wealth advisory business for years. We have an average of 25 years' experience as investment counselors, during which time we've seen trends come and go, often as fads.

"So, it is with the use of mutual funds. Many advisors believe they can pick and choose mutual funds with the same accuracy as they can individual company managements. But I haven't found that to be the case. Too often I've seen mutual fund managers become filters between investors and the companies they own. Yes, there are a lot of good mutual fund managers out there, but there are far more *bad* fund managers. No mutual fund manager can outperform their industry index or market index over a long period of time. *But*, they are paid to do just that!

"We prefer to avoid mutual fund fees and simply invest directly in the same quality of companies that the fund manager would buy. We can call up the company any day and ask our questions directly of the company's management. We can never have such access with a fund manager."

James nods agreement, and quickly interjects that he has to know the company or companies where he's investing his money. And, if he and his wife work with you, he'll have some specific ideas of where investment capital should be put.

"That's great," you say. "I welcome your input. I have some clients who put aside their 'hot' money so they can invest a small part of their portfolio in their ideas."

James feels you have addressed him face on, which he likes.

You continue. "This mutual fund issue goes to another problem we have with using funds in your accounts. It's the CYA issue. As a firm, we feel that too many investment advisors who are charged with managing individual client money choose to use mutual funds in client accounts because it allows them to hire and fire mutual fund managers if there are performance issues. If poor performance develops, the underperformers can be identified and the advisor exits. The client is told of the poor performance and the action taken, but it takes much longer, perhaps years, before the advisor's investment process and his ability to pick mutual funds is ever questioned."

You then explain that your firm feels it has a fiduciary duty to clients.

"You are asking us to invest your capital. Therefore, it's our responsibility to put your interests ahead of ours and to take actions that treat you accordingly. We would feel compromised, in a fiduciary sense, if we bought mutual funds, because we would not have control over what happens to your money; it would be handled by an intermediary, a mutual fund manager. It's hard enough to honor fiduciary duties when investing in individual companies. It's nearly impossible, in our opinion, when we invest in mutual funds."

You go on to explain that mutual funds have yet another downside for large investors. Many advisors, you note, use mutual funds to develop intricate asset allocation schemes in pursuit of what is called the "efficient frontier." This involves pursuing an ever more efficient group of asset classes and representative mutual funds to get the best combination of fund managers who, together, due to low correlation coefficients between funds over time, are supposed to provide the client with better performance than can be achieved by owning simple combinations of stock indexes like the S&P 500 and low-risk groups of Treasury bills.

"We've seen plots of how this is supposed to work, based on historical analyses, and it looks impressive, but it is all based on history," you warn. "These asset classes all maintain their low correlation with each other in backward-looking tests, and the mathematics hold true. But applying it going forward often doesn't work. That's because when it comes to the performance of mutual funds (as with all investments) history never repeats itself."

James likes what he hears. "Go back and tell me more about the fiduciary issue," he asks.

A fiduciary duty, you explain, is the highest level of responsibility that governs an investment advisor's actions on behalf of his or her clients. "When we're hired by a client, we work as that person's agent and must always make decisions in the client's best interest. This includes a duty of loyalty, but also a duty of care. The client's interests are, in fact, held above the interest of the advisor. Obviously, all conflicts of interest are to be avoided."

James quickly agrees that he sees how important an advisor's fiduciary duty is to building a sense of trust between the advisor and a prospective client.

Explaining Your Firm's Wealth Advisory Mission and Vision

"So, tell me more about how you go about choosing companies to invest in. What are the criteria?" James asks.

"Great question!," you respond. "Our vision here focuses on buying good quality companies for our clients whose financials and management are strong and whose growth prospects are promising. The company's stock must be reasonably valued relative to these growth prospects. We prefer pursuing this objective to getting involved in esoteric searches for mutual funds, lying on some mythical efficient frontier which might or might not materialize in a certain timeframe."

"Hmmmm . . ." you hear James say to himself.

You continue. "And here's one more thing to consider. How many people do you know who talk with pride or affection about owning some bond fund? Or even some stock fund? People don't!

"But, they *will* tell you if they own a particular stock, especially if it has done well. A client's pride of association can become even clearer if he or she owns a small cap or mid-cap name, especially if it isn't a household name. If its performance has been good, it becomes great cocktail party chit-chat. We wouldn't say this is where the best investment work is done. Our point is that investing brings with it a pride of association with really good companies that rarely exists when someone buys a mutual fund index."

"Investing can be a very emotional experience," you tell James and Serena.

As the advisor, you stop there, for a moment, to give your prospective clients a chance to react to what you're saying. They clearly like what they're hearing.

You then shift gears to talk about how individuals often approach decisions about investments in different ways. In the case of a couple, you note that sometimes one party or the other (often the major breadwinner) tends to be the driver of the conversation and tries to come to closure about investment decisions relatively fast. But in other cases, a couple may go back and forth and discuss possibilities and investment options almost endlessly, without coming to firm decisions. Still others have conversations that go all over the place ("kitchen sink conversations," you call them) in which one party or the other puts a lot on the table for the couple to discuss, seemingly in a random way without moving the conversations to a decision-making point.

You assure James and Serena that there are many ways couples make decisions about their investments. There's no one "right" way, and people may even change roles as a conversation proceeds—sometimes driving a conversation, sometimes opposing, sometimes endorsing what their partner has said, and sometimes appearing to defer or "bystand" from taking a firm position of their own.

Again, you assure the couple that such interpersonal and conversational dynamics are normal, and speak to the unique human natures of the individuals having the discussion.

James and Serena now appear to have said everything they wanted to say to you and seem to be soaking in all that you have shared with them. They both seem impressed with your style of engagement and the approach that the firm takes to building portfolios for clients. You've answered their questions and addressed their concerns. James realizes that the ultimate destination in using mutual funds in client portfolios is the broad use of index funds. This was an option he never found attractive because he couldn't fully control what he owned. Instead, someone who constructed the index did.

He senses that you have a depth and maturity with investing that he's not seen in other advisors he's met. He also realizes that you are advocating in favor of an anachronistic approach to investment planning that involves active investing. James like this and feels it shows courage, rectitude, and self-confidence on your part.

James now asks for a few minutes so that he and Serena can talk. You're a little surprised that they only want a few minutes because you've thrown a lot at them today, including a new approach to investing with which they weren't previously familiar. In the past, you've found that prospects often require a week or more to fully digest what you say to them during prospect meetings. Then again, James, in calling for a little privacy with his wife, is used to making important decisions with limited data. So, you leave the room.

James and Serena are left alone with one another.

What follows over the next 20 minutes is a pattern of conversation and decision-making on their parts that has been their norm since high school. She expresses her feelings, becoming emotional about all that you brought up about values, family culture and traditions, legacy planning, "doing the right thing" for the children, planning for the future, and so forth. But, she feels overwhelmed with information and doesn't want to make any hasty decisions about the firm with whom they currently invest their money.

"Shouldn't we talk to other firms? Get even more information before we decide?" she asks him.

James gets impatient with her. He listened intently to you, took your gauge, and sensed that you'd spent considerable time and care developing your comprehensive approach to the wealth management process. He's impressed, more than he thought he'd be. You conveyed intellectual heft, as well as solid business experience and perspective. He likes the fact that you and your firm "buck the crowd" in your approach to investment counseling and he respects the backbone that that requires.

As he shares this with Serena, he remarks that she seemed to like you, as an advisor, as well. Serena acknowledges this, saying that she liked being asked about her childhood, her family, her personal values, and how she met James. "I was tempted to tell him our entire story," she tells her husband, "But then realized that you didn't want to hear it yet again!"

James and Serena grow quiet. They've both played specific roles in the conversation they've just had with one another. It is a long-standing pattern of interaction. James has always been the practical one of the two of them, and Serena has typically deferred to him on matters of business and finance. For his part, he has usually deferred to her on other topics, such as the children, family, and home.

In this case, both parties feel they've gotten something important from you: a sense that you understand them. And so they decide: they will retain you as their advisor.

Looking Back: Analyzing an Advisor-Prospect Conversation

While the above client scenario is a case study, it's actually a synthesis of many such initial meetings that I've held with prospects and clients over the years. I share it with you because it's my firm belief that the way we set the stage initially with clients, and the way they respond to us, determines the outcomes (and success) of such meetings. Are professionalism and credibility established? Is chemistry forged? Is rapport built? Most important, are the beginnings of trust created even in an initial meeting with a client or prospect? For us, as wealth advisors, keeping these goals in mind, and attending to the interpersonal dynamics required to make them a reality, is a full-time job.

That's why, in the remainder of this chapter, I will talk about what it takes to build strong, healthy, and highly functional relationships with our clients regardless of their hero type. As you saw in the case study just presented, the advisor managed to build a connection with James and Serena in the course of just one get-acquainted meeting. He asked them questions about their personal and family values, about their investment and retirement goals, and then explained how his firm typically works with clients to invest their capital for them.

He went on to talk in depth about his firm's approach to "old-fashioned" investing, and why he and his colleagues put such a high premium on providing fiduciary care to all their clients. This served to engage James, and to comfort Serena, the result being that by the end of the meeting they decided to work with the advisor.

While obviously a case study for illustrative purposes, the vignette offered clear direction as to specific steps *all of us,* as advisors, need to take to connect with clients, build rapport, establish credibility, and forge a sense of trust.

So, what are the key building blocks that advisors need to be mindful of, in building strong working relationships with clients? (See Figure 9.1.)

■ ESTABLISH CREDIBILITY

As a top priority, an advisor needs to demonstrate his or her professional credentials to the prospect or client as a relationship is just being formed. Professional training, certifications, and other evidence of professional expertise are paramount, as is the ability to connect personally and easily with the clients with whom you work—because clients don't just hire credentials, they hire *people.*

So what, in fact, do you have to offer your clients as an advisor? To answer that question, I suggest you do an inventory of your professional background, skills, and experience. What do you consider to be your greatest strengths and assets as an advisor? What's unique?

How Are You Unique as an Advisor?

In his book, *The Consultant's Calling, Bringing Who You Are to What You Do*, Geoffrey Bellman offers advice and wisdom that wealth advisors are wise to embrace.[2] He asks the question: Why do clients [in any profession] actually hire us? And then he offers a list of reasons. They hire us because of our:

experience	friendship	support
eyes	vision	contacts
age	reputation	authenticity
wisdom	information	perspective
accomplishment	approval	objectivity
values	skills	insight
products	personality	compassion
expertise	guts	credibility

Authors Steve Yearout, Gerry Miles, and Rick Koonce have added still more "consultant qualities" to this list, including stories, humor, concern, confidentiality, empathy, and creativity, among others.[3] Understanding what you have to offer your clients as an advisor will do a great deal to fortify your professional self-confidence. Moreover, it's a great way to distinguish yourself from your professional colleagues, and to build a positive and professional brand.

▪ "CONTRACT" WITH YOUR CLIENT

In my view, the single most important task for any advisor to accomplish in his or her initial meetings with a new client or prospect is to have deep and wide-ranging discussion about the client's values, family history, life philosophy, and long-term life goals. In many cases, the conversations that advisors have with clients may be unlike any the client or prospect has had before. Indeed, advisors often discover that clients lack an even basic vocabulary for talking about such topics, until encouraged to do so as part of a holistic approach to wealth management discussions. In the case study, it's revealed that James and Serena were a bit surprised, at times, by the conversational tack the advisor took with them, but ultimately they were pleased that he was attentive to them and strived to understand their wishes.

Frame Expectations

Early meetings with prospects or new clients also need to focus on answering clients' initial questions, allaying potential concerns, framing expectations, and establishing good chemistry and rapport. Here I'm talking about "contracting" not in a legalistic sense, but in the sense of aligning yourself with your client, sharing with them what your firm's philosophy about investing is, and explaining why you embrace this philosophy as well.

Sometimes, initial contracting can be as basic as establishing good chemistry and rapport with a client in the early stages of a working relationship. On the other hand, it can sometimes be quite formal and structured, if you are working with a wealthy couple or family where other professionals, including lawyers, accountants, estate planners, and others are parties or stakeholders in the discussions about investing and wealth management that you have with your client(s).

In any case, it's critical to substantive contracting at the beginning of a client-advisor relationship to firmly anchor the relationship and create strong alignment between the advisor and the client. Doing this in low-stakes circumstances is far preferable to trying to build a relationship of trust and understanding when the markets are roiling or the client's portfolio experiences a market correction.

Hold Regular Reviews

A healthy client-advisor relationship necessarily entails regular review of financial, investment, and wealth management goals with the client, be it an individual, couple, or family. This means it's critical that you take the opportunity, at least on an annual basis, to query and explore with your clients their wealth management goals and objectives. In my experience, the Four-Player model can be an invaluable tool here. There will be times, for example, when it will be important for you to drive the conversation (as a *Mover*); times when it will be important to be a listener (act as a *Follower*); times when it will be important to simply let the client express his or her views, opinions, and concerns and reflect them back (be a *Bystander*); and times when it will be important to question, challenge, or invite further conversation by being an *Opposer* in dialogue with your client. The Four-Player model is a powerful client engagement tool. If you master its nuances and intricacies conscientiously, you will find it to be a powerful mechanism for navigating the conversational "waters" with clients both in low-stakes and high-stakes situations. It will help you to know when to be assertive and challenging, when to be deferential and/or supportive, when to be inquiring, and when to move conversations to closure.

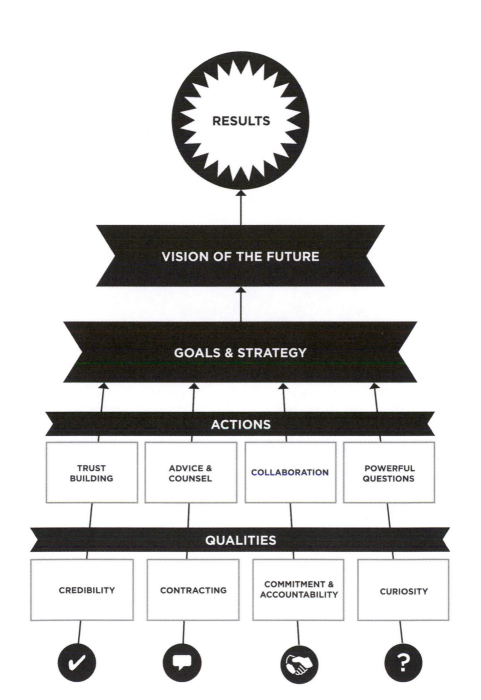

Figure 9.1   Building Blocks of Successful Advisor-Client Relationships.

■ EMPHASIZE COMMITMENT AND ACCOUNTABILITY

Clearly, as an advisor begins to work with a client, it's vital that he or she communicate his or her interest in and commitment to working with the client. This goes beyond paying mere lip service to professional guidelines; it should include a strong personal statement about fiduciary responsibility. In the case study, the advisor went out of his way to speak to the fiduciary responsibility that both he and his firm had when it came to serving the needs of his clients, in fact, putting the needs and interests of the clients above all else. If you are not intimately acquainted with the fiduciary responsibilities that are entailed with whatever professional credentials or certifications you hold, I strongly encourage you to familiarize yourself with them.

Be Present to the Client

Professional accountability goes hand in hand with personal commitment to clients. To me, accountability is about adopting an attitude of stewardship and servanthood in the work I do on behalf of clients. You know from my background and from my self-identification as a Protector personality (see Chapter One) that I believe it is critically important that I be accountable to clients and put their interests foremost. This goes beyond fiduciary responsibility to include stewardship, which I discuss, in depth, in Chapter Ten.

■ BE CURIOUS

As you know, I became a wealth advisor because of my keen interests and curiosity, both about the financial markets and about the motivations of people who invest in the markets. In my opinion, curiosity is absolutely essential to the work that we do as investment advisors. It's incumbent on us therefore that as part of serving our clients, we get to know them on as intimate a level as we can.

Part of being curious about our clients entails using what leadership coaches sometimes call powerful questions, questions that are open-ended and that invite a client or prospect to share their thoughts, ideas, and feelings with you in depth. As the case study highlighted, the advisor asked James and Serena questions about themselves and about their wealth that they were not accustomed to. Elsewhere in this book, I've described the eight key questions I like to ask clients. This process is sometimes referred to as appreciative inquiry (another term I borrow from the coaching world) as it entails a commitment to fully understanding not only the client's current thinking but also helping the client to think in strategic, long-term ways about the management of his or her wealth.

Appreciative Inquiry Helps the Client to Articulate His or Her Goals

In his book *Wealth in Families,* Charles Collier, former senior philanthropic adviser at Harvard University, points out that there are many kinds of wealth that people possess, including financial, social, intellectual, and human.[4] "There is more to . . . wealth than the financial dimension. *Human capital* refers to who individual family members are, and what they are called to do; *intellectual capital* refers to how family members learn and govern themselves; *social capital* denotes how family members engage with society at large, and *financial capital* stands for the property of the family." Thus, people of financial means are well served if they are asked to articulate the various kinds of "wealth" that they possess and to develop a vision around how such wealth is to be used. Collier poses a number of key questions that advisors need to ask wealthy families who are their clients. Similar questions can and should be directed to clients who are individuals and couples as well. Here are some examples I've come up with:

1. Do you have a "vision" for your wealth and how you want to use it? If so, what specific goals or priorities do you have?
2. What core values and principles do you think are important to bear in mind when developing investment and estate plans?
3. How do values such as achievement, knowledge, diversity, hard work, generosity, creativity, compassion, spirituality, justice, integrity, honesty, service, respect, and love influence you when it comes to thinking about your wealth?
4. What priorities do you wish to include in your wealth management plans relative to financial inheritances by siblings, children, grandchildren, and others?
5. What responsibility, if any, do you feel you have to society or to causes and interests beyond your family and extended family?

In my view, you will be doing your clients and prospects a big favor if you ask powerful questions and have expansive conversations with them as you go about helping them develop long-term investment and wealth management plans. Why? Because you will be helping them to fully actualize their lives and realize the full potential of their wealth to better themselves as well as others. Collier notes that a person's approach to wealth is a statement of what they stand for. It becomes a statement of who they are.

■ BUILD TRUST

One of the most difficult challenges for any advisor is to build a relationship of trust with a client. Building client trust entails both basic and complex steps. Being ethical, keeping client information private; assuring confidentiality; and providing clients with objective advice, information, and counsel are clearly all critical. It sounds a bit trite, but be a person of good character. As the late John Wooden, former basketball player and UCLA basketball coach put it: "Be more concerned with your character than your reputation, because your character is what you really are, while your reputation is merely what others think you are." Also, acknowledging failure and mistakes openly and forthrightly, when they occur, is essential to maintain credibility and humility. Indeed, I encourage you to exercise humility in service to your clients. It is a great defense against professional narcissism. Dealing with individuals of great social stature and wealth can be a heady experience, especially for younger advisers, so it's important to keep your feet on the ground and never take yourself too seriously.

Emphasize Integrity

What else is critical to the trust building process? Bryan Olson, CFA, and Mark Riepe, CFA, are authors of an article called "Using Behavioral Finance to Improve the Adviser-Client Relationship."[5] They cite 21 actions advisors should take to build credibility and trust with clients. Some are basic and obvious, such as "Establish and communicate an understandable corporate investment philosophy and a disciplined process" to clients. Also, "Avoid making overconfident statements to clients." Other recommendations are more subtle. "Be cautious about risk-tolerance assessments performed during or near periods of extreme market movements," they caution.

Olsen and Riepe know what they're talking about. How many of us, in the depths of the 2008 financial crisis, wanted to run away from stocks altogether? Certainly many clients were willing to throw in the towel. It was an exhausting time for clients and advisors alike. If you had asked many clients, who started with advisors at that time, about their risk tolerance, you would have heard many of them express a clear preference for bonds or hedge funds. But had you then gone back to those same clients a year later, they probably would have indicated a significantly stronger risk tolerance for stocks.

Olson and Riepe also believe it's important to learn if your client had previous relationships with advisors that were not satisfactory. "Past experiences, good and bad, may influence the client's perception of an adviser's intention or actions," they write. Prospective clients often seek out new advisors because of past poor relationships. So, it's critical for the new advisor to understand what went wrong. He or she can then work sensitively with that client to "set [clear] expectations, communicate the asset management process the advisor will follow, and reduce the odds of disappointment down the road."[6]

If you are meeting with someone who has worked with an advisor before, and perhaps did not have a pleasant experience, be ready. Gently probe the client as to their needs, hopes, goals, and desires in working with you. Sometimes, the most important needs and desires lie buried in the client. So, you may need to do some gentle digging to expose them to view.

Educate the Client on the Perspective of Time

Lastly, Olsen and Riepe encourage advisors to "adopt broad frames when discussing performance" with clients. There's tremendous wisdom in this recommendation. From your own experience in holding portfolio performance meetings with clients, you know that they sometimes focus too much attention on the few individual stocks in their portfolio that have underperformed, instead of taking a big picture view of the portfolio's performance as a whole. (It's analogous to what happens in parent-teacher meetings when parents focus on their child's one bad grade, instead of looking at the larger picture of the child's classroom performance!)

In these instances, advisors need to steer conversation toward discussion of the client's portfolio as a whole. At the same time, the portfolio's performance needs to be set in the context of the economy's current health, which is always influenced by factors such as central bank policies, international financial uncertainty, volatility in emerging markets, changing exchange rates, political developments (e.g., coups, terrorism), and other factors.[7]

Still other dynamics that contribute to the building of high levels of client trust are a number of "high touch" factors including the ability of the advisor to personally connect with his or her clients, to display empathy and understanding, and to help the client believe he or she is being listened to in an authentic fashion. The Family Office Exchange (FOX) based in Chicago, which helps high net worth families, representatives of family offices, and wealth advisors discharge their respective wealth management responsibilities, has just published research in this important area. It found that while product offerings are quite similar from one firm to the next, the realm of client experience remains a frontier yet to be fully leveraged with clients. Still, many firms (and their advisors) are endeavoring today to offer their clients "white glove" client experiences similar to those that consumers have grown to expect with Apple and Nordstrom.[8]

For more information on this, you may want to check out the FOX website at www.familyoffice.com.

▪ ENCOURAGE COLLABORATION

Ideally, as advisors, we want our relationships with clients to be "co-equal." In other words, we're not simply there to be subject matter experts (SMEs) but also as partners with our clients. Obviously, the degree to which clients will want to partner with us in helping to design portfolios and create investment plans will vary. But, it's my firm view that this process and the relationship itself should be as much of an interactive and collaborative partnership as possible. I have had some clients who want nothing more than an annual meeting where the general investment strategy is reaffirmed. In the case study though, James indicated that were he and Serena to work with the advisor, he would want to offer input into investment choices and decision-making, and the advisor wisely welcomed this as evidence of desired active engagement by the client in the investment planning process.

▪ PROVIDE ADVICE AND COUNSEL

Up to now, I've spoken of the advisor-client relationship almost as a co-equal relationship of peers. And to some extent, that's exactly what a well-designed advisor-client relationship is and should be: both parties co-equal partners to discussion of the client's wealth management and investment goals. Yet clearly, given the specialized expertise and product knowledge of wealth advisors and financial consultants, the advisor-client relationship necessarily requires that the advisor also play a consultative role with his or her clients. Advisors should work with the client to develop and articulate wealth management goals and objectives, performance expectations, and metrics by which portfolio performance will be developed. The advisor should be ready with worksheets for developing investment plans and portfolio options. He or she can and should also offer the resources of his or her firm on behalf of the client, for example, by providing client education materials, ancillary services, and online resources to clients, as requested and appropriate.

▪ ARTICULATE GOALS AND STRATEGY

Based on the discussions you have with clients, and the trust and rapport you establish, the time eventually comes when it's important to discuss and commit to financial goals. As part of laying the foundation for a client's investment and wealth management plans, I like to invite the client, at a certain point in our conversations to provide me with a set of their financial goals—at a high level. These goals are always based on the conversations that the two of us have already had, but I think it's important that the client use their own language to formulate goals relative to their financial objectives. These goals then become part of the investment policy statement that is developed for each client and each relationship or account. Developing investment policy statements is a highly collaborative process that should be periodically revisited on a mutually agreed-to timetable.

■ FORGE A VISION OF THE FUTURE

As you and your client develop investment and estate planning goals, and as you hold discussions with your clients about their values, family history, and priorities, a vision of the future for the client's investment plans begins to emerge. This purpose is usually derived after significant conversations over a period of months and has tremendous implications for the client and you in helping the two of you stay on course with wealth management goals and objectives over the long term. But the visioning process is not a one-time event. In my experience, a client's vision for their wealth typically evolves over time, as needs change or a family ages. Thus, advisors and clients are likely to have periodic re-visioning discussions over a period of years. During these meetings it's important to listen carefully to your clients, on many levels. Not just for the words they share with you, but also the tone of voice, affect, and body language they use in expressing themselves to you.

I believe that helping clients develop a personal vision for their wealth is critical to framing a client's wealth management goals and priorities and putting them into a meaningful context for both the wealth holder and those close to them, including spouses, siblings, children, grandchildren, and others to understand. After all, discussion of these topics will help family members fully understand how assets are managed and how estate plans are developed. As an advisor, you have a tremendous opportunity to act as a critical sounding board and conversation partner with clients who, in many cases, will need help in articulating their values about their wealth and their priorities for its use. As Collier notes, "Substantial financial wealth, whether created or inherited, has the capacity to transform the wealth holder. Many wealthy individuals rethink the meaning of their money, indeed their lives, in light of the freedom and empowerment their money provides them."[9]

■ MAINTAIN APPROPRIATE PROFESSIONAL BOUNDARIES

Finally, I want to say just a word about the importance of establishing and maintaining appropriate professional boundaries with clients at all times. I can't emphasize strongly enough the importance of you doing this, both for the sake of your career and the welfare of your clients.

As advisors, we often are privy to a great deal of personal information, family secrets, financial records, and other intimate information about people's lives. We must deal with grieving families and with spouses who have lost husbands, wives, partners, or significant others. In such situations, we are sometimes put on pedestals by individuals who are emotionally fragile, who over-identify with us, or who are looking to transfer (unconsciously) their love and grief to people beyond their immediate family.

The relationships we have with our clients typically are *not* symmetrical, which simply adds to the challenge. While we are there to provide financial assistance to people who need it, our clients often are wrestling with a variety of emotional, psychological, and even sexual/intimacy needs that come to the surface in moments of emotional vulnerability and life transition. Sometimes clients become overly dependent on us emotionally. Sometimes too, advisors get too close to their clients.

Always Take the Temperature of the Room

As a Protector who wants to serve as a steward to others, my own impulse to take care of others can be very strong. This is how I am wired. At times, I have to keep my own emotions for a client in check, notably when they present themselves to me as either Survivors or Protectors.[10] Over the course of my career, there have been times when I've worked with female clients who seem to welcome the sense of protection that I intuitively offer in my work. These are potentially dangerous situations which, as a Protector, I want to caution my fellow advisors about.

I have never succumbed to the temptations of these situations. First, I can't imagine a more damaging way to limit or end a career than to become romantically involved with a client. If I'm hired to provide advice to a client, how can I possibly do my job objectively if I'm romantically involved with that person? Second, to become romantically involved with a client would obviously damage my marriage and violate the promises I have made to my wife. I would never want to risk destroying the generous gift of love and faith she has placed in me. By honoring her, I validate what is most important in my life.

When Things Get Awkward

Sometimes, no matter how unwanted it is, an advisor can become the object of unwanted attention or affection from a client, as occurred on one occasion when a client of mine (a wealthy widow who'd recently lost her husband of 50 years) expected that a sexual liaison would be part of our working relationship. She was in her late 70s at the time. I was a young man, just getting started in my career as an advisor. Her actions toward me (including the writing of an erotic "love" letter) made me wince and forced me to share details of the incident with my colleagues in my firm, and to seek their guidance in how best to deal with it. When I shared my story with my colleagues, we jointly decided that thereafter I would always have one other person with me when meeting with and advising this client. Over time, I ultimately shifted much of my work to this colleague, and to others.

My advice to you is this: When you are counseling others about very personal and private topics, such as wealth and estate planning, and when either the client or counselor is emotionally vulnerable or even immature in judgement, it can be a recipe for catastrophe. Not only does it bring up issues of ethics, but it potentially can create a manipulative and dangerous situation for both parties involved. I offer counsel here especially to younger wealth advisors who may just be starting out in their careers. As advisors, you are likely to learn many intimate details of your clients' lives and be put in positions in which confidences must be kept and privacy respected. It can be a very heady experience, as a young advisor, to be a counselor to wealthy and sometimes famous people who are accustomed to getting their way and who (sometimes) are master manipulators that have learned to exert power and control over others.

If you find yourself in situations where you are uncomfortable, or are concerned that you could be violating ethical or professional standards or crossing interpersonal boundaries, err on the side of caution. Seek out a senior colleague in your firm for advice and counsel. Don't blame yourself or believe that you brought the situation on. And don't try to ignore what's going on. Instead, take note of what is happening and act with prudence and maturity.

Chapter Conclusions

This chapter has discussed critical components in establishing credibility and building trust with clients. Clearly, the relationship building process with clients is critical, if we are to understand their needs and help them achieve their investment and wealth management objectives. As with investing itself, the dynamics associated with effective client relationship building and management are both emotional and interpersonal in nature. And yet, your full and intentional engagement in this process can optimize the client-advisor relationship and assure the development of investment plans and estate arrangements that are fully aligned with the client's wishes, goals, and objectives for their wealth.

CHAPTER TEN

On Stewardship and Servant Leadership

You're gonna have to serve somebody.

—Bob Dylan

As you know by now, my focus and priority as a wealth advisor is on being of service to my clients. The "call" to serve others vocationally emerged early in my life, as the consequence of childhood experiences of love and loss, and as the result of the gracious love and caring that certain individuals showed to me in my formative years, which helped to shape me into the Protector personality I am today.

I have, in many respects, "recovered" from my early childhood experiences of "imperfect love." Or, perhaps it's more accurate to say that I've journeyed a sufficient enough distance in my life to be able to look back on those early childhood events with both perspective and insight. Today, I am no longer the hurt, eight-year-old little boy that I spoke of in the Preface, but a reasonably mature, full-grown adult. I have found my life's work—my passion—as a wealth advisor. I am aware of my strengths and vulnerabilities, of my resilience and grit, but also of my doubts and fears, the dark flecks of character that assert themselves in my life at times, the chinks in my emotional armor that remain to this day. I am, like all of us, a work in progress. But more than many, I suspect, I am a perpetual sleuth in pursuit of myself.

Wrestling with Angels, Demons, and Gremlins

I would be less than honest, however, if I didn't acknowledge that, at times, I still wrestle with my demons and struggle to create a fully formed vision and version of myself as an adult, and as a wealth advisor. In moments of doubt and questioning, I can succumb to my shadow. I've spoken of the human shadow at various points in this book, about what happens when any human being (of any hero type) finds themselves in the dark zone. A client's whole demeanor changes when the loss, or potential loss, of financial assets triggers painful memories from their childhood and evokes concerns that the past may repeat itself. The *Fixer* becomes hard, vindictive, and demanding; the *Survivor,* a willing even obsessive martyr to a cause; the *Protector* a victim/avenger who looks for someone to blame for the situation they find themselves in. In some cases, it's you, the advisor. As I noted in Chapter Five there are many triggers that can evoke the shadow—the fear of failure, poverty, shame, or humiliation. Other unknown demons and gremlins perhaps cause mischief as well.

In moments when my clients go to the dark zone, they may try to take me there too. At those points I'm careful and mindful to hold myself back from the abyss; to practice mindfulness and presence, not only in front of the client but also *with* myself. For example, I've been startled, even hurt at times, when a brazen client has spoken harshly to me. I can begin to doubt my abilities as an advisor, to question my approach with clients, my understanding of others, my capacity to help others, or my ability to ground myself in what may have become a stressful or emotionally difficult interpersonal situation with another person. This, despite the fact I have been working in my field for over 25 years!

Making Sense of the Shadow

To make meaning of my own shadow (my doubts, fears, insecurities, etc.) in such moments, I remind myself of where these feelings came from. They stem from my family of origin, my earliest memories and experiences of pain and loss, of feeling powerless to protect myself around "powerful" adults, and from other dark places. Once I connect those dots, I can make the *conscious* choice to move beyond my eight-year old childhood self, the old tapes, the sense of powerlessness and all the rest, to focus on the present moment and the actualization of my *adult* self. The person I am today.

Emerging from my shadow I ultimately return to the light zone, giving credence to the idea that from the dark side of one's psyche can come strength; what Richard Strozzi-Heckler describes as the "warrior spirit"—the ancient archetype of war that embodies self-knowledge, self-awareness, compassion, and wisdom as well as the ability to take effective action when necessary.[1] Understanding this quality about my own nature has given me great insights into how to live a more intentional and purposeful life. It also enables me to help those clients, who have slipped into the dark zone, to remove themselves from its grip in situations of high stress and high stakes.

Developing the capacity to psychologically regroup and to move on in the face of challenge or adversity requires that all of us have what I refer to as "a firm intention." Robert Greenleaf, in a wonderful essay titled, "Education and Maturity," contained in his book *The Power of Servant Leadership,* offers some wonderful insights (and hard-earned wisdom) on what it means to be a mature and grounded adult. The pursuit of maturity, he says, doesn't end with one's childhood or young adult years. It is a task we work on throughout our lives. Much of what we are called to do is to make sense of, and derive meaning from, our life experiences; to harvest them for the good, to take what we like and leave the rest, transmuted and strengthened by every new experience that comes our way. "Every life, including the most normal of the normal, is a blend of experiences that build ego strength, and those that tear it down . . . . As good a definition as I know is that maturity is the capacity to withstand the ego-destroying experiences and not lose one's perspective in the ego-building experiences," he writes.[2]

Greenleaf says that to prepare ourselves for personal growth and positive action in life we must commit ourselves to a single word: inspiration, or (to use the Greek word) *entheos,* which comes from the same roots as enthusiasm, and which means "possessed of the spirit" or "the power actuating one who is inspired." His recommendation resonates deeply in my brooding, self-reflective core. For me, inspiration means many *other* things including intention, motivation, focus, desire, and—especially—service. All these words provide me with a pathway to action and life purpose.

Bringing the Principles of Servant Leadership to My Work

Greenleaf affirms the importance of *all* of us developing not only mindfulness and self-awareness as we grow (mature), but also intention and purpose. To this end, he wrote extensively about "servanthood" throughout his life, and the principles he espoused resonate deeply in my heart—as the basis and framework by which I choose to serve others as a wealth advisor. Indeed, they help infuse my work with enduring meaning.

Here are ten traits that Greenleaf describes as key attributes of a servant leader. I invite you to consider how you might incorporate these very same traits into your own advisory work with clients.

The Servant Leader:

1. Has a great capacity to listen. To me, the ability to listen to my clients is perhaps the foremost skill that I need to bring to my role as a counselor-advisor. Each client I have is unique; each with his or her own formative life experiences and one-of-a-kind emotional template. A seminal element in the "contracting" process I undertake with each new client is to commit myself to listening to them, to understanding their stories, fears, hopes, and dreams. Early conversations often focus on a person's earliest memories of how someone in their family (a parent, grandparent, or someone else) first spoke to them about wealth. In other cases, clients will share with me photos or family mementos that are emblematic of how they feel about their family of origin, its history, legacy, and values. When I work with couples and families, in particular, it's not unusual for family members to share stories and reflections based on cherished family heirlooms such as family Bibles, old photographs, newspaper clippings, and other memorabilia that may harken back to an earlier time, to the time of the family's wealth creator.

Tools such as the Four-Player model provide a wonderful (and powerful) conversation device with which to "set the table" with clients, as a *Bystander*, and to use powerful questions as the basis for understanding clients at a deep level. In Chapter Nine, I referred to this practice as "appreciative" (also called humble) inquiry. By setting the stage for discussion, and by artfully toggling back and forth, playing the parts of *Bystander, Mover, Follower* (and yes, even *Opposer* at times), I commit myself to listening to my clients with the intention of understanding them at as deep a personal and emotional level as I can. When we make this kind of commitment to our clients, we are truly being in service to them.

2. Displays empathy toward others. As a wealth advisor, it is imperative that I be able to empathize with my clients, regardless of their hero type and the way they physically (somatically) present themselves to me when I meet with them. It is our ability to put ourselves in the shoes of others that enables us, in the end, to serve our clients to the greatest extent, to connect, and to customize investment and estate planning plans and outcomes that are fully aligned with their goals, priorities, and wishes.

3. Builds community. Often, conversation about wealth management goals includes mention of others in the client's life (spouses, partners, family members, extended family, estranged parties, etc.) when discussing topics such as bequests, legacy gifting, multigenerational wealth transfer, and estate planning. As an advisor, you become a de facto community builder, mediating conversations and building an atmosphere of inclusivity and trust that often brings parties together—within a marriage, household, or family.

4. Acts as a healer. Greenleaf believed that the "healing of relationships is a powerful force for transformation and integration."[3] By virtue of the intimacy and proximity a financial advisor has with clients, you are in a position to help individuals deal with and work through their feelings and emotions with regard to wealth; to help resolve life-long issues and concerns relative to money, and to help individuals forge goals and plans that serve not only their needs and wishes, but also the welfare of their loved ones (spouses, partners, children, and grandchildren).

5. *Is self-aware.* I've noted from the outset of this book that developing keen self-awareness is key to your success as a wealth advisor. This means understanding your own hero type, your own engagement style, and your own language of communication (be it *power*, *meaning*, or *affect*) and having the facility to work in other languages and styles, depending on the client in front of you. That's why I encourage you to develop your "multi-lingual" talents as a wealth advisor, in order to meet your client—*any* client—where they are, and to understand the emotions behind their actions and the life experiences that shape how they show up in the present.

6. *Is committed to people.* I'm in the wealth advisory business to serve my clients, to help people. I'm not in this business simply to push financial products on clients and prospects. I'm here to help clients develop wealth management goals and plans that are tightly aligned with their personal beliefs, priorities, and values. At times, this may require me to go against the popular (and political) wisdom of doing whatever a firm might want me to do with a client or refusing to put margins and results above client desires and goals. Each of us, as advisors, must make a judgment call about boundaries and integrity. Generally speaking, I know myself, trust myself, and have learned to listen to myself. The integrity of the advisor-client relationship is paramount to me. While the goals and priorities of Fixer, Survivor, or Protector clients may vary, what's key is that the plans we put in place mirror the goals and priorities of the individual, couple, or family with whom we are working.

7. *Brings foresight to the relationship.* Foresight is an important trait, born of experience and maturity, that enables a wealth advisor to speak honestly and authentically in client-advisor meetings (and sometimes in intra-firm meetings and situations) even when doing so doesn't necessarily reflect the wishes or desires of other parties present. For example, clients may wish me to promise them a certain reliable rate of return on an investment, to which I normally say, "I cannot promise such returns" or, "We can put plans in place, but the market sometimes has a mind all its own." Similarly, firms that I have been associated with in the past sometimes put pressure on me to hold to a company or firm line about which products to use, or what perspective to share with clients as my own. I always reserve the right to be the final judge of my own integrity with clients. Call it integrity of

conscience. My own view is that if I don't bring integrity and authenticity to my relationships with clients and colleagues, I'm little more than a shill and a fraud for causes and purposes beyond me.

8. *Is persuasive.* Dealing persuasively with clients of different hero types requires use of different communications approaches, strategies, and tools on my part. Throughout this book, in various case studies and scenarios, I've provided examples of how I use my influence and professional credibility to persuade clients to take deliberate and client-focused courses of action. It goes without saying that this is a crucial part of the wealth advisory process. We are not in our jobs simply to listen to clients—as important as that is. There comes a time when we must take on active *Mover, Follower,* and *Opposer* stances to bring client conversations to closure and to help clients make critical wealth management decisions.

9. *Is a great conceptualizer.* As with great leaders who work with their organizations to create compelling visions of the future, effective wealth advisors work closely with clients to help them visualize and achieve their dreams. Through our efforts at listening, inquiry, use of empathy, and appropriate advice and counsel we help clients frame their wealth management goals and values in terms relevant and compelling for them. You'll recall that in Chapter Five I offered up eight questions that I will ask new clients about the goals they have for their wealth. Such questions are always asked for the purpose of identifying a client's life values and/or determining the priorities they have for their wealth. Frequently, I find that clients have never been invited or encouraged to think about their wealth in these terms, but helping clients conceptualize what they want to do with their wealth is foundational to putting goals and objectives in place that match their priorities, personalities, and values.

10. *Is a powerful steward of others' interests.* To me, wealth advisory work is all about stewardship. Each of us is in the business of safeguarding the wealth of others, helping our clients to conserve it, grow it, and use it to the specific ends that they desire. To me, as a Protector, this is wonderful work. But it can be rewarding for advisors of *any* hero type, if we continuously keep the needs and interests of our clients in mind. We can be stewards in working with individuals, couples, and families. As noted, couples and families present more dynamic complexity than individuals, but each of the three types of clients I've described represents a unique system with which we must deal. Noted leadership expert and consultant Peter Block, author of numerous books including *Stewardship,* and *The Empowered Manager*, defines stewardship as "'holding something in trust for another.'"[4] I couldn't agree with him more! Regardless of the type of client (individual, couple, or family) with whom I'm working!

Motivating Our Clients to Action and *Inspiration*

There is a strong spiritual strain to Greenleaf's thinking about "servanthood." It reminds me of the Quakerism of my youth. It is caring, compassionate, and most definitely counter-cultural. His invocation—and *invitation*—to me to adopt the qualities of a servant in working with clients is perhaps something that will resonate with you as well.

If inspiration (*entheos*) is at the heart of Greenleaf's advice to us as advisors, I believe it is also sage counsel for us to offer our clients. For if we can inspire our clients to act boldly (with inspiration) and to go in pursuit of their hopes and dreams, then we will most certainly fulfill our calling and requirements as wealth management professionals.

So, how does one do that?

As noted elsewhere in this book, it begins by engaging our clients in discussion about their personal values, and what they see as the meaning and purpose of their wealth. In many cases, discussions about values begin with a discussion about roots. It is not a coincidence that, as a wealth advisor, I have developed a keen interest in genealogy over the years. I have long been associated with the New England Historic Genealogical Society (NEHGS) and the Society of Colonial Wars (SCW). NEHGS supports the study of one's ancestors and genealogy, placing them in historical context. SCW is a group of men whose forebears served in some capacity during the American Revolution or during the colonial period in our country. Through my involvement with both groups, I have met and become friends with many fine people who, through exploration of their family roots, have discovered much about their family history, legacy, and values. It has also provided much cherished context for the lives they then choose to live today.

In Service to Clients

Helping our clients explore (and sometimes discover) their roots is a powerful way to be of service, not only to wealth creators who are interested in understanding the roots of their own motivations and passing on specific values to subsequent generations. It can also be a powerful exercise through which those who have inherited wealth as members of what author Charles Collier calls Gen 2, Gen 3, and Gen 4 can connect with the ideas, values, and beliefs of the family's original wealth creator.

Another way that we, as wealth advisors, can be of service to our clients is to help them with issues of family governance. The cultivation, conservation, growth, and transfer of wealth from one generation to others can be a daunting task and requires the intelligent use of sophisticated estate planning tools. Lee Hausner and Douglas Freeman, among others, have written in detail about the different kinds of wealth (*human, intellectual, financial,* and *social*) that wealthy individuals, couples, and families must manage—adroitly and with careful forethought, if wealth is to last beyond a single generation. Effective management of wealth is also addressed by Jay Hughes in *Family Wealth* and its sequel, *Family, the Compact Among Generations,* in which he emphasizes the importance of wealthy individuals, couples, and families embracing the tasks of family governance against the backdrop of an evolving and ever more complex trust and estate planning landscape.

Still others have written insightfully about the challenges of managing and maintaining one's wealth, once one has achieved it. In *Strangers in Paradise: How Families Adapt to Wealth Across Generations,* James Grubman speaks of "immigrants to wealth" (wealth creators) and "natives" who are born to it. The challenges facing individuals in both categories can be complex and are often misunderstood by others, he says. "Immigrants" to the world of wealth "have to learn new rules, new responsibilities, and even some new language, all of which require special knowledge. There will be many guides around who say they can help, but truly experienced guides will be difficult to find."[5] Lee Hausner expands on the challenges of "natives" and "immigrants" alike in *Children of Paradise: Successful Parenting for Prosperous Families.*[6] Her prescriptions concerning stewardship and sound parenting when a family is blessed by affluence are "medicines" that wealthy parents of multiple generations can employ to avoid confusion and hurt around issues of love, money, accomplishment, and entitlement. Without a "capacity to value money, children do not acquire the ability to *manage* it," she writes. "As adults, their ignorance can lead to reckless spending, careless investing, and, in the most extreme cases, the squandering of an entire family fortune."

What of Happiness, Significance, and Success?

Ah, these are perhaps the most profound topics of all, when it comes to the work we do with our clients! Clearly, wealth does not buy happiness. Nor does success. In my career as an advisor, I have known both wealthy and successful people who are not happy, for a variety of reasons.

In his book, *The Happiness Advantage,* Shawn Achor provides a new model for understanding human happiness, based not on accomplishments, the acquisition of things, or even financial and professional success. For Achor, happiness is defined as "the joy we feel striving after our potential."[7] Achor quotes Barbara Frederickson of the University of North

Carolina as saying that the ten most common positive emotions are "'joy, gratitude, serenity, interest, hope, pride, amusement, inspiration, awe, and love.'"[8] These are all good feelings, but Achor writes that happiness is far more than simply these good feelings. It is wrapped up in our striving to realize our fullest potential, and thus is connected with Greek philosophical writings about *Eudaimonia*, or "human flourishing." Aristotle's *Nichomachean Ethics,* for example, explains that pursuing happiness involves living a virtuous life.

Living a virtuous life isn't necessarily easy, at least not all of the time, but it *is* within our locus of control. "We are left with a choice," says Achor, "to use [our] finite resources to see only pain, negativity, stress and uncertainty" in the world around us. Or, "to look at things through a lens of gratitude, hope, resilience, optimism, and meaning."[9] It is my belief that human flourishing, set in the context of living a virtuous life, and associated with pleasure, engagement, and meaning, is the surest path we can travel toward living a full and good life.

Conclusions

Throughout this book, I have strived to explain how and why human emotions are the basis of all investing and why people's attitudes about money, wealth, status, and self are inextricably tied together in unique and often compelling ways. As a wealth advisor, you have a wonderful ringside seat from which to observe human nature, learn from it, and advise others not only about wealth and money but also about matters of family, success, significance, generativity, and legacy. The ideas I've shared with you in this book—about human motivations, emotional templates, behavioral economics, and hero types—are simply my ways of talking about and understanding the human condition. They are lenses through which I make meaning of the world around me and find my purpose in it.

It is my hope that this book has provided insights, ideas, and tools to help you become a more effective wealth advisor, by understanding both yourself and your clients in new and deeper ways. If you can pursue your work with a mix of curiosity, wonder, drive, and, as Robert Greenleaf suggests, *inspiration*, you will do your clients a great service and bring your best personal and professional self to the work you do.

So that's it. I began this book by talking about emotions, and I conclude by talking about them as well. It is my firm desire that, by reading this book, you will find new passion and purpose in your work, and that you be able to use the ideas I've shared here as a springboard of service to your own clients.

As you conclude this book, please know that I would be delighted to hear from you. You can reach me at the following email address: chriswhite@ theemotionalinvestor.net.

And, to learn more about *Working with the Emotional Investor,* please check out my website: www.theemotionalinvestor.net.

With Admiration and Respect,

Chris

Epilogue

Man's main task is to give birth to himself.

—*Erich Fromm*

Thank you for taking time to read this book! Ultimately, this book is about stewardship, service, and love. The writing of this book, for me, has been a search for and journey toward a mature, adult understanding of love. Love that I ultimately and intentionally choose to bring to my personal relationships today—most especially my wife and family, but also to those whom I serve as a wealth advisor. Thus, I want to close with a favorite poem of mine, written by the poet George Herbert. I hope its invitation resounds with you as it does with me.

> LOVE bade me welcome; yet my soul drew back,
>   Guilty of dust and sin.
> But quick-eyed Love, observing me grow slack
>   From my first entrance in,
> Drew nearer to me, sweetly questioning   5
>   If I lack'd anything.
> 'A guest,' I answer'd, 'worthy to be here:'
>   Love said, 'You shall be he.'
> 'I, the unkind, ungrateful? Ah, my dear,
>   I cannot look on Thee.'   10
> Love took my hand and smiling did reply,
>   'Who made the eyes but I?'
> 'Truth, Lord; but I have marr'd them: let my shame
>   Go where it doth deserve.'
> 'And know you not,' says Love, 'Who bore the blame?'   15
>   'My dear, then I will serve.'

'You must sit down,' says Love, 'and taste my meat.'
    So I did sit and eat.

George Herbert. 1593–1632
Source: Bartleby.com

Thinking, Fast and Slow: The Differences in Two Philosophies of Trading

Back in the early 1990s, I covered the steel industry as part of my analytical responsibilities at CIGNA Investments. At the time, the industry was going through tremendous change as steel production began to shift away from reliance on large, integrated steelmakers like U.S. Steel, Bethlehem Steel, and Inland Steel to small, more operationally agile mini-mills. Large steel makers produced high-end materials for use in making cars and appliances. Mini-mills, on the other hand, focused on manufacturing lower-grade steel products such as rebar and steel bar, used in construction and plate steel. The large steel manufacturers were constrained by high fixed costs for labor, pension coverage, and facilities. Mini-mills, on the other hand, had relatively low operating costs, allowing them to quickly change production levels based on market demand.

As I analyzed the industry, I came to favor Nucor, an inventive mini-mill, for long-term investment over U.S. Steel and Bethlehem Steel. I saw Nucor as a "long-haul" market player because it demonstrated an ability to quickly adjust to price pressures and market demands, while old-time market players were getting badly beaten up in the marketplace, forced to keep production facilities open and running at high levels to cover costs, even when prices sagged.

So, I took my recommendations to buy Nucor to one of CIGNA's leading fund managers, a guy I'll call George. George was an aggressive manager, and I thought that if anybody in the firm would side with me about Nucor, he would. As a long-term investment, I thought it couldn't be beat.

So, I told him, "Buy Nucor!"

George looked at me and said, "Nah, I'm going to buy Bessie (Bethlehem) Steel."

"Why?" I asked disbelievingly.

"Because not many people know Nucor," he said. "And, if money managers get wind that steel prices are going up, they'll buy what they know." (He meant the big, traditional industry players that had been around for decades.)

In retrospect, this proved to be an important lesson for me in behavioral finance: *People buy what they know, what they are familiar with, even if a company is heavily burdened with problems.*

George continued with his impromptu behavioral finance tutorial. "The other reason I'm going to buy Bessie is because the stock has been so badly beaten up during the current market downturn," he said. "Look at the current valuation: It's cheap! Especially when you compare it to Nucor which is a couple of PE points higher."

I countered that I still thought Nucor was worth it in the long term, and that in five or ten years the company's stock would be worth far more than that of any of the traditional players.

"That might happen," he said. "But I want the pop," George said, increasingly annoyed. "I want to see the 'dead cat bounce' of everything eventually pouring back into traditional steel stocks. People will buy the cheapest stuff with the dirtiest, most problematic financials," he said. "Because they want market/price leverage to work for them on the upside just as it may have worked against them on the downside."

George then regaled me with stories about how short-term investors often "bottom fish" in hopes of buying stocks that are "dogs" and seeing them rebound before quickly selling them off. In retrospect, George's observations about human behavior in a changing price market proved to be highly accurate. He correctly intuited that investors, on seeing that the price of Bessie Steel had been so badly beaten up, would buy the stock in anticipation of it going up again the future. As indeed it did! That ultimately gave George the short-term "pop" he was looking for, and helped contribute to his fund performance numbers that year.

For my part, my long-term approach to thinking about the market had me avoiding Bessie and preferring Nucor for its long-term potential. Nucor's qualities lent itself to becoming a good *company* to own rather than a good *stock* to own in the short term. Ultimately, Nucor's stock price did very well, but in the short-term world of my friend George, Bessie's performance certainly proved him right for short-term gains.

To give you some perspective on this, take a look at the share price graph for Nucor (NUE) and U.S. Steel (USX). Bethlehem Steel is no longer publicly traded (need I say more?), but look carefully back at the early 1990s.

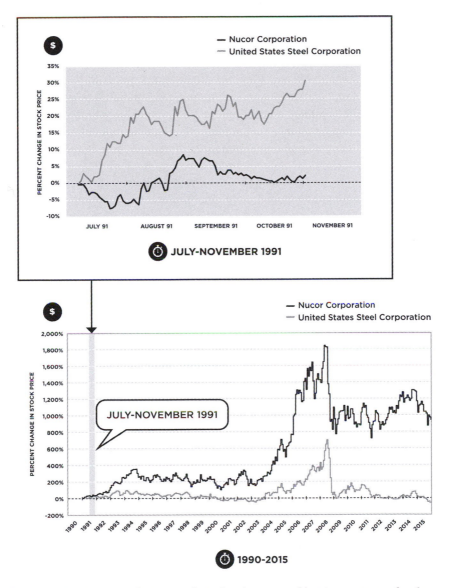

Figure A.1 Nucor and U.S. Steel. In the short term (that is over two calendar quarters) the "Thinking Fast" approach to stock picking shown in the upper chart highlights U.S. Steel Corporation handily outperforming Nucor Corporation. But over the longer-term, the lower chart shows that the "Thinking Slow" selection of Nucor Corp. clearly beats U.S. Steel.

There was, in fact, a quarter or two when USX stock outperformed NUE. But over the longer-term, NUE has clearly outperformed USX. And as noted, Bessie is nowhere to be seen!

So, who's right? It all depends on your point of view, your goals, your game plan for the future, and your risk tolerance. In other words, how people think about, and emotionally connect with, their investments strongly determines their attitude about designing a portfolio. A short-term investor (somebody who thinks fast) is more likely to feel they own a group of stocks. A long-term investor (somebody who thinks slow) is more likely to think they own a group of businesses!

In this case, "thinking fast," as George was inclined to do, causes a person to move toward owning a portfolio of stocks with short holding periods, higher transaction costs, higher taxes, and potentially frenetic portfolio management required. Many people (investors and advisors alike) enjoy operating in this caffeinated market environment. For my part, I believe that "thinking slow" is a saner approach to managing the money of high net worth clients. Why? The obvious reasons are lower trading costs and lower taxes. Beyond these reasons, though, in my experience, most individuals find it easier to relate to businesses than to stocks.

Regardless of whether a client takes a short-term or long-term approach to investing, *what* they buy is often based on emotions. Example: Some clients have an emotional (negative) reaction to owning Wal-Mart because of the company's past labor practices. The stock is often undervalued because many clients view the company in a negative light. Yet this can make it a very attractive purchase for other clients who are perfectly comfortable with how the company is managed.

Over the short term, an investor can certainly take some profits and call it a day. But over the longer term, approaching investments as though you are buying businesses is ultimately more remunerative and psychologically rewarding.

Applying Principles of Behavioral Finance to Understanding the Ups and Downs of Stock Prices

Quality tools for charting, understanding, and forecasting the financial markets are relatively few in number and often questionable in their reliability. However, there is one firm whose indices I believe help detail the subtle yet powerful behavioral dynamics at work in the marketplace, impacting everything from analysts' earnings estimates to stock prices to the behaviors associated with buying and selling stocks at various points in a market cycle. The firm MPT, Inc. of Seattle is a leading provider of quantitative investment research, used primarily by institutional money managers and plan sponsors. I have found it to be valuable in managing money for high net worth clients.

MPT, which stands for Market Profile Theorems, uses various models that look at the market from different perspectives. Three of these models, the *Insider model*, the *Earnings model*, and the *Technical model* have special interest to me insofar as they help explain the emotions and behaviors often at play behind the setting of earnings estimates by analysts and the prices at which stocks are eventually bought and sold. These models also offer a fascinating backstage look at the dynamism of stock pricing, based on the interplay between different parties operating in the financial marketplace.

▶ *MPT's Insider model helps wealth advisors and investors to better understand and interpret what insiders from a company may be thinking about their company's vitality and short- and long-term market prospects.* Insiders, such as a company's CEO, CFO, COO, CTO, and board members, all have a substantive, forward-looking grasp of the company's future growth prospects, its emerging product markets, potential new sources of revenue, long-term profitability, and current cash flows within the company. MPT's Insider model works to determine and interpret what these corporate insiders think about their company's current revenue prospects. Are insiders buying up or selling off their stock? The Insider model identifies (by company):

- Individuals undertaking transactions. (Who in the C-suite is buying or selling stock? The role of the transactor in the company dictates the weight given to a transaction.)
- The date of transactions. (More recent buys and sells are given a greater weight than older ones.)
- The size of transactions. (Transactions of over 10,000 shares are given a higher weight.)
- Other factors that provide context for stock purchases and sales by a company's C-Suite leadership team.

▶ *A second MPT model, the firm's Earnings model, measures corporate earnings from six key perspectives.* For example, the model captures the company's current year expected earnings, as estimated by Wall Street analysts, and earnings estimates for the subsequent two years (referred to as FY0, FY1, and FY2). MPT also monitors earnings estimate changes, surprises in reported earnings each quarter, and standard unexpected earnings (SUE). Finally, MPT monitors, on a daily basis, actual earnings reports for emerging market, industry, and individual stock trends. These numbers and their trends are used to monitor the earnings health of a company.

▶ *Finally, MPT's Technical model captures the actual change in price in a stock and reflects actions taken by institutional and retail investors to buy or sell the stock.*

Each of the three main models I've mentioned is given a ranking from 1 to 10, with 10 being the most favorable outlook from the point of view of insider activity, earnings revisions, or stock price. Each of the aforementioned models is part of a larger, seven-factor model that MPT uses to measure and gauge stock performance across over 5,000 companies, 59 industry groups, and 16 economic sectors.

So, why do I have such high respect for MPT's financial markets modeling tools? Simply, MPT's multidimension model set is based on behavioral finance and the premise that:

- Corporate insiders, either by buying or selling company shares, provide initial signals as to how attractively priced they view their company's stock. As such, insiders can influence the insight and work of Wall Street analysts who issue buy and sell recommendations on stocks. (Behaviorally, insiders can be seen as the "smart" money at the table.)

- Wall Street analysts who follow a company are usually the second most knowledgeable group of people about a stock. They provide published and private forecasts of corporate earnings, based on their information sources, but it often takes analysts time (weeks or months) to incorporate insider insights and knowledge and other data into formal earnings estimates and recommendations.
- Institutional portfolio managers and retail investors are sometimes the last to receive timely and accurate market and stock information, given the time it takes for information to reach them from diverse sources. And, it can take them weeks to incorporate new information into their portfolios.

As you can see, there is a hierarchy of information that creates a cascade of behaviors from insiders to Wall Street analysts to portfolio managers. The careful observer, using MPT, can understand the nuances of these patterns and invest accordingly.

Notes

Preface

1. The buying, holding, and selling of securities, currency, or commodities in different markets or, in derivative forms in order to take advantage of differing prices and values for the same asset.

Chapter One

1. Jason Zweig, *Your Money & Your Brain* (New York: Simon & Schuster, 2007), 132.

2. Investors hate experiencing losses. Consequently, most investors do whatever they can to avert loss, against all odds or logic. Through their research, Kahneman and Tversky found evidence that the pain an investor feels with a modest loss is about twice the satisfaction he or she experiences with a modest gain. From my observations of clients over the years, I think that the 2:1 ratio of pain felt versus satisfaction experienced persists, even in the realm of large losses and gains. The hero-typology discussed in this book provides a more nuanced and accurate description of loss-aversion dynamics as experienced by each hero type. More about this in Chapter Five.

3. Jason Zweig, *Your Money & Your Brain* (New York: Simon & Schuster, 2007), 14.

4. Ibid., 15.

5. Ibid., 17.

6. Jason Zweig, "Your Money and Your Brain," *Money*, September 2007, 104.

7. Ibid., 106.

8. Ibid., 107.

9. Ibid.

10. Ibid.

11. Ibid.

12. Ibid., 108.

13. Ibid.

14. Richard Davidson (with Sharon Begley), *The Emotional Life of Your Brain* (New York: Hudson Street Press, 2012), 4–6.

15. Ibid., 6.

16. David Kantor, *Reading the Room* (San Francisco: John Wiley & Sons, 2012), 11.

17. Ibid., 11–12.

18. Ibid., 56. Kantor notes that when people speak in the meaning domain, "it is to test and cement [their] understanding of [their] identity, try out new theories, gather more information, and learn from those around [them.]"

19. Ibid., 49.

20. Kantor refers to these engagement styles as "operating systems."

21. David Kantor, *Reading the Room* (San Francisco: John Wiley & Sons, 2012), 206–221.

22. Ibid., 213.

Chapter Two

1. Jason Zweig, *Your Money & Your Brain* (New York: Simon & Schuster, 2007), 66.

2. Ibid., 6.

3. Ibid., 7.

4. Here I would recommend high-quality stocks with good management and sound financials.

5. State Street Center for Applied Research, "The Folklore of Finance: How Beliefs and Behaviors Sabotage Success in the Investment Management Industry" (Boston, 2015), 14.

6. Ibid., 14–15.

7. Ibid.

8. Ibid., 15.

9. Ironically, State Street itself is a purveyor of exchange-traded funds (ETSs) that mimic these indices.

10. State Street Center for Applied Research, "The Folklore of Finance: How Beliefs and Behaviors Sabotage Success in the Investment Management Industry" (Boston, 2015), 15.

11. Ibid.

12. Ibid.

13. For further reading on this controversy, I suggest you read *Reckless Endangerment* by Gretchen Morgenson and Joshua Rosner; *Hidden in Plain Sight* by Peter Wallison; and *Free Our Markets* by Howard Baetjer, Jr. (see this book's Bibliography for these publication details).

14. State Street Center for Applied Research, "The Folklore of Finance: How Beliefs and Behaviors Sabotage Success in the Investment Management Industry" (Boston, 2015), 16.

15. Ibid., 17.

16. Ibid., 31.

17. The State Street report contains good brief descriptions of these biases on page 31. You can also access these definitions at the following URL: http://www .statestreet.com/content/dam/statestreet/documents/Articles/CAR/Folkloreof Finance_report.pdf

18. "The tendency to imbue people or objects with certain qualities based on perceived value rather than objective data." (Source: mattyford.com/blog/2014/4 /4sway-value-attribution-and-diagnosis-bias)

19. The psychology of money is also a factor, of course, when the leaders of companies speak at industry conferences, at shareholder meetings, or to Wall Street analysts. In such moments, it's important to assess the tone and body language of the individuals or "experts" speaking, just as it is when listening to outside mutual fund managers or to "for hire" business consultants who may be advising you and/ or others with whom you work.

Chapter Three

1. You may use other terms to describe what you do, such as investment manager, trustee, or portfolio manager.

2. David Kantor, *Reading the Room* (San Francisco: John Wiley & Sons, 2012), 23–26.

3. Ibid., 49–59.

4. An important clarification here. The designations of *Mover, Follower, Opposer,* and *Bystander* are not absolute categories of people. Nobody plays any of these roles to the exclusion of others. These descriptions refer instead to the kinds of "action stances" people are most likely to use in conversation in low-risk situations. Think of it as being a person's behavioral default setting. With training and conscious effort, anyone can learn to employ any of these stances at different times, often benefiting the quality of conversation and decision-making.

5. David Kantor, *Reading the Room* (San Francisco: John Wiley & Sons, 2012), 11.

6. David Kantor, interview by Rick Koonce, Cambridge, MA, September 24, 2015.

7. David Kantor, *Reading the Room* (San Francisco: John Wiley & Sons, 2012), 130.

8. Each of us carries elements of all three types in us, according to Kantor, but we "tend to express ourselves predominantly through one or maybe two of these heroic modes" (Ibid., 206).

9. David Kantor, interview by Rick Koonce, Cambridge, MA, September 24, 2015.

10. James Grubman, *Strangers in Paradise: How Families Adapt to Wealth Across Generations* (Lexington, KY: FamilyWealth Consulting, 2013), xi.

11. The Four-Player model is applicable in both low-stakes and high-stakes settings. In low-stakes situations, individuals are likely to be flexible in the roles they play in conversation. But, as stakes rise, roles potentially become more stilted.

Stuck Movers and Opposers become more dominant. Disabled Bystanders become more common, made ineffective by Movers or Opposers. More players simply choose to become Followers in order to survive.

Chapter Four

1. Kantor refers to engagement styles as operating systems. I use the term "engagement style" because it is more relevant to understanding the nature of client-advisor interactions. That said, the descriptions of Open, Closed, and Random systems are drawn from Kantor's work on group dynamics.

2. David Kantor, *Reading the Room* (San Francisco: John Wiley & Sons, 2012), 82–95.

3. Each style provides a unique window into how a client conducts themselves in conversation with others.

4. The experience of loss is perhaps the most central event in defining how a person responds, as an adult, to financial losses, threats of such losses, or anticipation of financial gains.

5. Bruce W. Tuckman, "Developmental Sequence in Small Groups," *Psychological Bulletin,* Volume 63, Number 6, 384–99

6. Augustus Napier, PhD with Carl Whitaker, MD, *The Family Crucible: The Intense Experience of Family Therapy* (New York: HarperCollins, 1978).

7. Eventually, however, the Schibasky children came to believe their parents' finances were being well managed and conserved through the active support provided by my firm.

8. The Social Styles Matrix, developed by Wilson Learning of Eden Prairie, MN, identifies four basic interpersonal styles that people display in one-on-one, social, or group settings: *Drivers, Expressives, Amiables,* and *Analyticals.* For more information on this social styles model, I suggest you read *The Social Styles Handbook: Adapt Your Style to Win Trust* (Nova Vista Publishing, 2011).

Chapter Five

1. According to Kantor, all human beings develop a predominant hero type based on early life experiences of love and loss. This hero type emerges in early adulthood, taking shape as the result of a person's life experiences and their interpretations of those experiences. A person's hero type seeks to answer key existential questions: How do I see myself in the world? How do I want to be known? To what will I commit my life's work? Will my work, and those in control, reward or reject my way of being? Will I be loved for my heroic self? And, who is the best person I can be in the world? While Kantor says these hero types become most evident in situations of high-stakes, they are actually nascent in us even in low-stakes situations. No one is a pure hero type. In situations of low stakes we can

exhibit behavior of more than one hero type, but in situations of high stakes, one hero type tends to be dominant. David Kantor, *Reading the Room* (San Francisco: John Wiley & Sons, 2012), 207.

2. Ibid., 174.

3. The Protector's experience with loss and gain is in line with Kahneman and Tversky's observations that for most people, losses are twice as painful as financial gains are pleasurable.

4. Richard J. Davidson (with Sharon Begley), *The Emotional Life of Your Brain* (New York: Hudson Street Press, 2012), 2.

5. Ibid.

6. Ibid.

7. I have found that childhood stories are sometimes volunteered in response to these questions and can be of great value in learning more about the meaning that a person ascribes to experiences of love and loss.

8. If you feel uncertain what your own hero type is, or what your client might be, give yourself some time, and refer to sidebar, Understanding the Hero Type That *You* Bring to Client Discussions. Applying and leveraging the tools in this book will take time to use with insight and skill.

9. Remember, no individual is a pure hero type. There is no absolute relationship between a person's hero type, language of communication and engagement style. Variations always exist in a person's emotional template. What is presented in this chapter is a generalized hero typology.

10. David Kantor, *Reading the Room* (San Francisco: John Wiley & Sons, 2012), 222–223.

11. For example, you may advise the client to buy stocks and increase the weight of equities in the portfolio just when the market has been selling off in a prolonged downturn. You may say that you can never "bottom-tick" the market, but when stocks are relatively cheap, they may be attractive for purchase and should therefore be owned more broadly.

12. But also remember that, in high-stakes situations, the Protector may want to sell everything after the market has already corrected. In such cases, you, as the advisor, may not understand this sentiment of wanting to give up and will need to work with the Protector to avoid this mistake. After all, the only investors who lose in a bear market are those who sell everything and never recover the value of the stocks they sold.

13. Be careful, however, not to be so conservative that you significantly underperform in an up market! One client I had told me repeatedly that he didn't want to lose money. So, we invested very conservatively. At the end of one particular year we were up 5% while the S&P 500 was up 10%. He was not satisfied because we, in fact, had underperformed. The amount of underperformance was likely an opportunity cost that he found painful to bear.

14. As a Protector counseling a Protector, be careful not be to be overly influenced emotionally by working with such a client. As a Protector myself, I recognize

that this can be difficult, and that my own tendency to be a steward and protect my clients needs to be weighed against the potential upsides of prudently chosen stocks and investments that may be new or appear initially risky to the client.

Chapter Seven

1. Lee Hausner and Douglas K. Freeman, *The Legacy Family* (New York: Palgrave MacMillan, 2009), 6–7.
2. Ibid.

Chapter Eight

1. For the uninitiated, Monte Carlo simulations are a projective modeling technique that can be used to forecast a portfolio's growth potential by manipulating various inputs (e.g., cash flows, tax obligations, likely inflation rates, and anticipated client lifespans) to project a portfolio's likely performance over a specified time period.

Chapter Nine

1. Incentive stock options or nonqualifying stock options.
2. Geoffrey Bellman, *The Consultant's Calling: Bringing Who You Are to What You Do* (San Francisco: Jossey-Bass Publishers, 1990), 123.
3. Steve Yearout, Gerry Miles, and Richard Koonce, *Growing Leaders* (Alexandria, VA: ATD Press, 2001), 219.
4. Charles Collier, *Wealth in Families* (Boston: President and Fellows of Harvard College, 2006), 8.
5. Bryan Olson and Mark Riepe, "Using Behavioral Finance to Improve the Advisor-Client Relationship," in *Behavioral Finance and Investment Management*, ed. Arnold S. Wood (New York: CFA Institute, 2010), 125–154.
6. Ibid., 137.
7. Ibid., 125–154.
8. Charles Grace, III, "The Power of the Client Service Experience," Family Office Exchange website. https://www.familyoffice.com/insights/power-client-service-experience.
9. Charles Collier, *Wealth in Families* (Boston: President and Fellows of Harvard College, 2006), 13.
10. I have seen other advisors who are Fixers act as if they can take care of their clients simply by telling them what to do. Survivors generally are more restrained in offering directive counsel, but sometimes the Survivor's sense of stability proves to be very attractive to the client who sees "broad shoulders" to lean on.

Chapter Ten

1. Richard Strozzi-Heckler, *In Search of the Warrior Spirit* (Berkeley: Blue Snake Books, 2007), x.

2. Robert Greenleaf, *The Power of Servant Leadership* (San Francisco: Berrett-Koehler, 1998), 63.

3. Ibid., 5.

4. Ibid., 7.

5. James Grubman, *Strangers in Paradise: How Families Adapt to Wealth Across Generations* (Turners Falls, MA: FamilyWealth Consulting, 2013), 3.

6. Lee Hausner, *Children of Paradise: Successful Parenting for Prosperous Families* (Los Angeles: Jeremy Archer, 1990), 21.

7. Shawn Achor, *The Happiness Advantage* (New York: Crown Business, 2010), 40.

8. Ibid., 40.

9. Ibid., 63.

Bibliography

Achor, S., (2010). *The Happiness Advantage*. New York: Crown Business.

Baetjer, H. (2013). *Free Our Markets: A Citizen's Guide to Essential Economics*. New Hampshire: Jane Philip Publications, LLC.

Baker, H. and Riccaiardi, V., eds. (2014). *Investor Behavior: The Psychology of Financial Planning and Investing*. Hoboken, NJ: John Wiley & Sons.

Bellman, G. (1990). *The Consultant's Calling: Bringing Who You Are to What You Do*. San Francisco: Jossey-Bass.

Brafman, O., and Brafman, R. (2008). *Sway: The Irresistible Pull of Irrational Behavior.* New York: Doubleday.

Brooks, R., and Richman, D. (2010). *The Charismatic Advisor: Becoming a Source of Strength in the Lives of Your Clients*. Boston: Eaton Vance Advisor Institute.

Budge, G. S. (2008). *The New Financial Advisor: Strategies for Successful Family Wealth Management*. San Francisco: John Wiley & Sons.

Chernow, R. (1998). *Titan: The Life of John S. Rockefeller, Sr.* New York: Random House.

Collier, C. (2006). *Wealth in Families*. Boston: The President and Fellows of Harvard College.

Daniell, M., and McCullough, T. (2013). *Family Wealth Management: 7 Imperatives for Successful Investing in the New World Order.* Singapore: John Wiley & Sons.

Davidson, Richard J., Ph.D., with Begley, Sharon. (2012). *The Emotional Life of Your Brain*. New York: Hudson Street Press.

Dryden, J. (2014). "Depression, Overwhelming Guilt in Pre-school Years Linked to Brain Changes." St. Louis, November 12, https://news.wustl.edu/news/pages/27670.aspx (Accessed November 22, 2014).

Eaton, L. (2014). "The Silent Value: Advice for the 21st Century." San Francisco: First Clearing, LLC, an affiliate of Wells Fargo & Company.

The Economist. (2015). "Old-fashioned Virtues: Patience, Distinctiveness, Thrift and Trust Still Count." Special Report: Family Companies. April 18.

Ellis, C. (1993). *Winning the Loser's Game.* New York: McGraw-Hill. Revised Edition.

Gitomer, J. (2008). *Little Teal Book of Trust: How to Earn It, Grow It, and Keep It to Become a Trusted Advisor in Sales, Business & Life.* Upper Saddle River, NJ: FT Press.

Goleman, D. (1998). "What Makes a Leader?" *Harvard Business Review* (November-December), 93–102.

Grace, C. "The Power of the Client Service Experience." Family Office Exchange website: https://www.familyoffice.com/insights/power-client-service-expe rience (Accessed October 24, 2015).

Graham, B. (1973). *The Intelligent Investor.* 4th ed. New York: Harper & Row.

Greenleaf, R. (1998). *The Power of Servant Leadership.* San Francisco: Berrett-Koehler.

Greenleaf, R. (2008). *The Servant as Leader.* Atlanta: The Greenleaf Center for Servant Leadership.

Grubman, J. (2013). *Strangers in Paradise: How Families Adapt to Wealth Across Generations.* Lexington, KY: FamilyWealth Consulting.

Hausner, L. (1990). *Children of Paradise: Successful Parenting for Prosperous Families.* Los Angeles: Jeremy Tarcher.

Hausner, L., and Freeman, D. (2009). *The Legacy Family.* New York: Palgrave MacMillan.

Hughes, J. (2004). *Family Wealth: Keeping It in the Family.* Princeton: Bloomberg Press.

Hughes, J. (2007). *Family: The Compact Among Generations.* New York: Bloomberg Press.

Kahneman, D. (2011). *Thinking, Fast and Slow.* New York: Farrar, Straus and Giroux.

Kahneman, D., Slovic, P., and Tversky, A., eds. (1982). *Judgment under Uncertainty: Heuristics and Biases.* London: Cambridge University Press.

Kahneman, D., and Tversky, A. (1979). "Prospect Theory: An Analysis of Decision-Making under Risk." *Econometrica* 47(2), 263–292.

Kahneman, D., and Tversky, A. (2000). *Choices, Values, and Frames.* Cambridge: Cambridge University Press.

Kantor, D. (2012). *Reading the Room.* San Francisco: John Wiley & Sons.

Kantor, D. (1999). *My Lover, Myself: Self-Discovery Through Relationship.* New York: Riverhead Books.

Kantor, D., and Lehr, W. (1975). *Inside the Family.* San Francisco: Jossey-Bass.

MacBride, E. (2015). "Emotions Count: The Brain Chemistry behind Investing." DIY Investing (blog), CNBC, January 21, http://www.cnbc.com/2015/01 /20/emotions-count-the-brain-chemistry-behind-investing.html (Accessed September 2015).

MacBride, E. (2015). "Emotions Count: The Brain Chemistry behind Investing." Fort Lee, NJ, January 21, http://www.cnbc.com/2015/01/20 (Accessed July 22, 2015).

Maslow, A. H. (1948). "A Theory of Human Motivation." *Psychological Review* 50(4), July, 370–396.

Meadows, D. (2008). *Thinking in Systems: A Primer.* White River Junction, VT: Chelsea Green Publishing.

Morgenson, G., and Rosner, J. (2011). *Reckless Endangerment: How Outsized Ambition, Greed, and Corruption Created the Worst Financial Crisis of Our Time.* New York: Times Books.

Napier, A. Y., with Whitaker, C. (1978). *The Family Crucible: The Intense Experience of Family Therapy.* New York: HarperCollins.

Rendon, J. (2015). "After Trauma, Scars but Also Strength." New York: *Wall Street Journal.* Dow Jones & Co.

Statman, M. (2013). "Investor, Know Thyself." New York: *Wall Street Journal.* Dow Jones & Co.

Statman, M. (2015). "Our Unconscious Investing Motives—And How They Get Us in Trouble." New York: *Wall Street Journal.* Dow Jones & Co.

Strozzi-Heckler, R. (2007). *In Search of the Warrior Spirit.* Berkeley: Blue Snake Books.

Sullivan, P. (2014). "Focusing on the Human Element of Estate Planning." *New York Times.*

Tuckman, B. W. (1965). "Developmental Sequence in Small Groups." *Psychological Bulletin* 63(6), 384–399.

Tversky, A., and Kahneman, D. (1991). "Loss Aversion in Riskless Choice: A Reference-dependent Model." Cambridge, MA: *The Quarterly Journal of Economics,* November.

Veres, R. (2014). "Crashing Through the Insurance Industry's Wall of Silence." Advisor Perspectives, March 11, http://www.advisorperspectives.com/news letters/2014 (Accessed June 28, 2014).

Wallison, P. (2015). *Hidden in Plain Sight: What Really Caused the World's Worst Financial Crisis and Why It Could Happen Again.* New York: Encounter Books.

Widger, C., and Crosby, D. (2014). *Personal Benchmark: Integrating Behavioral Finance and Investment Management.* San Francisco: John Wiley & Sons.

Wilson Learning Center. (2011). *The Social Styles Handbook: Adapt Your Style to Win Trust.* Herentals, Belgium: Nova Vista Publishing.

Wood, A., ed. (2010). *Behavioral Finance and Investment Management.* Charlottesville, VA: The CFA Institute.

Wray, H. (2015). "To Thine Own Self: The Psychology of Authenticity." New York: *The HuffingtonPost.com*, March 25. (Accessed November 8, 2015).

Zweig, J. (2007). *Your Money & Your Brain.* New York: Simon & Schuster.

Zweig, Jason. (2007). "Your Money and Your Brain." *Money,* September, 104–109.

Index

Accountability, 162

Achor, Shawn, 178, 179

Action propensity, 50

Action stances, 38. *See also* Kantor's Four-Player model of human interaction

Advisor. *See* Wealth management advisor

Advisor/client hero type pairings, 78–86; fixer/fixer, 80; fixer/protector, 81, 82; fixer/survivor, 80–81, 82; overview, 79*f*; protector/fixer, 84–85; protector/protector, 86; protector/survivor, 85–86; special hero pairings, 82; survivor/fixer, 82–83; survivor/protector, 82, 83–84; survivor/survivor, 83

Affect dimension: bystander, 42; communicate "in affect," 15, 41, 53; follower, 41; mover, 41; opposer, 42

Alan and Suzanne (fixers), 100–103

American International Group (AIG), 25

Anchoring, 96–100

Anchoring bias, 33

Anticipation vs. realization of gain, 23

Anxiety, 142–143, 144

Aphorism: Buffett, Warren, 25; money, 27

Apple, 165

Appreciative inquiry, 163, 174

Aristotle, 179

Ashley and Leonard (protectors), 132–137

Asset allocation discussion, 64

Attention style, 11

Author. *See* White, Chris

Autocratic family system, 57

Availability bias, 33

Backward-looking patterns, 29

Behavioral finance, 28

Behavioral propensities profile (BPP), 43–44

Beliefs about money, 26–29, 193n.19

Bellman, Geoffrey, 159

Bethlehem Steel, 184

Bias, 33, 34

Biology of emotion, 10–11

Blaming, 33

Block, Peter, 176

"Bottom fish," 184

BPP (behavioral propensities profile), 43–44

Brain, 9–11

Brain-biology-belief-behavior connection, 21–22

Brain's seeking system, 10
Breaking the ice, 151–152
Buffett, Warren, 25
Business consultants, 31, 193n.19
Bystander, 38, 39, 40*f*; affect
dimension, 42; meaning
dimension, 42; power dimension,
42
Bystander role, 85, 92–95, 104, 106,
137

Caffeinated market environment, 186
Case studies: Alan and Suzanne,
100–103; Ashley and Leonard,
132–137; Cavanaughs, 149–157
(*see also* James and Serena
Cavanaugh); dreamy David,
115–119; Harrison family, 63–64;
Jeremy and Ash, 138–141; Jessica,
99; Jill, 127–131; Joseph, 96;
Madeleine and Lucas, 141–143;
Malcolm and Deborah,
philanthropists, 119–122;
Ossenfeldts, 90–95; Quentin, the
good steward, 110–115; Schibasky
family, 60–61; Stanley, 97–98
Celera Genomics Group, 10
Change in personality from low- to
high-stakes situations, 45–47, 73*f*
Childhood stories, 12, 14, 43, 44
*Children of Paradise: Successful
Parenting for Prosperous Families*
(Hauser), 178
Chrysler, 25
Client: change in personality from
low- to high-stakes situations,
45–47, 73*f*; emotional profile,
75–76; mood swings, 46*f*; people
buy what they know, what they are
familiar with, 184; personal values,
152–153; psychological
healthiness, 59–60; psychological
system, as, 4, 34. *See also*
Client-advisor relationship

Client-advisor relationship: case
study, 149–157 (*see also* James and
Serena Cavanaugh); difficult
situations, 59; form, storm, norm,
and perform, 58–59; psychological
healthiness of client, 59–60;
romantic involvement with client,
168–169; sifting and sorting
process, 58. *See also* Relationship
building
Client anchoring, 96–100
Client scenarios. *See* Case studies
Closed engagement style, 16, 54–55,
56*f*
Cognitive dissonance, 33
Collaboration, 166
Collier, Charles, 163, 167, 177
Commitment to client, 162
Commitment to others, 4–5, 144,
175
Communicate "in affect," 15, 41, 53
Communicate "in meaning," 15, 41,
53
Communicate "in power," 15, 39, 53
Community building, 174
Compassion, 4–5
Complexities of human nature, 87
Conceptualizer, 176
Confirmation bias, 33
Conservatism bias, 33
Consultants, 31, 193n.19
*Consultant's Calling, Bringing Who You
Are to What You Do, The* (Bellman),
159
Continental Insurance, 23–24
"Contracting" with client, 34,
159–160, 174
Control, 95, 106
Conversation stances, 44. *See also*
Kantor's Four-Player model of
human interaction
Corporate insiders, 188–189
Couple (husband and wife)
situations, 65

Credibility, 158–159
"Crosses they bear," 109
Cuomo, Andrew, 32
Curiosity, 162–163

Danger of advisor hubris (folklore of knowledge), 32–33
Dark zone, 17, 46*f*, 172
Davidson, Richard J., 11, 75
Deborah and Malcolm (philanthropists—survivors), 119–122
Decision fatigue, 33
"Developmental Sequence in Small Groups" (Tuckman), 194n.5
Disposition effect, 34
Dividends, 30
Dodd, Chris, 32
Dodd-Frank Act, 32
Dreamy David (survivor), 115–119
Dunlap, Al, 89
Dylan, Bob, 171
Dynamism of human relationships, 87
Dysfunctional system, 60

Early "contracting" with clients, 34
Earnings call, 30
Earnings model, 188
Economic downturn (2008–2009), 25, 31
Economy's current health, 165
Egalitarian family system, 57
"Elephants in the room," 100
Emotion: biology of, 10–11; defined, 4; positive, 179
Emotional bandages, 5
Emotional fingerprint, 11
Emotional intelligence, 47
Emotional Life of Your Brain, The (Davidson), 11, 75
Emotional quotient, 33
Emotional scars, 22
Emotional styles, 11, 75

Emotional tapes, 22
Emotional template, 5, 13, 22. *See also* Kantor's model of formation of emotional template
Empathy, 174
Empowered Manager, The (Block), 176
Empowerment, 144
Endnotes, 191–197
Endowment effect, 33
Engagement style, 15–16, 53–66; adapting your style to client's personality, 55–57; case study (Harrison family), 63–64; case study (Schibasky family), 60–61; checklist of items to attend to, 66; closed, 16, 54–55, 56*f*; couples, 65; families, 62–64; multigenerational situation, 62, 63; open, 16, 54, 56*f*; overview, 56*f*; random, 16, 55, 56*f*; when clients have clash of engagement styles, 65
Entheos (inspiration), 173, 177
Eudaimonia (human flourishing), 179
Evolutionary biology, 4

False comfort thinking, 30–32
Family, The Compact Among Generations (Hughes), 178
Family business administration, 122
Family Crucible: The Intense Experience of Family Therapy, The (Napier/Whitaker), 194n.6
Family governance, 177
Family Office Exchange (FOX), 165, 166
Family Wealth (Hughes), 178
Family wealth management discussions, 62–64
Fear, 25, 72
Fictionalized case studies. *See* Case studies
Financial capital, 163
Financial parenting, 122
Firm intention, 173

Fixer, 5, 6, 17, 67–68, 76, 89–107;
   anchoring, 96–100; author
   suggestions, 104–107; bystander
   role, 92–95, 104, 106; case study
   (Alan and Suzanne), 100–103;
   case study (Jessica), 99; case
   study (Joseph), 96; case study
   (Ossenfeldts), 90–95; case study
   (Stanley), 97–98; charming and
   charismatic, 75; communicate "in
   power," 75; control, 95, 106;
   conversational timing, 106; dark
   zone, 46*f*; delivering a difficult
   message, 105–106; "elephants in
   the room," 100; Four-Player
   model, 106; intermediate zone,
   46*f*; Jekyll-Hyde transformation,
   104; light zone, 46*f*; pain from
   loss, 72; persistence, 100;
   preferred engagement style, 106;
   required skills/personal traits, 107;
   roadmap (guidelines), 76; shadow
   side, 172; tough stand, 105;
   well-known fixer personality
   (Patton), 68
Fixer-Fixer pairings, 80
Fixer-Protector pairings, 81, 82,
   138–139
Fixer-Survivor pairings, 80–81, 82
Folklore of finance, 29–33; folklore of
   false comfort, 30–32; folklore of
   knowledge, 32–33; folklore of
   time, 29–30
Folklore of knowledge, 32–33
Folklore of time thinking, 29–30
Follower, 38–39, 40*f*; affect
   dimension, 41; meaning dimension,
   41; power dimension, 41
Foresightedness, 175
Formation of emotional template. *See*
   Kantor's model of formation of
   emotional template
Formative life stores (childhood
   stories), 12, 14, 43, 44

Four-Player model. *See* Kantor's
   Four-Player model of human
   interaction
Four types of capital, 121
FOX (Family Office Exchange), 165,
   166
Framing bias, 33
Frank, Barney, 32
Frankl, Victor, 109, 110
Frederickson, Barbara, 178
Free Our Markets (Baetjer),
   192n.13
Free-wheeling family system, 57
Freeman, Douglas, 121, 122, 178
Fromm, Erich, 181
Full and good life, 179
Functional system, 59

Gambler's fallacy, 33
Gandhi, Mahatma, 109, 110
Genealogy, 62, 177
General Motors, 25
Good feelings, 179
Graham, Benjamin, 3
Gray zone, 17, 46*f*
Greed, 25
Greenleaf, Robert, 173, 174, 177,
   179
Growing Leaders (Yearout et al.),
   196n.3
Grubman, James, 48, 178

Happiness, 178–179
Happiness Advantage, The (Achor),
   178
Harrison family, 63–64
Hauser, Lee, 121, 122, 178
Healing of relationships, 174–175
Healthy, functional human "system,"
   59
Herbert, George, 181, 182
Herding, 34
Hero pairings. *See* Advisor/client hero
   type pairings

Hero types, 16–18, 67–87; advisor understanding his/her own hero type, 74; determining client's emotional profile, 75–76; development of one's hero type, 71*f*; existential questions, 194n.1; Fixer, 17 (*see also* Fixer); generalized hero type, 195n.9; hero pairings, 78–86 (*see also* Advisor/client hero type pairings); low-stakes vs. high-stakes situations, 195n.1; Protector, 17 (*see also* Protector); specific type not evident until stakes become high, 74; Survivor, 17 (*see also* Survivor)

Heuristics, 33

Hidden in Plain Sight (Wallison), 192n.13

Hierarchy of information, 188–189

High-stakes situations, 26, 44–45, 46*f*, 89

"High touch" factors, 165

Hindsight bias, 33

Home bias, 33

Hughes, Jay, 178

Human brain, 9–11

Human capital, 163

Human flourishing, 179

Human happiness, 178–179

Human seeking system, 10, 23

Humble inquiry, 174; appreciative inquiry, 163, 174

Husband and wife situations, 65

Illusion of control bias, 33

In Search of the Warrior Spirit (Strozzi-Heckler), 197n.1

Indices, 30–31

Individuation, 59

Insider model, 187–188

Inspiration (*entheos*), 173, 177

Institutional portfolio managers, 189

Integrity, 164–165, 175

Integrity of conscience, 176

Intellectual capital, 163

Intelligent Investor, The (Graham), 3

Intention and purpose, 173

Intermediate zone, 46*f*; gray zone, 17, 46*f*

Interpersonal confidence, 47

Interpersonal dynamics, 37–50, 86, 106, 138

Intrinsic uncertainty of investing, 33

Investment manager, 193n.1. *See also* Wealth management advisor

James and Serena Cavanaugh, 149–157; breaking the ice, 151–152; firm's wealth advisory approach, 153–155; firm's wealth advisory mission and vision, 155–157; personal values, 152–153

Jekyll-Hyde transformation, 104

Jeremy and Ash (protectors), 138–141

Jessica (fixer), 99

Jill (protector), 127–131

Joseph (fixer), 96

Journey to selfhood, 71*f*

Kahneman, Daniel, 6–8, 72

Kantor, David, 5, 12–17, 25, 43, 67

Kantor's Four-Player model of human interaction: bystander, 39 (*see also* Bystander); family discussions, 64; follower, 38–39 (*see also* Follower); mover, 38 (*see also* Mover); opposer, 39 (*see also* Opposer); overview, 40*f*; when/how used, 43

Kantor's model of formation of emotional template: level I (hero types), 16–18; level II (engagement style), 15–16; level III (language of communication), 15; level IV (childhood stories), 14–15; overview, 13*f*

Koonce, Rick, 159

Language of *affect,* 15, 41, 53
Language of communication, 15
*Language of Emotions,
    The* (McLaren), 3
Language of *meaning,* 15, 41, 53
Language of *power,* 15, 39, 53
*Legacy Family: The Definitive Guide to
    Creating a Successful
    Multigenerational Family, The*
    (Hauser/Freeman), 121
Lehman Brothers, 25
Life experiences, 4, 5, 71*f*
Life legacy, 121–122
Light zone, 17, 46*f*
Listening, 173–174
Long-term investor, 186
Loss aversion, 6, 7*f,* 22
"Love bade me welcome" (Herbert),
    181–182
Low-stakes situations, 25–26, 44
Low- to high-stakes situations,
    45–47, 73*f*

Madeleine and Lucas (protector),
    141–143
Malcolm and Deborah
    (philanthropists—survivors),
    119–122
Mandela, Nelson, 109
Market folklore. *See* Folklore of
    finance
Market Profile Theorems (MPT), 31,
    187–189
Mascotte, Jake, 24
Mature and grounded adult, 173
McLaren, Karla, 3
Meadows, Donella H., 53
Meaning dimension: bystander, 42;
    communicate "in meaning," 15, 41,
    53; follower, 41; mover, 41;
    opposer, 42
Mediator, 65, 135
Meeting agenda, 64
Mental accounting bias, 33

Miles, Gerry, 159
Millionaire, The (TV), 125
Mindfulness, 173
Missional family system, 57
Money, 26–29, 193n.19
Monte Carlo simulations, 142,
    196n.1
Mother Teresa, 70
Mover, 38, 40*f;* affect dimension, 41;
    meaning dimension, 41; power
    dimension, 41
MPT, Inc., 187–189
Multigenerational situation, 62, 63

NEHGS (New England Historic
    Genealogical Society), 177
Neuroeconomics, 9
Nevil, Dorothy, 37
New England Historic Genealogical
    Society (NEHGS), 177
Newton, Isaac, 21
Nichomachean Ethics (Aristotle), 179
Nordstrom, 165
Notes (endnotes), 191–197
Nucleus accumbens, 9
Nucor, 185

Object relations theory, 14, 22
Olson, Bryan, 164, 165
Open engagement style, 16, 54, 56*f*
Operating systems, 194n.1. *See also*
    Engagement style
Opposer, 38, 39, 40*f;* affect dimension,
    42; meaning dimension, 42; power
    dimension, 41
Ortega y Gasset, José, 67
Ossenfeldts (fixers), 90–95
Outlook style, 11
Outside managers, 31, 193n.19
Overconfidence, 33, 34

Pain felt versus satisfaction
    experienced, 72, 191n.2
Panksepp, Jaak, 10, 23

Patriarchal family system, 57
Patton, George, 68
People buy what they know, what
    they are familiar with, 184
Performance review, 64
Personal story and identity, 14
Personality development, 14
Persuasiveness, 176
PetSmart, 98, 98*f*
Portfolio management tools, 64
Portfolio manager, 193n.1. *See also*
    Wealth management advisor
Positive emotions, 179
Power dimension: bystander, 42;
    communicate "in power," 15, 39,
    53; follower, 41; mover, 41;
    opposer, 41
Power of Servant Leadership, The
    (Greenleaf), 173
Preservation of wealth, 143
Professional accountability, 162
Professional boundaries, 168–169
"Prospect Theory: An Analysis of
    Decision Under Risk" (Kahneman/
    Tversky), 7
Protector, 5, 6, 17, 69–70, 76,
    125–145; anxiety, 142–143, 144;
    author suggestions, 143–145;
    beneficiaries, 144; case study
    (Ashley and Leonard), 132–137;
    case study (Jeremy and Ash),
    138–141; case study (Jill),
    127–131; case study (Madeleine
    and Lucas), 141–143; commitment
    to others, 144; communicate "in
    affect," 75; dark zone, 46*f*;
    empowerment, 144; high-stakes
    situations, 126, 144; intermediate
    zone, 46*f*; light zone, 46*f*; low-
    stakes situations, 126; preservation
    of wealth, 143; "process"
    investment options in open-ended
    way, 144; risk aversion, 126;
    roadmap (guidelines), 77;

self-righteousness, 145; shadow
    side, 72–73, 172; "spoiled,"
    "elitist," or "entitled," 145; "talk
    Protectors down," 126; victim
    avenger, 70; well-known protector
    personality (Mother Teresa), 70
Protector-Fixer pairings, 84–85
Protector-Protector pairings, 86
Protector-Survivor pairings, 85–86
Psychology of money, 26–29,
    193n.19

Quakerism, 177
Quarterly earning results, 29–30
Quentin, the good steward (survivor),
    110–115

Random engagement style, 16, 54,
    56*f*, 123
Reading the room, 28, 100
Reality repeating itself, 22
Recession of 2008–2009, 25, 31
Reckless Endangerment (Morgenson/
    Rosner), 192n.13
Reflective brain, 9
Reflexive brain, 9
Reflexive thinking processes, 9
Regret aversion, 33
Regular reviews, 160
Regulation and disclosure practices,
    31–32
Relationship building, 158–169;
    adopt broad frames when
    discussing performance, 165;
    advice and counsel, 166;
    appreciative inquiry, 163;
    collaboration, 166; commitment
    and accountability, 162;
    "contracting" with client, 159–160;
    credibility, 158–159; curiosity,
    162–163; frame expectations,
    159–160; goals and strategy,
    166–167; "high touch" factors, 165;
    integrity, 164–165; overview, 161*f*;

Relationship building (*cont.*)
  professional boundaries, 168–169;
  regular reviews, 160; romantic
  involvement with client, 168–169;
  trust building, 164–166; vision of
  the future, 167–168. *See also*
  Client-advisor relationship
Representativeness bias, 33
Resilience style, 11
Retail investors, 189
Riepe, Mark, 164, 165
Risk aversion, 8, 126
Risk-related indices, 30
Rockefeller, John D., 23
Romantic involvement with client,
  168–169
Roots (genealogy), 177
Rosenblum, Mary, 149

Saint-Exupery, Antoine de, 125
"Salt away gains," 74
Same-sex couple (protectors),
  138–141
Same-sex couple situations, 65
Schibasky family, 60–61
SCW (Society of Colonial Wars),
  177
Self-attribution bias, 32
Self-awareness, 173, 175
Self-awareness style, 11
Self-control bias, 33
Self-sacrifice, 124
Sensitivity to Context style, 11
Servant leadership: commitment to
  others, 175; community building,
  174; conceptualizer, 176; empathy,
  174; foresightedness, 175; healing
  of relationships, 174–175;
  listening, 173–174; persuasiveness,
  176; self-awareness, 175;
  stewardship, 176
Shackleton, Ernest, 68, 69
Shadow/shadow side, 17, 70–74,
  172; dark zone, 17, 46*f*, 172

Short-term investor, 186
Short-termism, 33
Slovic, Paul, 10
Social agility, 47
Social capital, 163
Social intuition style, 11
Social styles, 105
*Social Styles Handbook: Adapt Your
  Style to Win Trust,* 105, 194n.8
Social Styles matrix, 66, 194n.8
Society of Colonial Wars (SCW), 177
S&P 500, 32
Special hero pairings, 82
Stanley (fixer), 97–98
State Street Center for Applied
  Research, 29, 30, 32, 33
Status quo bias, 33
Stay the course (stick-to-it-iveness),
  123
Steel industry, 183–186
Stewardship, 4–5, 176, 178
Stewardship (Block), 176
Stewart, Potter, 3–4
Stock market indices, 30–31
Stock market turbulence (August,
  2015), 25
*Strangers in Paradise: How Families
  Adapt to Wealth Across Generations*
  (Grubman), 48, 178
Strozzi-Heckler, Richard, 172
Style of social engagement, 53. *See
  also* Engagement style
Survivor, 5, 6, 17, 68–69, 76,
  109–124; author suggestions,
  122–124; case study (dreamy
  David), 115–119; case study
  (Malcolm and Deborah,
  philanthropists), 119–122; case
  study (Quentin, the good steward),
  110–115; charitably and even
  selflessly inclined, 123;
  communicate "in meaning," 75;
  critical capital accounts
  (intellectual, human, and social

capital), 122; "crosses they bear,"
109; dark zone, 46*f*; famous
survivor personalities from history,
69, 109; fatalistic, 75; intermediate
zone, 46*f*; light zone, 46*f*;
long-term investment focus, 124;
low-stakes circumstances, 123;
loyal clients, 123–124; mission
"beyond financial capital," 121;
random engagement style, 123;
roadmap (guidelines), 76–77; "salt
away gains," 74; self-sacrifice, 124;
shadow side, 73–74, 172; stay the
course (stick-to-it-iveness), 123;
world of meaning and causes, 109
Survivor-Fixer pairings, 82–83
Survivor-Protector pairings, 82, 83–84
Survivor-Survivor pairings, 83
System, 53
System One thinking, 8
System Two thinking, 8

Technical model, 188
Thinking, Fast and Slow (Kahneman),
8
Thinking fast, 183–186
Thinking in Systems: A Primer
(Meadows), 53
Thinking slow, 183–186
Thinking types, 8
"Thrill of the chase," 23
Tight and secretive family system, 57
Trust building, 164–166
Trustee, 193n.1. *See also* Wealth
management advisor
Tversky, Amos, 6–8, 72

Uncertainty of investing, 33
Unhealthy, dysfunctional system, 60
Unified field theory, 18
U.S. Steel, 185
"Using Behavioral Finance to Improve
the Adviser-Client Relationship"
(Olson/Riepe), 164

Value at risk (VaR), 30
Value attribution, 34
Values, 152–153, 177
Victim avenger, 70
Vignettes. *See* Case studies
Virtuous life, 179
Vision of the future, 167–168
Visioning exercises, 64

Wall Street analysts, 189
Walmart, 186
Warrior spirit, 172
Wealth creation and conservation, 122
Wealth in Families (Collier), 163
Wealth management advisor:
adapting your engagement style to
client's personality, 55–57; astute
observation of clients, 34; early
"contracting" with clients, 34;
family meetings, 62–64; fixer,
196n.10; mediator, as, 65, 135;
personal inventory (questions to
answer), 48–49; portfolio
management tools, 64; questions
to ask to ascertain emotional profile
of client, 75–76; skills/personal
traits, 4–5, 47, 107, 159; survivor,
196n.10; understanding your own
engagement style, 57; understanding
yourself as a system, 47–48. *See
also* Client-advisor relationship
Wealth transfer, 122
Welch, Jack, 89
Whitaker, Carl, 59, 60
White, Chris: behavioral finance guy,
as, 28; "calling" to serve others,
171; e-mail address, 180;
engagement style, 58; integrity and
authenticity, 176; "perpetual sleuth
in pursuit of myself," 171;
Protector tendencies, 5, 85;
website, 180; "when brazen client
spoke harshly to me," 172
"White glove" client experiences, 165

Wilson Learning, 66, 105
Wooden, John, 164
World of meaning and causes, 109
www.familyoffice.com, 166
www.theemotionalinvestor.net, 180

Yearout, Steve, 159
Your Money and Your Brain (Zweig), 9,
    21

Zweig, Jason, 9–11, 21, 22

ABOUT THE AUTHORS

Chris White (author), CFA, is a senior investment counselor at Hemenway Trust Company, LLC, a New Hampshire–chartered wealth management firm. An experienced wealth management advisor and strategist, Chris has invested on behalf of individuals, families, and institutions for over 25 years. During this time he has worked with hundreds of individuals, couples, and families, developed a keen sense of human nature, and come to understand how human emotions, life experience, and family history (more than rationality) typically drive decisions people make about their money—be it in planning for retirement, building an investment portfolio, or undertaking multi-generational wealth management. He is a chartered financial analyst and a member of the CFA Institute, the Boston Security Analysts Society, and the Boston Economics Club. An avid sailor, Chris lives with his wife in Boston. You can reach him at TheEmotionalInvestor.net.

Richard Koonce (collaborator) is an accomplished author and interviewer who has written or co-written six previous books. A former print and broadcast journalist, he is a professional certified executive coach and communications consultant based in Philadelphia. Reach him at www.richardkoonce.com.